FINAL JOURNEY

FINAL JOURNEY

THE UNTOLD STORY OF FUNERAL TRAINS

NICOLAS WHEATLEY

The
History
Press

To my daughters
Laura and Olivia.

First published 2020

The History Press
97 St George's Place, Cheltenham,
Gloucestershire, GL50 3QB
www.thehistorypress.co.uk

British Library Cataloguing in Publication Data.
A catalogue record for this book is available from the British Library.

ISBN 978 0 7509 9433 0

Typesetting and origination by The History Press
Printed and bound in Great Britain by TJ Books Limited, Padstow,
Cornwall.

CONTENTS

FOREWORD

This fascinating book is full of interesting historical facts concerning the manner in which the deceased through time were transported to their final resting place. Railways in particular played a prominent role in such events and I personally was involved in one such sombre movement. Operation 'Hope Not' was established in advance of the demise of Sir Winston Churchill and was known to but senior officials responsible for its overall execution. At Nine Elms depot, my driver, Alfred Hurley, and I were briefed by the Southern Region management on the part that we had been selected to perform. The funeral arrangements were precise and fitting for this 'great man'. Our part, on the footplate of the 'Battle of Britain' locomotive bearing his name, was the last significant use of a steam locomotive to perform such a prominent role.

James (Jim) Lester – 70A

James (Jim) Lester was the then 22-year-old fireman on steam locomotive 34051 *Winston Churchill* that hauled the funeral train for Sir Winston Churchill from Waterloo to Long Handborough, Oxfordshire, on 30 January 1965. Further details of this event are contained in Chapter 7.

ACKNOWLEDGEMENTS

The author would like to thank an enormous number of people whose contributions have made this book possible. There are too many to name them all individually and the names of some the author either never knew or has unfortunately forgotten. However, the input of three people in particular has been crucial. The idea for this book developed over a period of time, following the author's purchase of the then third edition of John Clarke's book on the Brookwood Necropolis Railway. A visit to Brookwood Cemetery was made in November 2004 for the 150th anniversary celebrations of its opening and five years later another a visit followed, which happily involved a meeting with John when he kindly signed a copy of his book, by then in its fourth edition. Little did either of us know that this seminal meeting would one day lead to the production of this book. John's considerable assistance along the way has been invaluable and much appreciated.

Critical to the book's production has been the support and assistance provided by Dr Brian Parsons, whose knowledge of the history of funeral directors in Great Britain is unrivalled. He has most generously shared both his knowledge and his researches in the records of funeral directors, particularly on the sending of coffins by train, which has been invaluable. Without his numerous contributions, including the provision of many historic photographs, this book would not have been possible. The author also owes a huge debt of gratitude to Dr Helen Frisby, not only for sharing her extensive knowledge of Victorian funerals but also for her encouragement and support during the long processes of researching and writing this book.

Amongst the many others whose contributions (direct or indirect) must be acknowledged are, in no particular order: Dr Tony Walter, Dr John Troyer and Dr Kate Woodthorpe (Tuckwell), all from the University of Bath; Dr Julie Rugg, organiser of the annual Cemeteries Colloquium at the University of York; the many staff of the Search Engine at the National Railway Museum, York; James (Jim) Lester, fireman on Sir Winston Churchill's funeral train; Colin Fenn, formerly of the Friends of West Norwood Cemetery; Robert Stephenson of the Friends of Kensal Green Cemetery: several senior people in The Brookwood Cemetery Society; Brian Janes of the Colonel Stephens Museum, Tenterden, Kent; Roger T. Price of the Bluebell Railway; various members of The Pullman Society, in particular Terry Bye; Maxine Barton-Hawkins and many other people at the Gloucestershire Warwickshire Steam Railway, where the author is a volunteer; the Great Western Trust, Didcot; John Brodribb of the South Devon Railway; Colin Marsden of Dawlish; Annette Everett, Business Manager and all her staff of the Railway Convalescent Home in Dawlish, where part of this book was written; Francis and Gill Crowther, friends of the author, whose support and encouragement has been much appreciated; the author's late parents, Dr Bernard and Mrs Marion Wheatley, whose deaths provided the finances needed to carry out the research and writing for this book; and last, but by no means least, Amy Rigg, Commissioning Editor at The History Press, for so astutely recognising the potential in this book and arranging for it to be published, together with the staff at The History Press for their patience and assistance during its production. Any errors occurring in the book remain the responsibility of the author.

The author would also like to acknowledge the assistance of everyone who has helped with supplying any of the numerous photos used in this book, in particular Luci Gosling of the Mary Evans Picture Library, Colin Panter of PA Media, Justin Hobson of SSPL and Jane Skayman at Mortons Media. Many of the photographs are of historical events, so their quality is not always as high as desired. However, their inclusion is justified by their depiction of events relevant to the topic and sometimes by their rarity. The author is also most grateful to all those people who have generously allowed him to use photographs of their loved ones experiencing a final journey on a heritage (or private) railway. All reasonable efforts have been made to trace copyright holders and to obtain permissions to use the images and photographs in this book. However, if any have been missed then anyone whose rights or permissions have not been properly acknowledged should contact the author via the publishers and steps will be taken to correct any shortcomings in a future edition.

INTRODUCTION

The steam locomotive puffed gently as it moved slowly out of the station, sounding a short but mournful whistle, pulling the train with its special van containing the mortal remains of a very important person. As the train headed towards London on that November evening, many people stood by the lineside paying their respects to a person they thought they might have known, even though probably no one present had ever met them. Who was that person and when did this event take place?

The truth is that we shall never know whose remains were being transported in the special van. They were the remains of one of a million or so British people killed in what was known at the time as the Great War but has now become better known as the First World War. What we do know is that the person was a soldier from the British Army, whose remains had been selected very carefully so that his name was not known. He was therefore given a new identity as the Unknown Warrior, by which name he has been known to millions in the United Kingdom and worldwide ever since. Within Britain he represents all of those fallen in the Great War, so he might have been the husband, brother, son, sweetheart or other loved one of any of the people who stood by the lineside paying their respects as the train travelled to London on that November evening.

The event took place in 1920, two years after the signing of the Armistice that ended the fighting of the Great War, though the conflict itself did not officially finish until the signing of the Treaty of Versailles on 28 June 1919. It is the anniversary of the Armistice that is commemorated each 11 November rather than the signing of the treaty and this has been the case ever since 1919. The special van was carrying the remains of the Unknown Warrior to London on 10 November for burial in Westminster Abbey the following day. This was as part of the first major national commemoration of the ending of the Great War, a day of events that included the unveiling by King George V of the Cenotaph in Whitehall. A wooden temporary structure had been erected in 1919, but when the procession to the Abbey passed down Whitehall it stopped for the King to unveil the stone monument that is so familiar today.

The role of the special van in the train conveying the Unknown Warrior's remains to London, and the procession taking his remains to the Abbey, provide an important illustration of the twin main themes of this book. The first is the functional role of railways in transporting the dead to their place of burial or at least to a station near to that place. The second theme is the way that the transportation of coffins by train is often part of the procession which forms an important part of the funeral ritual.

The special van used to transport the remains of the Unknown Warrior had been built by the South Eastern & Chatham Railway (SECR) at its Ashford (Kent) works, as the prototype of a new type of four-wheel luggage-carrying van. Painted umber with yellow lettering and given the number 132, it was originally known as the 'Special Van'. It was specifically selected, when only a few weeks old, to perform its first duty of being used in May 1919 to transport the remains of Nurse Edith Cavell from Dover to London. She was being repatriated to England after having been executed by the Germans in occupied Belgium in October 1915. Nurse Cavell had been running a hospital caring for sick and injured soldiers and had assisted in the return to Britain of over 200 soldiers. Having been found guilty of what the Germans considered to be treasonable behaviour, she was executed by firing squad on 12 October 1915, thus becoming the most famous British woman to lose her life as a direct result of the Great War.

Her execution caused a major outcry internationally at the time and her repatriation when the Great War was over provided a focal point for the early days of remembrance and commemoration with which we are so conversant today. Such was the impact of this event, and the role of Van 132 as part of it, that the van itself became known as the 'Cavell Van'. Indeed that name was later attached by generations of railwaymen to variations of the design of the four-wheel luggage van, which was produced in great numbers by the Southern Railway from 1923 and by British Railways until as late as 1951.

Remarkably, the original Cavell Van had been used in another high-profile repatriation only a few weeks after its solemn duties in the service of Nurse Cavell. In July 1919 it was used to transport the mortal remains of Captain Charles Fryatt on part of his final journey, on the section from Dover to London. Captain Fryatt was not a military man but was the master of a ship operated by the Great Eastern Railway during the Great War on the sea crossing from Harwich, Essex, to the Hook of Holland, in what was then neutral Netherlands. In brief, his claim to fame is that he was alleged to have rammed a German submarine whilst escaping from being captured by it. Unsurprisingly, the Germans took exception to this action and subsequently captured and executed Captain Fryatt, in July 1916.

The Prime Minister at the time, Herbert Asquith, described his execution as 'murder' and a massive outrage followed, both at home and internationally. Like Nurse Cavell before, he was regarded as a martyr and his repatriation to England, and subsequent burial in Dovercourt, near Harwich, was accompanied by considerable ceremony. Again, the SECR brought out the Cavell Van and used it for the Dover to London part of Captain Fryatt's final journey. After a service in St Paul's Cathedral and a road journey to Liverpool Street Station, he was taken by his former railway employers, the Great Eastern Railway (GER), by train to Dovercourt, Essex. That part of his final journey used the GER's hearse van, No. 512, a six-wheeled vehicle that had been converted from a passenger carriage originally built in 1892. Coincidentally, that was the same hearse van that been used a few weeks earlier for Nurse Edith Cavell's final journey from Liverpool Street Station to Norwich, where she was buried just outside the eastern end of the magnificent cathedral in that fine city.

Sadly, the Great Eastern Railway's van 512 has not survived into preservation, though somewhat miraculously the original Cavell Van, the SECR's

SECR Van 132 (later known as the Cavell Van) in ex-works condition as built at Ashford Works, 1919. (Courtesy of Brian Janes, Colonel Stephens Museum)

Van 132, has survived. It is now restored and is on display as a memorial to Nurse Edith Cavell, Captain Charles Fryatt and the Unknown Warrior, usually located at Bodiam Station on the Kent & East Sussex Railway, though it has been displayed in other locations to commemorate specific events. In October 2015 it had been on display in Norwich for two weeks to commemorate the centenary of Nurse Cavell's execution and in the summer of 2018 it spent several weeks on display at Arley Station on the Severn Valley Railway as part of that railway's commemorations of war-time events. In late October 2018 the Cavell Van was displayed on the Harbour Arm in Folkestone in remembrance of when it was used to take the coffin for the Unknown Warrior to that port, so that it could be taken to France to collect the Warrior's remains for repatriation to the UK. More recently, in July 2019 the Cavell Van spent two weeks in Harwich as part of the commemorations for the centenary of the repatriation of Captain Fryatt's remains.

Another railway van that was used as a hearse to transport the remains of an even more famous person has also survived, equally miraculously, and is in the ownership of the Swanage Railway Trust. Having been under the care of the National Railway Museum, where it was on display initially in York from January 2015 and then later at the museum's Locomotion branch in Shildon, it is now in the care of the One:One Collection based in the former Hornby factory warehouse in Margate, Kent. The van moved there in early September 2019, but the venue is not currently (January 2020)

Funeral train of Sir Winston Churchill leaving Waterloo, 30 January 1965.
(Photo from Chris Lade Archive, Courtesy of Nick Lade, via Terry Bye)

open to the public on a regular basis, though its owners hope to develop it as a visitor attraction in the future.

This van, known by its British Railways designation as S2464, is better remembered as the van in which the coffin containing the body of Sir Winston Churchill was transported on 30 January 1965 from Waterloo Station to Handborough in Oxfordshire. From that station he was taken by motor hearse for burial in the nearby churchyard at Bladon, close to Blenheim Palace where he had been born in 1874.

The three uses of the Cavell Van and Churchill's funeral train are probably the most famous occasions when railways were used to transport the coffins of important but non-royal people. There were also several occasions when trains were used as part of important royal funerals, firstly for Queen Victoria in 1901, then for her son King Edward VII in 1910, followed by King George V in 1936 and finally King George VI in 1952. The funeral in 1979 of Earl Mountbatten should be added to that list, for although he was not a monarch he was related to the Royal Family and his funeral train, from Waterloo Station to Romsey, was the last time a private funeral train ran on the main line.

However, until British Rail stopped transporting coffins by train in 1988, the railway network had been used since its early days to carry the coffins of deceased ordinary people all over the UK, on their final journeys to a place of burial that had some significance to them or their loved ones. This book explores why that was done, how it was done by the railways (and sometimes by tramways), and provides more information about the use of trains in the funerals of the people already mentioned. It also takes a brief look at the lives of some of the many people already identified who had their final journeys by train, and many more are bound to be identified in the future.

There are examples of coffin transport that took place in England, Wales, Scotland and Ireland, with a couple of examples in the Isle of Man also included. Although the transport of coffins on the main line is no longer permitted, there are numerous occasions when heritage railways, and even a couple of miniature railways, have provided ceremonial final journeys for their respected volunteers or other people with significant links to the line. It is even possible to pay for a private funeral train on a narrow-gauge railway in Derbyshire, as will be described in Chapter 13.

The definition of a funeral train for the purposes of this book is one that is carrying a coffin, so trains (usually on heritage railways) on which a person's ashes are placed into a steam locomotive's firebox and blown through the chimney are excluded. Similarly, trains merely displaying a wreath in memory of a person who has died are also excluded. To record comprehensively either type of train would be an almost impossible task and is outside the scope of this book.

The story of funeral trains in the British Isles has never before been told in a comprehensive manner and there are some extraordinary tales to be recounted. Many of the people involved are famous names even now, such as the first Duke of Wellington – the 'Iron Duke' – (1852), George Hudson, 'The Railway King', (1871), Prime Minister William Gladstone (1898), Dr Thomas Barnardo (1905), Florence Nightingale (1910) and the suffragette Emily Wilding Davison (1913) to name but a very few. Others were famous in their day but are now largely and undeservedly forgotten, for example Britain's first non-white circus proprietor, William Darby (1873) who under his stage name 'Pablo Fanque' is commemorated in a Beatles song on their 'Sergeant Pepper' album.[1]

Many others whose coffins were transported by train, with greater or lesser degrees of ceremony, include victims of accidents, such as those killed in the Salisbury train crash in 1906, the Quintinshill railway accident in 1915 and the victims of the R101 airship disaster in 1930, and indeed the R38 airship crash before that in 1921. However, there were also hundreds, indeed thousands, of other people whose coffins were transported by train, without great ceremony, simply to get them 'home' for burial in a place that was of significance to them or their loved ones.

Read on to find out more about these people and about some of the many others whose final journey was by train. How the railways undertook this solemn transport, what equipment was used, its legacy and some quirks and curiosities related to how coffins were transported are a few of the topics covered by this book. As a mixture of railway and social history, covering an aspect of the use of trains that has never previously been addressed in this manner, this unique book is not an academic study of either railway operations or funeral transport. However, it aims to provide an insight into an area of railway activity that was affected by, and in turn influenced, the development of funeral and burial practice.

Nevertheless, the book is not just about history because the ceremonial transport of coffins still occurs on some heritage railways and has occasionally taken place on a recreated tramway. There are even three examples of railway enthusiasts, one of them very well known, who were privileged enough to have their coffin ceremonially transported on their own private railway in the grounds of their estate. To find out who they were, read on!

1

DEATH AND RAILWAYS

Thou know'st 'tis common; all that live must die
Passing through nature to eternity.

Statement by the Queen, in Shakespeare's *Hamlet*

During the nineteenth century, railways changed the world. They changed how, and how far, people travelled, where they worked, how they worked, how they spent their recreational time, the food they ate and virtually all other aspects of the ways people went about their daily activities. In short, railways changed people's lives, but what should not be overlooked is that railways also changed people's experience of death.

This was a change not just because railway accidents were the cause of death for many people, but also because of what happened to their bodies after their deaths. In total, thousands of people were killed in countless accidents all over the United Kingdom, and it took many decades before safety measures that are now regarded as essential, such as proper signalling and continuous brakes on all coaches and wagons, were introduced. Often these changes were only introduced after a terrible accident, such as the ones at Abbots Ripton,[1] in which fourteen people were killed in two collisions between three trains, and at Armagh,[2] which left eighty people dead. Even after these changes train accidents still occurred, killing railway workers and passengers alike, with two notable accidents, at Quintinshill, near Gretna in Scotland, in 1915 and Harrow and Wealdstone in 1952, each resulting in over one hundred fatalities. The former was the UK's worst-ever railway accident in terms of loss of life, with over 200 fatalities, mostly troops on their way to fight in Gallipoli during the Great War. The latter was the UK's worst peacetime railway accident. It is perhaps no coincidence that each accident involved three trains, with a third train crashing into the wreckage of an initial collision between two trains, one of which was stationary.

The development of railways in Britain, from the opening in 1830 of the Liverpool & Manchester Railway,[3] enabled people to travel further and faster than they could by horse alone or even by horse and stagecoach. The transformational impact of this on the life of the country cannot be underestimated. In the early nineteenth century this was characterised as 'the annihilation of space and time', whereby people could travel the same distance in a shorter time or a greater distance in the same amount of time. One writer on the history of railways[4] discusses this concept in greater detail and there are many books and TV programmes than cover the general impact of railways on so many aspects of Victorian life. However, this book is the first general study of how death and burial were also affected by the development of railways.

By enabling people to travel, live and work away from their 'home' area, i.e. where they had been born or brought up, the spread of railways unwittingly meant that large numbers of people died away from a place with which they had a familial connection. Nevertheless this did not override a deep and enduring human desire to be laid to rest near to home, wherever that was. Often this was not necessarily a desire articulated by the deceased themselves, but was a wish on the part of their surviving loved ones, those responsible for organising the funeral and subsequent burial.

However, the railways also provided opportunities for bodies to be transported much greater distances than was possible by horse-drawn vehicles. This enabled bodies to be buried in a greater choice of places than merely in the churchyard nearest to where the person had died.

In countless cases the availability of train services enabled bodies to be transported 'home', for example to a family burial plot[5] or for burial in a cemetery where being interred conferred or reinforced some social status, e.g. Kensal Green in west London, West Norwood in south London, or later in Brookwood near Woking. Sometimes the place of burial conferred or reinforced an even greater status, on a national scale, for example being buried in Westminster Abbey or St Paul's Cathedral, both in London.

Nowadays, in the twenty-first century, when air travel has enabled people to journey even further from home for work, holidays or just for adventure, there is still a desire by the relatives of those dying abroad to repatriate their bodies for burial or cremation in the UK. In effect this is just a modern way, using the currently available technology, of dealing with the same issue that railways dealt with, from their early days until motor hearses and cremation diminished and then terminated the role that railways played in the transportation of the dead.

The link between railways and death has a very long history, for it pre-dates even the tragic and well publicised accident that befell William Huskisson MP[6] (1770–1830) at the opening of the Liverpool & Manchester Railway in September 1830. Huskisson was a senior political figure, having been President of the Board of Trade (1823–27) and Leader of the House of Commons (1827–28), though he did not hold any government office at the time of his death. Years earlier an accident took place on the Middleton Railway near Leeds, when a 13-year-old boy named John Bruce was reported[7] to be the first member of the public killed by a steam locomotive, whilst running along the tracks. In February 1813 *The Leeds Mercury* reported the accident, saying it 'should be a warning to others'.

Sadly that warning was not heeded by William Huskisson, who disregarded instructions from the railway company not to disembark from the train in which he was travelling. Having stepped down from his train, apparently to exchange greetings with the then Prime Minister, the Duke of Wellington, he could not get back into his carriage in time to avoid being knocked down and injured, ultimately fatally, by the pioneer locomotive *Rocket*, which was being driven on the parallel track by the famous railway engineer Joseph Locke. One cause of this accident was that *Rocket* had no brakes, a deficiency which persisted in locomotive design and construction

21

for several decades, with the similar lack of brakes on coaches also being the cause of many later fatal accidents.

Although William Huskisson has gone down in railway history as being the first passenger to be killed in a train accident, he was not the first person whose coffin was transported by train. After the accident he was transported at the then unprecedented speed of 30mph to the home of a local vicar in Eccles where he died later that same day. His body was taken by horse-drawn hearse back to Liverpool, where he was buried in St James's Cemetery. Having been the Member of Parliament for Chichester, Sussex, from 1812 to 1823, a large statue of him dressed as a Roman senator was later erected in Chichester Cathedral.

Curiously, coffin transport by train later features in relation to three elements of this story. After his death in 1852 at Walmer Castle, where he had an official residence as Warden of the Cinque Ports, the Duke of Wellington's body was transported by train from Deal station to London. There he was given a lavish State funeral followed by burial in St Paul's Cathedral. *Rocket*'s driver at the time of Huskisson's accident, Joseph Locke, died in 1860 at Moffat in Dumfriesshire, Scotland, and his body was returned to England by train to allow his burial in Kensal Green Cemetery in west London. Finally in relation to this story, Chichester Cathedral became the last resting place of Prince Edward of Saxe-Weimar, whose body was taken to Chichester by train from London in 1902. The Prince was not a member of the British royal family, though he was the nephew of Queen Adelaide, consort and later widow of King William IV. The Prince's coffin was accompanied on his final journey by the Prince of Wales, later King George V, whose own coffin was transported by train from Paddington to Windsor after his death in 1936.

The early link between railways and death that was created by William Huskisson's accident did not put people off travelling by train and soon railways were being built all over the country. Although initially developed to carry freight, receipts from which exceeded revenue from passengers until well into the twentieth century, Victorian people delighted in travelling by train, with one famous actress and later writer of the time, Fanny Kemble (1809–93), describing her experience of train travel on the Liverpool & Manchester Railway in 1830 as being 'like flying', saying she 'had a perfect sense of security, and not the slightest fear'. A contemporary

Whig politician, Thomas Creevey (1768–1838), who became famous post-humously for the publication in 1903 of his 'Creevey Diaries', had spoken in similar terms in 1829. He described a trip on Stephenson's *Rocket* as 'it is really flying' though he expressed a concern that 'it is impossible to divest yourself of the notion of instant death to all upon the least accident happening.'[8] Considering the fatal encounter between *Rocket* and William Huskisson the following year, this concern seems remarkably prescient.

However, as people were to discover when powered aviation became a reality for humans after the first flight by the Wright Brothers in 1903, the technology of the early forms of these mechanised transports – trains and aircraft – was prone to failure and accidents, often fatal. Some of the earliest recorded fatalities involved railway workers, for example Thomas Port, who died in August 1838. He was a guard on the London & Birmingham Railway, which had been extended from London to Bletchley in June 1838 and was officially opened in September 1838. Port's job involved passing along the outside of the train's carriages, which in those days did not have internal corridors, to check passengers' tickets. With an almost tragic degree of inevitability, he fell from a moving train near Harrow in north-west London and was severely injured as the train passed over him. His father, from Staffordshire, touchingly arranged for his grave, in the churchyard of nearby Harrow-on-the-Hill, to be marked with a headstone that records in some detail the manner of his death. The writing on the headstone is worth setting out, as it shows the rather florid, even gruesome, language used in early Victorian descriptions of accidents.

THOMAS PORT'S HEADSTONE – Harrow-on-the Hill, London. (Unknown author, 1838)

TO THE MEMORY OF
THOMAS PORT
SON OF JOHN PORT OF BURTON UPON TRENT
IN THE COUNTY OF STAFFORD
HAT MANUFACTURER
WHO NEAR THIS TOWN HAD BOTH HIS LEGS
SEVERED FROM HIS BODY BY THE RAILWAY TRAIN

WITH THE GREATEST FORTITUDE
HE BORE A SECOND AMPUTATION BY THE SURGEONS
AND DIED FROM LOSS OF BLOOD
AUGUST 7TH, 1838 AGED 33 YEARS

Bright rose the morn and vig'rous' rose poor Port
Gay on the train he used his wonted sport.
Ere noon arrived his mangled form they bore,
With pain distorted and o'erwhelmed with gore:
When evening came to close the fatal day,
A mutilated corpse the sufferer lay.

History has been enriched by John Port's ability to memorialise his son in this way, though it is noticeable that the father has taken the opportunity to credit himself on the headstone almost as prominently as his son's name. Sadly, Thomas Port's widow and two children do not receive a mention on the headstone, as is often the case with memorials to people killed in accidents.

Another example of a fatal accident in the early days of the railways took place at Bromsgrove, Worcestershire, on the Birmingham and Gloucester Railway on 10 November 1840. A locomotive named *Surprise* (previously named *Victoria* but later renamed *Eclipse* after a new boiler was fitted)[9] was being assessed for purchase when its boiler exploded, no doubt causing both consternation and surprise, as well as several injuries. More seriously, it also caused the deaths of Thomas Scaife and Joseph Rutherford, respectively the driver and fireman of the locomotive, though in the language of the time they were both described as 'engineer'. They were buried in the nearby churchyard of St John the Baptist church, and two adjacent headstones were erected in 1841 and 1842. The one for Joseph Rutherford was 'erected by his affectionate widow' in 1841 and, clearly with a degree of co-ordination, a headstone of very similar design for Thomas Scaife was erected 'at the joint expence [sic] of his fellow workmen' in 1842.

Curiously, the locomotive depicted on the headstones is not *Surprise*, a British-built 0-2-2 well-tank design, as perhaps this would have perpetuated bad memories of the accident. Instead the locomotive shown

Headstones in St John's churchyard, Bromsgrove, Worcestershire, to victims of a boiler explosion in 1840. (© Nicolas Wheatley)

in mirror image on the headstones is an American-built Norris 2-4-0 design that was only introduced to the Birmingham and Gloucester Railway in 1842. In trials in the US the design had proved itself capable of hauling trains up steep inclines, so it was suitable for hauling trains up the steep Lickey Incline that runs northwards from Bromsgrove. The headstones are made of soft sandstone, which is prone to deterioration, but given their historic value they have been restored several times since they were erected. A photo taken soon after a more recent restoration appears above, but it is worth setting out the wording of these wonderful memorials to the lives lost in the early days of unsafe railway technology.

BROMSGROVE HEADSTONE POEMS (unknown authors, 1840)

Thomas Scaife's headstone reads:

SACRED

TO THE MEMORY OF THOMAS SCAIFE.

Late an Engineer on the Birmingham and Gloucester Railway
Who lost his life at Bromsgrove Station by the Explosion of
An Engine Boiler on Tuesday the 10th of November 1840.

He was 28 Years of Age, highly esteemed by his fellow workmen
For his many amiable qualities, and his Death will long be lamented
By all those who had the pleasure of his acquaintance.

The following lines were composed by an unknown Friend
As a Memento of the worthiness of the Deceased.

My engine now is cold and still.
No water does my boiler fill:
My coke affords its flames no more
My days of usefulness are o'er
My wheels deny their note speed.
No more my guiding hands they heed.
My whistle too, has lost its tone.
My valves are now thrown open wide.

My flanges all refuse to guide.
My clacks also once so strong
Refuse to aid the busy throng
No more I feel each urging breath
My steam is now condens'd in death
Life's railway's o'er each station past.
In death I'm stopped and rest at last.
Farewell dear friends and cease to weep.
In Christ I'm SAFE, in Him I sleep.

Joseph Rutherford's headstone reads:

SACRED
TO THE MEMORY OF
JOSEPH RUTHERFORD
LATE ENGINEER TO THE BIRMINGHAM AND
GLOUCESTER
RAILWAY COMPANY

Who died Nov 11th 1840 Aged 32 Years

Oh! Reader stay, and cast an eye
Upon this Grave wherein I lie
For cruel Death has challenged me.
And soon alas will call on thee:
Repent in time, make no delay
For Christ will call you all away.

My time was spent like a day in sun.
Beyond all cure my glass is run.

It will be noted that the deaths of Thomas Port, Thomas Scaife and Joseph Rutherford were all followed by burial in a nearby churchyard. It is not clear where their home towns or villages were, but the earliest identified (so far) transport of a coffin by train was in 1840, from London to Derby. This will be covered in greater detail in Chapter 2.

It was not only railway workers who lost their lives in train accidents in the early days. Shortly before 7.00 a.m. on 24 December 1841, an accident occurred in Sonning Cutting near Reading when a heavily laden luggage (goods) train ran into a blockage caused by an embankment which had slipped on to the track a few hours earlier. There were three open waggons carrying thirty-eight passengers, described as being 'chiefly of the poorer class', coupled between the tender of the locomotive and the following luggage waggons. The accident was reported in *The Times* newspaper on Christmas Day under the headline 'Frightful Accident on Great Western Railway'. Altogether nine people were killed and the accident was widely reported at the time. An inquest into the deaths of the eight people killed at the scene was held within only a few days, but one passenger died six days after the accident, so another inquest was held, giving the story added coverage in the press and no doubt impressing upon the minds of early Victorians that railways could be dangerous. This was the first major accident on the developing railway network at the time and was a rare mass casualty event on the Great Western Railway, which later generally had a safety record that was better than many other railway companies.

Another accident that would have alarmed early Victorian railway travellers occurred not in Britain but outside Paris, France, in May 1842, though it was widely reported in the UK and across Europe. A heavily laden train was carrying people who had been at celebrations at the Palace of Versailles marking King Louis Philippe's saint day back to Paris. An axle on the leading of two locomotives broke, causing a derailment. This resulted in the fire being spilled from the engine and when the rest of the train passed over the initial wreckage the carriages caught fire. The continental practice at the time was to lock the doors from the outside and many people were thus trapped inside the burning carriages. The fire was so intense that the number of casualties could not be definitively stated, but estimates of the number of deaths vary from 52 to 200 and it was the world's worst railway accident at the time.

It was not surprising therefore that Victorian travellers developed a wariness, if not a fear, of train travel, though that did not put them off travelling in ever greater numbers. Advice was provided to people on how to use trains, for example in the 'Handy Guide to Railway Travel', which was published in 1862 and contained a chapter entitled 'how to act in cases of threatened accidents'. This book was reprinted in facsimile form in 2010, with a cartoon on the cover that was first published in the popular satirical *Punch* magazine, in 1852, with the title *Railway Undertaking*. This shows an undertaker offering his business card to a nervous-looking traveller, thus reinforcing any fears of an accident befalling him that the traveller may have already had.

For reasons that probably need further research, excursion trains feature prominently in major accidents throughout the nineteenth century. In 1870 an excursion train hit a wagon that had derailed when its axle broke, resulting in sixteen deaths in the ensuing accident near Newark,

Cartoon from *Punch*, 1852, Vol XXIII. An undertaker offers a puzzled traveller a business card: a comment on the dubious safety of rail travel. (Mary Evans Picture Library, 10724739)

Lincolnshire. This led to another popular magazine of the time, *Tomahawk*, publishing on 9 July 1870 a cartoon called *Waiting for the Excursion!* showing a skeleton dressed as a railway worker holding a lamp at a darkened station whilst a train approaches from the distance. The skeleton appears to be holding a lever for some points visible on the track, perhaps intending to derail the excursion train thereby causing some casualties.

Only four years later, on Christmas Eve 1874, the Great Western Railway (GWR) suffered its worst ever accident in terms of loss of life, though strangely this accident is not mentioned in some histories of the GWR. No fewer than thirty-four people lost their lives when a part of a heavily laden train bound for Birkenhead, via Birmingham Snow Hill, taking many people home for Christmas derailed at Hampton Gay, near Shipton-on-Cherwell, north of Oxford. A metal tyre had broken on the wheel of an old carriage that had been added to the scheduled service to accommodate the extra travellers. By an unfortunate twist of fate the derailment took place on an embankment next to where the railway crossed the River Cherwell and the Oxford and Birmingham canal. Although the derailed carriage crossed the river bridge, it plunged down the embankment, taking some of the other carriages with it, one of which fell into the canal. Many of the dead were taken to the paper store of nearby Hampton Gay mill, but some of the injured were transported by train back to Oxford. Sadly three died on the way and their bodies were kept in the second-class waiting room at Oxford station until the inquest was held a few days later. Afterwards many corpses were taken by train back to their home communities in the north, enabling them to complete their final journey, and only one victim, Benjamin Taylor from Wolverhampton, is buried in the churchyard of St Giles, Hampton Gay.

There were many other serious railway accidents in mid-Victorian times, including Clayton Tunnel (1861, twenty-three dead), Thorpe (Norwich), (1874, twenty-five dead), Abbots Ripton (1876, fourteen dead) and the Tay Bridge disaster (1879, estimated seventy-five dead) to name just a few of the well-known worst ones. Worse than any of these, however, was the Armagh accident in 1889, in what is now Northern Ireland, when no fewer than eighty people were killed, many of them children on a Sunday school outing. Another accident occurred in June 1897 to an excursion train returning from Barmouth, on the mid-Welsh coast, to Royton, near

Oldham in Lancashire. On a stretch of line near Welshampton, in North Wales, the train derailed initially causing nine fatalities, whose remains were returned home by train the following day. A further two people died in hospital and their remains were probably sent back home by train later. Although only the last two of these accidents specifically involved excursion trains, it is not surprising that there was a fear of railway travel amongst some Victorian people.

Indeed, even Queen Victoria herself, who first travelled by train from Slough in 1842, to go back to London after staying at Windsor, was still wary of trains thirty years later. On 3 October 1873 she is recorded[10] as having written to her least favourite Prime Minister[11] stating:

> The Queen must again bring most seriously & earnestly before Mr Gladstone & the Cabinet the very alarming and serious state of the Railways. Every day almost something occurs & every body trembles for their friends & for every one's life … There *must* be fewer Trains, - the speed must be lessened to enable them to be stopped easily in case of danger & they must keep their time.

Once again *Punch* was able to feed into these fears with a cartoon showing passengers queuing to buy tickets for an excursion train which are being sold by a skeleton dressed as a railway worker. Taking its title from a notice on the side of the ticket office wall – 'There and Back' – the cartoon is entitled *There and (Not) Back*.

Despite this, the railway historian Wolfgang Schivelbusch opines that 'the ever present fear of a potential disaster remained, however, only until the railroad had become part of normal everyday life. By the time Western Europe had culturally and psychically assimilated the railroad, that is, by the mid-19th century, these anxieties had vanished.'[12] However, this view is not borne out on the evidence of *Punch*'s cartoon published in September 1878.

Part of the problem lay with the attitude of the railway companies themselves, which were slow to adopt and implement safety systems. The high (or low) point of this attitude was stated in chilling terms by the response from Frederick Slight, the Secretary of the London Brighton & South Coast Railway (LB&SC) to the report by Captain Tyler of the Board of Trade[13] following his investigation into the Clayton Tunnel accident.

Cartoon from *Punch*, 1878. Rail Accident Risk/There and (not) Back. A satirical comment on the remarkably high accident rate of excursion trains. (Mary Evans Picture Library, 10091754)

He had recommended improved signalling and the introduction of an absolute block system, whereby trains would not permitted to enter a section of line until it had been confirmed by telegraphic means that any preceding train had cleared that section. The response was that:

> my board feel bound to state frankly that they have not seen reason to alter their views which they have so long entertained on this subject and they still fear that the telegraphic system of working recommended by the Board of Trade will, by transferring much of the responsibility from the engine drivers, augment rather than diminish the risk of accident. Indeed they think it is open to grave doubt whether the circumstances of the serious collision in question do not, when fairly considered, tend to prove that the increasing practice of multiplying signals, and thus lessening the responsibility of the engine driver who is in charge of the motive power, and whose own life is at stake, has not resulted in reducing rather than increasing the safety of railway locomotion.[14]

The railway company were clearly of the view that the responsibility for safety should rest with the drivers, whose lives were at stake, rather than fall on the railway company to provide a safe form of operating, requiring more signalling. Thankfully this attitude did not prevail and the LB&SCR did agree to give the block system a 'fair trial' on part of their line.

Another aspect of this problem was the way that railway employees – 'servants' in the language of the time – were forced to work long hours, which could result in compromises to safety. Shifts of more than twelve hours were commonplace and being on duty for many more hours than that was not unusual, even in safety-critical roles such as signalling and driving. This sometimes led to serious accidents such as at Thirsk, North Riding of Yorkshire (1892, ten dead, signalman was exhausted due to death in family) and Eastleigh (1890, driver asleep, see below). Eventually this led to strikes in the early 1900s and the introduction of shorter working hours, but by then several accidents had taken place in which fatigue was determined to be a factor.

One of these was an accident at Eastleigh in 1890 when the driver and fireman are thought to have fallen asleep or nearly so. This led to yet another cartoon in *Punch*, this time depicting the fate of the driver,

PUNCH, OR THE LONDON CHARIVARI.—October 4, 1890.

"DEATH AND HIS BROTHER SLEEP."

Shelley.

(See Major Marindin's Report to the Board of Trade on the Railway Collision near Eastleigh.)

Cartoon from *Punch*, 1890. *Death and his Brother Sleep*. A ghostly shrouded figure haunts a collapsed train driver whilst Death drives the train. (Mary Evans Picture Library, 13048074)

entitled *Death and his Brother Sleep*. The cartoon shows the driver slumped on the floor of the locomotive whilst a ghostly shrouded figure (Death) is in charge of the train. It was produced by no less a person than Sir John Tenniel, perhaps now more famous for his illustrations of the *Alice in Wonderland* stories by Lewis Carroll than for his cartoons for *Punch*, though he drew more than 2,000 cartoons for *Punch* over a fifty-year period as its principal political cartoonist.

Along with this cartoon *Punch* published a hard-hitting poem questioning who was in charge of a train when the driver had fallen asleep through exhaustion, concluding that 'Death is in charge of the clattering train'.

DEATH AND HIS BROTHER SLEEP by 'Queen Mab'. (From *PUNCH, OR THE LONDON CHARIVARI*, 4 October, 1890)

(Major Marindin, in his Report to the Board of Trade on the railway collision at Eastleigh, attributes it to the engine-driver and stoker having 'failed to keep a proper look-out'. His opinion is, that 'both men were asleep or nearly so' owing to having been in duty for sixteen hours and a-half. 'He expresses himself in very strong terms on the great danger to the public of working engine-drivers and firemen for too great a number of hours' – *Daily Chronicle*)

Who is in charge of the clattering train?
The axles creak, and the couplings strain.
Ten minutes behind at the Junction. Yes!
And we're twenty now to the bad – no less!
We must make it up on our flight to town.
Clatter and crash! That's the last train down
Flashing by with a steamy trail.
Pile on the fuel! We must not fail.
At every mile we a minute must gain!
Who is in charge of the clattering train?

Why, flesh and blood, as a matter of course!
You may talk of iron, and prate of force:

But, after all and do what you can,
The best -and cheapest- machine is Man!
Wealth knows it well, and the hucksters feel
'Tis safer to trust them to sinew than steel.
With a bit of brain, and a conscience, behind,
Muscle works better than steam or wind.
Better, and longer, and harder all round:
And cheap, so cheap! Men superabound
Men stalwart, vigilant, patient, bold;
The stokehole's heat and the crow's-nest cold,
The choking dust of the noisome mine,
The northern blast o'er the beating brine,
With dogged valour they coolly brave;
So on rattling rail, or on wind-scourged wave,
At engine lever, at furnace front,
Or steersman's wheel, *they* must bear the brunt
Of lonely vigil or lengthened strain.
Man is in charge of the clattering train!

Man, in the shape of a modest chap
In fustian trousers and greasy cap;
A trifle stolid, and something gruff,
Yet, though unpolished, of sturdy stuff,
With grave grey eyes, and a knitted brow,
The glare of sun and the gleam of snow
Those eyes have stared on this many a year.
The crow's feet gather in mazes queer
About their corners most apt to choke
With grime of fuel and fume of smoke.
Little to tickle the artist taste-
An oil-can, a fist-full of "cotton waste",
The lever's click and the furnace gleam,
And the mingled odour of oil and steam;
These are the matters that fill the brain
Of the Man in charge of the clattering train.

Only a Man, but away at his back,
In a dozen cars, on the steely track,
A hundred passengers place their trust
In this fellow of fustian, grease, and dust.
They cheerily chat, or they calmly sleep,
Sure that the driver his watch will keep
On the night-dark track, that he will not fail.
So the thud, thud, thud of wheel upon rail
The hiss of steam-spurts athwart the dark.
Lull them into confident drowsiness. Hark!

What is that sound? 'Tis the stertorous breath
Of a slumbering man-and it smacks of death!
Full sixteen hours of continuous toil
Midst the fume of sulphur, the reek of oil,
Have told their tale on the man's tired brain,
And Death is in charge of the clattering train!

Sleep - Death's brother, as poets deem,
Stealeth soft to his side; a dream
Of home and rest on his spirit creeps,
That wearied man, as his engine leaps,
Throbbing, swaying along the line;
Those poppy fingers his head incline
Lower, lower in slumber's trance;
The shadows fleet, and the gas-gleams dance
Faster, faster in mazy flight.
As the engine flashes across the night.
Mortal muscle and human nerve
Cheap to purchase, and stout to serve
Strained too fiercely will faint and swerve.
Over-weighted, and underpaid,
This human tool of exploiting Trade,
Though tougher than leather, tenser than steel,
Fails at last for his senses reel,
His nerves collapse, and, with sleep-sealed eyes,

Prone and helpless a log he lies!
A hundred hearts beat placidly on,
Unwitting they that their warder's gone;
A hundred lips are babbling blithe,
Some seconds hence they in pain may writhe,
For the pace is hot, and the points are near,
And Sleep hath deadened the driver's ear;
And signals flash through the night in vain,
Death is in charge of the clattering train!

One can only hope that *Punch's* efforts to highlight the plight of railway servants caught in a culture of excessively long hours contributed towards improvements in their working conditions. Nevertheless, many people would pay with their lives for the gaps that existed between the benefits of train travel and the safe operation of railways that was so desperately lacking for many decades. How the impact of death on the railways was brought into a more positive role, with the development of cemeteries that were served – or planned to be served – by railways is the subject of Chapter 3. Before reaching that destination, however, it is necessary to examine the nature of funerals and what role trains played in funeral transport in the next chapter. This will provide an opportunity to consider 'what is a funeral train?'

2

FUNERALS, TRANSPORT AND BURIALS

The dread of something after death,
The undiscover'd country from whose bourn
No travellers return, puzzles the will.

Hamlet, in Shakespeare's eponymous play.

In this book it is important to understand what constitutes a funeral train, as essentially there are two types. The first is a special train used for the ceremonial transport of a coffin as part of a funeral of a high-status individual, such as for various monarchs and, most notably, as the funeral train for Sir Winston Churchill in 1965. The second type is an ordinary train, part of which is used to transport a coffin to a funeral, or from a funeral to a place of burial, referred to in this book as functional transport. Examples of each type of transport, ceremonial and functional, occur many times in this book as do some variations on each type.

This book does not cover the modern practice of placing a person's ashes in the firebox of a steam locomotive, so as to blow and scatter them through the chimney. Nor does it cover the practice of displaying a wreath on the front of a locomotive to commemorate the death of a particular individual, usually one who had a connection to the railways during their lifetime. Occasionally such people have special memorial trains run in their honour, often carrying unique headboards and sometimes giving their years of birth and death. Examples of both practices are easy to find, but to record them all would require a database the size of which would be enormous, and is outside the scope of this book.

It is, however, within its scope to examine the nature of funerals, including the different types that are encountered in this book and their component parts, which have a bearing on the type of train transport involved. In the UK there are essentially three types of funeral, the most important being state funerals, which have to be approved by Parliament and are paid for by the State. Not surprisingly, they are generally reserved for monarchs and other very significant individuals of national stature, such as Sir Winston Churchill. Of slightly lesser importance are ceremonial funerals, many features of which are similar to state funerals but are pro-vided for a wider range of individuals whose life, or the circumstances of their deaths, merits a public funeral. Often part of the cost of these is paid for from public funds of one source or another. However, by far the most common type of funeral is a private one, where the mourners are invited by the family of the deceased or whoever else is arranging the funeral, and attendance is generally restricted to those invited.

All three types of funeral are what anthropologists[1] would describe as 'Rites of Passage', such as christenings, confirmations, bar mitzvahs, graduations, weddings and several others. All involve a ceremony that marks a transition from one stage of a person's life to another and are accompanied by certain rituals, social gatherings and very often the sharing of refreshments. The unique aspect of funerals is not that they mark a transition event in a person's life but that they mark the transition between the person's life on earth and their life in the hereafter, wherever that is believed to be. In the early twenty-first century the role of organised religion and religious belief has much diminished compared to previous centuries and the role of many funerals has been changing to celebrations of the deceased's life.

In the past, however, and even now for many people, the religious aspects of traditional funerals carried great importance. These include the committal of the soul of the deceased to God and the expectation of resurrection in the future. The Christian liturgy for funerals in the Church of England[2] covers these with specific wording that is used by vicars at funerals, even if the significance of the wording is not always widely understood or its meaning appreciated by all of the mourners. Similarly, other Christian denominations, and indeed other religions, have ritual wording to cover the transition of the souls of their dead from this life to the hereafter.

Other components of funerals are also important, such as confirming the death of the person, providing an opportunity for the mourners to say goodbye, to pay their respects and to provide a focus for people to grieve and comfort each other. Funerals also are often the occasion when those left after the death start to reform their social groups or hierarchies. Another important part of funerals is the procession, an opportunity to display the deceased's coffin, if done in a glass-sided hearse (whether horse-drawn or motor vehicle), which contributes to confirming the death of the person. The procession also allows people not attending the funeral to pay their respects to the deceased as the procession – in funeral terms known as a cortege – passes by. The greater the distance travelled by the cortege, and the more important the deceased person was, the greater the numbers of people who might line the route to pay their respects. Many of these aspects underlie the way trains have been used in funerals, especially the larger ceremonial events, for example the large numbers of people who paid their respects at the lineside when the funeral trains of various monarchs and for Sir Winston Churchill passed by. These are matters that will be covered in greater detail in later chapters.

After any death and funeral there is a requirement to 'dispose' of the body. Whilst this term is not in everyday use by the general public, it is the preferred term used by the funeral industry and others[3] to describe what must be done to the deceased's corpse to avoid causing a nuisance to the health of the living. Though not many people think about this aspect of death, the inevitable decomposition of a body means that it must be dealt with in a way that prevents harm to the living. Initially this can be by embalming, but later must be by burial or, ever increasingly from the late nineteenth century onwards, by cremation.

Since the beginning of civilization, special places have been set aside by almost all societies for the disposal of their dead, most commonly by burial but sometimes by cremation or, very occasionally, by other methods such as 'sky burials' where bodies are left out to be consumed by birds of prey. Although sky burials have never featured in Western civilization, cremation was a practice known as far back as prehistoric times. For example, many special urns, called cists, containing cremated human remains have been found at Stonehenge; indeed cremation is the form of disposal favoured by certain religions, e.g. Sikhs. However, until the reintroduction of cremation in England in the very late nineteenth century, which did not really become significant until well into the twentieth century, the main method of disposal of the dead in Britain was by burial.

The need to bury bodies in a special place gave rise immediately to the need to transport the deceased from where they died to that special place. Over many centuries how this was done changed, according to the technology of the times and how far that technology enabled the dead to be transported, at a realistic cost. Once Christianity had spread across the country, with churches and their surrounding churchyards – commonly known as 'God's Acres' – people would be buried in the churchyard of the parish where they lived; indeed they had a right under church law to be buried there. By the thirteenth century it was the norm for people to be buried in the churchyard of their local church, though until about the mid-nineteenth century this did not guarantee an individual plot in perpetuity, as would be expected today.

If they died within the parish boundaries, their coffins would be carried to the churchyard by their relatives, friends or other surviving parishioners, known historically as a 'walking funeral'. However, if the parish covered a large area, for example in rural areas, or if a person died in another parish, there would be recognised 'corpse roads' along which coffins could be carried to reach the churchyard where the burial was to take place. Some vestiges of these corpse roads still exist, though they are no longer used to transport coffins, being retained as historical reminders of past practices. Examples can be found in the Lake District, between Rydal and Ambleside, and in Gloucestershire where there were two corpse roads leading to Blockley, one from Aston and the other from Stretton-on-Fosse, which is actually in Warwickshire.

Sometimes the corpse road itself no longer exists but features along its route still survive. One such case can be found in Hanbury, Worcestershire, where Bridge 34 over the Worcester & Birmingham Canal is marked on several maps as 'Coffin Bridge'. Apparently the promoters of the canal (built between 1792 and 1815) were obliged to provide this bridge to maintain continuity of a footpath, which no longer exists but is believed to have been a corpse path, that led from Huntingdrop to the nearby (now closed) church at Hadzor. The bridge was constructed in 1815 but was deliberately built too narrow, at only 3ft, for the local farmer to take his vehicles across, it being just wide enough for a coffin to be taken across on a wheeled bier.[4]

As technology developed, horses and carts were used to transport coffins, though obviously this also required recognised routes, often early forms of roads. These were not the well-constructed and tarmac-covered structures that would be recognised today, but this method of transport enabled coffins to be transported greater distances. Indeed the development of roads that were maintained by the payments charged for their use – the original turnpikes – led to the growing ability of people to travel greater distances more easily, either on horseback or in the developing network of stagecoaches, which were an early form of public transport. Although canals started to spread across the country during the latter part of the eighteenth century, these were rarely used for passenger transport and were too slow for use as funeral transport, given the problems of decomposition in the days before embalming.

There were, however, some exceptions to the general rule that people were buried locally to where they died, but this depended very much on the status of the individual and the ability of their survivors to pay the necessary transport costs. One example is Admiral Lord Nelson, whose famous death during the Battle of Trafalgar in 1805 was well recorded. His remains were repatriated to the UK in a barrel of brandy, an unusual but apparently effective preservative, to enable him to be buried as the nation's hero in St Paul's Cathedral.

A much earlier long-distance coffin transport resulted in a railway connection that is perhaps largely forgotten these days. Following Queen Eleanor of Castille's death at Harby, Nottinghamshire, in 1290, her husband King Edward I arranged for the transport of her body to London for burial in Westminster Abbey. Her final journey took twelve days and stone crosses were later erected in several places where the body and its accompanying cortege had rested overnight. The last and most elaborate of these 'Eleanor

Crosses', as they became known, was erected in London, in a location outside the Royal Mews, Charing, near the top of what is now Whitehall. The area later became known as Charing Cross but the actual cross itself was demolished in 1647. When the South Eastern Railway Company built its new terminus in 1864 near to the area it became, and is still, known as Charing Cross station and in 1865 a new cross was erected in front of the railway's hotel. Probably few people using Charing Cross station realise that its name derives from a monument to a Queen who made her final journey over 700 years ago using the technology of the time. Sadly no one who made their final journey by the Victorian technology of a train has ever been memorialised in such a significant manner.

Until the mid-nineteenth century, for most people burial would have been in the churchyard of the local parish church; indeed, as noted above, people had a right to be buried in the churchyard of the parish where they lived. For many centuries this did not cause any problems, as bodies decomposed at least as fast as more people were buried and the population of the country was largely spread out, with few towns having a large number of inhabitants, especially outside London. Additionally, most of the people who died were not wealthy enough to be memorialised with stone monuments that took up valuable space in the burial ground. In rural areas there was always the option of extending the churchyard into adjoining land if it became full.

However, the development and spread of railways across the UK virtually coincided with changes in burial practice, particularly the practice of interment in individual graves, which had started in the late seventeenth century and had become the norm by mid-Victorian times. The development of railways also coincided with, and to some extent influenced, the development of new types of burial locations, such as garden cemeteries, as mentioned in Chapter 3. The practice of burying people in individual graves in the churchyard of the parish where they lived or died started to cause many problems when the industrial revolution that commenced in the late eighteenth century led to rapid increases in population and a greater concentration of people in urban areas.

This population growth had many negative impacts in urban areas, particularly in terms of overcrowded housing, inadequate supplies of clean water and poor sanitation, and forced people to live in such close proximity to each other that the spread of diseases was almost unstoppable. This caused an increase in the death rate and, as there were greater numbers of people living in urban areas, it also caused a considerable pressure on churchyards in those areas for the burial of the dead. This led to the serious overcrowding of some churchyards, with some horrific cases of corpses being disturbed by later burials, bones being spread around, dreadful odours were released and distressing sights were commonplace in many churchyards in urban areas, particularly in London. The details of these occurrences are well recorded in contemporary studies, such as George Alfred Walker's *Gatherings from Grave Yards*, published in 1839, and more recently have been detailed in several books, for example Catharine Arnold's *Necropolis: London and its Dead*.[5]

Eventually the need for more burial space was recognised, although the Church of England did not provide it and it fell to the expanding range of private enterprise to meet the demand. In due course, a series of large cemeteries was built in what were then the outskirts of London. In total seven new burial facilities were provided by private companies, and these became known as the 'magnificent seven', being cemeteries at Kensal Green (1833); West Norwood (1837); Highgate (1839); Brompton, Abney Park and Nunhead (all 1840); and Tower Hamlets (1841). Other new cemeteries were built by private enterprise in other parts of the country, such as The Rosary in Norwich (opened in 1819 but little used for many years), St James' in Liverpool (1829) and the Necropolis in Glasgow (1832). These were all close enough to the centres of population for the deceased who were to be buried in them to be transported there by horse-drawn hearses.

However, almost contemporaneously with the development of these cemeteries, the railway network was developing, providing more links between cities, such as Liverpool to Manchester (1830), London to Birmingham (1838), London to Bristol (1841) and Birmingham to Gloucester (1840), then on to Bristol (1845). Many other routes were completed, especially during the 'Railway Mania' of the mid 1840s. No fewer than 6,220 miles of railway were built, having been authorised between 1844 and 1846, before economic forces caused the collapse of investment in railway projects. However, investment was gradually revived, though on a lesser scale, and railways continued to be built all over the country until the network reached its zenith in the early 1900s, when the UK had over 22,000 miles of lines – the current total is about 11,000 miles.

As a result of this expansion of the railway network, virtually every town of note, and a great many smaller communities, were served by, or were close to, a railway line. This enabled people to travel relatively easily to or from a previously unreachable number of places. It also enabled a limitless range of goods and produce to be transported between anywhere that had a station, or at the very least a siding where goods could be loaded or unloaded. It was not long before it was realised that the dead could also be transported by train, either back to their 'home community' or to a place of burial that had some significance to them or their relatives.

The earliest records of coffin transport by train may not have survived, but Dr Brian Parsons is to be congratulated and thanked for having found a record in the archives[6] of Westminster City Council of a coffin that was transported from London to Derby in 1840. This is, so far, the earliest documented example of a coffin being transported by train, though the deceased required a convoluted final journey to reach their destination. Nowadays it would be a straightforward trip from St Pancras station up the Midlands main line to Derby. However, this route was not available in 1840, so the coffin was transported on the London and Birmingham Railway from Euston station[7] to Rugby, then probably changed trains to travel on the Midlands Counties Railway via Leicester before eventually reaching Derby. The route to Leicester from Rugby opened only on 1 July 1840, so the transport of a coffin on 22 August 1840 was almost certainly the first time a coffin had been transported on this line. The cost is recorded as being £6 16s, a considerable sum for the time, so the deceased must have been a person of some importance for their relatives to pay for this repatriation. The transportation was organised by the London funeral firm of William Garstin, whose records are now held in Westminster Archives. William Garstin had been founded in 1834 and became undertakers to London society in the nineteenth century, which underlines the importance of the deceased whose coffin was transported in 1840.

Another early example of coffin transport by train involved a member of the royal family. Indeed, this has been noted as the first time a member of the royal family had their coffin transported by train.[8] In November 1844 Princess Sophia Matilda of Gloucester died aged 71 at her home, the Ranger's House, in Blackheath in south-east London. She was a great-granddaughter of King George II of the United Kingdom through the

THE FUNERAL PROCESSION OF THE PRINCESS SOPHIA LEAVING HER HOUSE, BLACKHEATH.

The 1844 funeral procession of Princess Sophia Matilda of Gloucester, leaving her home, The Rangers House, Blackheath, London. (Mary Evans Picture Library, 10114814)

male line of descent. This entitled her to burial in St George's Chapel, Windsor, and her remains were taken by train from Paddington station to Slough. The train could not proceed to Windsor, as did many later royal funeral trains, as the branch from Slough to Windsor Central station was only built in 1849. A further significance of the Princess's funeral was that the procession from Blackheath was depicted in an engraving which appeared in the *Illustrated London News*.

This image is the earliest so far discovered of a funeral that involved the transport of a coffin by train and was no doubt produced because of the status of the deceased. The size of the procession is particularly impressive, another reflection of the Princess's royal status. Many, though not all, later royal burials in Windsor were preceded by the transportation there of the deceased's coffin by train, the most recent ceremonial royal funeral train being that for King George VI in 1952,[9] which will be covered in greater detail later in Chapter 6. However, in December 1956 the body of Princess

Marie Louise of Schleswig-Holstein (1872–1956), a granddaughter of Queen Victoria, was taken by train from London to Windsor in a coach within the royal train, possibly the same vehicle as used to transport the late king's coffin. This event was not, however, accompanied by as much ceremony as would be expected for a monarch's funeral train.

There is other evidence that some coffins were already being transported by train during the 1840s. A Report by the General Board of Health, published in February 1850, led to the Bill which became the Metropolitan Interments Act in August 1850, proposed in Conclusion 4:

> That, considering the river as a highway passing through the largest extent of densely-peopled districts, the facilities for establishing houses of reception on its banks, the conveniences arising from the shorter distances within the larger portion of the same area for the removal of the bodies to such houses of reception, the advantages of steam-boat conveyance over that by railway in respect of tranquillity, and the avoidance of any large number of funerals at any one point at any one time, and of any interference with the common traffic and the throng of streets: and, lastly, taking into account its comparative cheapness, it is desirable that the chief metropolitan cemetery should be in some eligible situation accessible by water-carriage.

Several points should be noted from this conclusion, including the introduction of the idea of 'houses of reception' and a 'chief metropolitan cemetery' to be located by the riverside 'accessible by water-carriage'. These will be considered further in the next chapter, but for now it is worth noting that the transport of the dead by steamboats was considered to have 'advantages ... over that by railway' in terms of tranquillity. Whether that would have been the case will remain a mystery as steamboats never became a significant means of transporting the dead. What is notable, however, is that even by the time this report was published in early 1850, the concept, and probably the developing practice, of transporting bodies by train was something that was important enough to be commented upon in an official report.

Further evidence of the early role of railways in the transportation of the dead comes from an unusual but quite charming memorial, inscribed with a poem entitled 'The Spiritual Railway', to be found in Ely Cathedral in Cambridgeshire. It is located just outside the door exiting from the south aisle. This memorial has been described as a tombstone,[10] though there is no evidence that it ever performed such a function. In a way very similar to the headstones in Bromsgrove churchyard (see Chapter 1), this memorial records the deaths of two locomotive crew killed on the railway, followed by a poem related to their fate. In this case the accident commemorated occurred on 24 December 1845, near Harling Road on the line to Thetford from Norwich in East Anglia. At the time of the accident the line to London through Thetford was the only route from Norwich to the capital, the direct rail line through Diss not being opened until 1849. The line between London and Norwich, via Cambridge, Ely and Thetford, had only been open since 30 July 1845, so this accident took place very early on in its existence.

In the official Board of Trade Report dated 1 January 1846 by C. W. Pasley (Major-General and Inspector-General of Railways), it is recorded that the train was the 11.30 a.m. departure from Norwich, and the accident took place about 12.30 p.m. on a long downward gradient of 1 in 200 towards London, between Harling and Thetford, about 8 miles to the west. In fact the Coroner's Death Certificate records the driver's place of death as Croxton. The cause of the accident was determined to be excessive speed going down the incline, causing the locomotive and tender to derail, with the front vehicles of the train coming off the rails. Only the front luggage van was destroyed, though the next two coaches, both second class, did overturn down the embankment. The Board of Trade report confirms that no passengers were seriously injured but the driver died instantly; the fireman was reported[11] to be terribly mutilated and died shortly afterwards.

The Coroner's Death Certificate dated 5 February 1846[12] gives the driver's cause of death as 'lost his life by the upsetting of a locomotive steam engine which was driven at an excessive and unnecessary velocity'. Although publicly blamed for the accident, this damage to the driver's reputation did not prevent the creation of the memorial plaque to him and his fireman. It is worth setting out the wording of the plaque and a photograph of it appears below on page 51.

In Memory of
WILLIAM PICKERING
Who died Dec 24 1845
AGED 30 YEARS

Also RICHARD EDGER
Who died Dec 24 1845
AGED 24 YEARS

THE SPIRITUAL RAILWAY

The Line to Heaven by Christ was made
With heavenly truth the Rails are laid,
From Earth to Heaven the Line extends
To Life eternal where it ends
Repentance is the Station then
Where Passengers are taken in,
No fee for them is there to pay
For Jesus is himself the way
God's Word is the First Engineer
It points the way to Heaven so dear
Through tunnels dark and dreary here
It does the way to Glory steer
God's Love the Fire, his truth the Steam
Which drives the Engine and the Train,
All you who would to Glory ride
Must come to Christ, in him abide
In First and Second and Third Class
Repentance, Faith and Holiness
You must the way to Glory gain
Or you with Christ will not remain
Come then poor Sinners, now's the time
At any Station on the Line
If you'll repent and turn from sin
The Train will stop and take you in.

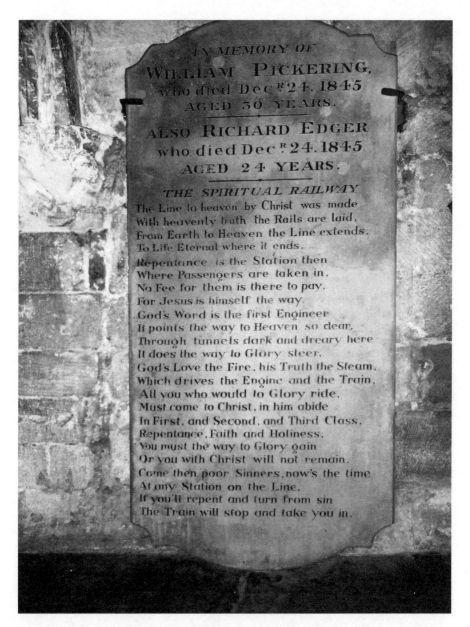

'Tombstone' monument in Ely Cathedral, Cambridgeshire to victims of railway accident in 1845. (Photograph © Nicolas Wheatley)

This memorial now survives as a wonderful early Victorian expression of the relationship between religion and the relatively new railways. It explicitly uses the metaphor of the railway to urge 'poor Sinners' to repent so that they can 'to Glory ride' using the train on 'the Line to Heaven'. Even though this memorial does not specifically record the transport of a coffin by train, its entreaties to use the railway to reach heaven would not have been misunderstood by the early Victorians.

This poem may be the first to use the metaphor of a train to take the deceased to heaven but such imagery has, like railways themselves, become embedded in people's psyche. There are other examples of the genre which have been used in twenty-first-century funerals in Chapter 14, together with a wistful poem about a train full of souls coming to take a person on their final journey, also in Chapter 14.

It has been suggested[13] that one of the functions of a funeral is to 'get deceased where they need to go and bereaved where they need to be'. The ritual, social and other aspects of the funeral, as mentioned above, contribute towards the bereaved achieving the latter part of this function, whilst the spiritual and religious aspects contribute towards the soul of the deceased achieving the first part. However, the role of funeral transport is crucial to enabling the body of the deceased to achieve the first part and the function that trains played in that role now forms the remainder of this book. The starting point is the proposal that cemeteries should be served by railway lines. Who made this proposal and the extent to which such links were developed, successfully or otherwise, is the subject of the next chapter.

3

CEMETERIES AND THEIR RAIL LINKS, ACTUAL OR PLANNED

Chapter 2 has covered the importance of transport as part of funerals and the need for transport after a funeral to take the body to a place of burial. It has been noted that coffins were transported by train from as early as 1840 and a member of the extended royal family had her coffin taken by train in 1844, only seven years into Queen Victoria's reign. The Queen herself became the first British monarch to have their coffin transported by train at the end of her long reign in 1901, but between these dates the railway network had expanded significantly and the use of trains to transport coffins around the country had become common place. Such transport was mostly of single coffins carried on ordinary trains, i.e. trains that were already scheduled in the timetable to run.

Almost contemporaneously with the development of the railway network, new forms of cemetery, which became known as garden cemeteries, were being established around the country. These were developed by private enterprise and included the Rosary Norwich (laid out in 1819 but the first burial was only in 1821), St James' Liverpool (1829) and the Glasgow Necropolis (1832). The great Scottish-born landscape designer John Claudius Loudon (1783–1843), who became the doyen of cemetery design, proposed that cemeteries should be developed around London. In

Luggage label, 'Bury, Midland Railway'. (Author's Collection)

a letter in 1830 to the *Morning Advertiser* he wrote: 'allow me to suggest that there should be several burial grounds, all, as far as practicable, equidistant from each other and what may be considered the centre of the metropolis.' These cemeteries would take the form of an arboretum and he elaborated this idea in *The Gardener's Magazine* in 1830 proposing that:

> ... a railroad and locomotive engine might convey corpses thither once a day and company [i.e. visitors] at all hours. Those who had near relations buried in the arboretum should be free of it for seven years; all others should pay a shilling each ... the poor soil would become enriched and the trees would thrive and at half the burial fees now taken the establishment would pay.

The concept of out-of-town cemeteries was not new, as the Romans often used to bury their dead alongside the roads leading in or out of towns. Much later Sir Christopher Wren, the architect of St Paul's cathedral, had proposed in 1711 that cemeteries be built on the outskirts of London, though this suggestion was never implemented.

Following the examples of new cemeteries in other towns, private companies started to develop large garden cemeteries around London, much as Loudon had proposed. The most well-known ones are the so-called 'Magnificent Seven' built around London between 1833 and 1841. The first of these was Kensal Green (1833), followed by West Norwood (1837), Highgate (1839), Abney Park, Brompton and Nunhead (all 1840) and finally Tower Hamlets in 1841. Some of these cemeteries, Kensal Green, Brompton and West Norwood in particular, became popular with the middle and upper classes, who were able to afford elaborate monuments over their graves. Kensal Green even became the final resting place of two members of the royal family: Augustus Frederick, Duke of Sussex (1773–1843) and later his sister, Princess Sophia (1777–1848), both children of the late King George III (reigned 1760–1820).

The development of these cemeteries did not, however, solve the problem of overcrowding in the churchyards in more central areas of the metropolis, which continued to receive more corpses for burial than they could accommodate without causing public health problems. The population of London had increased from just under one million in 1801 to over two and a quarter million by 1851, with a corresponding increase in annual burials, from 49,900 in 1838 to 55,500 in 1851. Despite the growth of London from 44,800 acres in 1838 to 78,000 in 1851, the total area of burial grounds remained relatively stable, at under 300 acres, resulting in the severe overcrowding of graveyards.[1] This led to the constant reuse of graves, often with existing buried corpses being desecrated and sometimes broken up and scattered around the burial ground.

Much has been written about these terrible occurrences, from contemporary social reformers, such as Dr George Alfred Walker, whose 1839 report *Gatherings from the Grave-Yards* included in its full title the words 'the unwise and revolting custom of inhuming the dead amongst the living'. Perhaps a better-known social reformer was Edwin Chadwick, whose 1843 Supplementary Report into the *Practice of Interment in Towns* led to the Public Health Act 1848 (see below). Even Charles Dickens[2] was sufficiently appalled to refer to the problems in his literary works. More recently the burial scandals of London in the early nineteenth century have been covered in books such as J.S. Curl's *Victorian Celebration of Death* (Second Edition 2002) and the more accessible book by Catharine Arnold, *Necropolis: London and its Dead*.[3]

What Loudon, and many others at the time, was concerned about was the cost of funerals for paupers, i.e. people of limited financial means, or who in modern parlance would be described as people from the lower socio-economic classes. It was his ideas that eventually led to the development of the large cemetery near Woking, the Brookwood Necropolis,[4] which became the only major cemetery in the UK to have its own dedicated railway service. It is worth analysing what Loudon proposed to understand how the railway service to Brookwood eventually came about. His proposals were set out in the book for which he is best remembered, a book which remains the most comprehensive work published on the design of cemeteries.

In *On the laying out, planting and management of cemeteries*, published shortly before his death in December 1843, Loudon expressed a view that the price of land in London for new burial grounds for paupers was too high. He wrote:

> the price of land, within ten miles of London, is much too high to admit of burying paupers singly in the London cemeteries: but one thousand, or even two thousand, acres of poor waste land, admirably adapted for burying-ground, might be purchased in the parishes of Woking, Chobham, Horsall, Perbright [sic, the modern spelling is Pirbright], Pyrford, & etc, at from £4 to £8 per acre.[5]

These are all places to the south-west of London, in the county of Surrey.

He made a suggestion 'with a view to the interment of the poor, of paupers, and of such persons as desire no monuments to their graves belonging to London'. He proposed temporary cemeteries to be leased for a period of twenty-one years, in which burials would cease after fourteen years and then after a further seven years would revert to their landlords 'to be cultivated, planted or laid down in grass, in any manner that may be thought proper'. The link with railways came in his view that:

> we see no objection for the taking of land for temporary cemeteries at a considerable distance from a town, provided it were on the line of a railway, as, for example, Bagshot Heath; and we can see no difficulty in the different districts of a city as London having a place of temporary deposit for their dead, whether paupers who paid nothing, or poor persons who paid moderately.[6]

One of the causes of ill health to poorer people at this time was the keeping of the corpses of family members in their homes until burial, which could take a week or more. This was a particular problem because in areas such as Whitechapel in east London, and indeed in many other poorer parts of the capital, nearly all the labouring classes lived in only one room, so corpses were kept in the same room where the residents slept and ate their meals. Many medical men at the time believed that 'miasma', something in the atmosphere caused by decaying organic matter (such as decomposing corpses) was a cause of sickness and death.

Loudon had seen on his travels, particularly in Frankfurt and Munich, Germany, that places for temporary deposit for the dead between the time of death and burial were 'found to add greatly to the convenience, economy and salubrity of persons having only small dwelling houses, and moderate incomes'. He went on to suggest that:

> were depositories of this kind established in the metropolis, it might be so arranged that a number of bodies should be conveyed to the place of interment at the same time, and this might be done with appropriate decency and respect in a railway or a steam-boat hearse. There are thousands of acres of the poorest gravelly soil, which the Southampton railway[7] passes through, that at present do not rent for more than 3 s[hillings] or 4 s[hillings] an acre, which would afford a cemetery for all the poor of London, and the rich also, for ages to come.[8] ... we can see no sufficient reason against having permanent monumental cemeteries, as well as temporary ones which are to have no monuments, laid out on poor soils at great distances from London, along the railroads, with cooperative railroad hearses, and other arrangements to lessen expense.

In his Introduction to the 1981 reprint of Loudon's book, Professor James Stevens Curl records that 'Loudon's advanced ideas often caused eyebrows to rise in certain quarters ... His practical notions for burying paupers out in the country near railway lines, afterwards reverting the land to agricultural use, caused offence.' Although Curl does not elaborate on why this was so, Clarke[9] records some comments from the Bishop of London expressed in 1842 before a Select Committee of the House of Commons, in which he gives his reasons for being against using railways for funeral traffic. Although speaking personally, the Bishop was effectively articulating the views of the religious establishment, i.e. the Church of England (Anglican) hierarchy. He stated: 'I consider it improper ... At present we are not sufficiently habituated to that mode of travelling not to consider the hurry and bustle connected with it as inconsistent with the solemnity of a Christian funeral.' As noted by Clarke,[10] the Bishop also found the idea of assembling a number of funerals from widely different social backgrounds in the same conveyance 'offensive' and believed that this would shock and injure the feelings of the bereaved. When asked his opinion concerning the carriage of more than one coffin, the Bishop replied:

> my impression is that they [the bereaved] would object ... It might sometimes happen that persons of opposite characters might be carried in the same conveyance, for instance, the body of some profligate spendthrift might be placed in a conveyance with the body of a respectable member of the church, which would shock the feelings of his friends; and however poor they might be, I think they would feel a pride that their relations should not be conveyed to the place of interment in the same carriage with the body of such a man.

These comments give a good insight not only into the contemporary views of the church on Victorian social-class distinctions but also into the impact of early railways on the public consciousness. As noted in Chapter 2, the 1850 Report of the General Board of Health preferred the use of steamboats to railways in terms of 'tranquillity' for carrying coffins, so the Bishop's objections to the 'hurry and bustle' of using railways for funeral transport still held some sway eight years after he expressed his views, even though some coffins had already been carried by trains by 1850. However, only a few years later some of Loudon's proposals were taken up in legislation and, eventually, by the development of Brookwood Cemetery itself. Nevertheless, the sentiments behind the Bishop of London's comments were, perhaps, one of the reasons why plans for another scheme for a rail-served cemetery, the proposed Knowle Necropolis near Birmingham, foundered (see below).

The living conditions of the poor in London had been the subject of studies by social reformers like Dr George Alfred Walker[11] (1807–1884) and

Edward Chadwick (1800–1890), whose work followed on from Walker's and whose famous Report,[12] published in 1843, alerted Victorian society to the need for reforms and improvements to public health, which were implemented by the Public Health Act 1848, and in funerals. Additional impetus was given to this need by several outbreaks of cholera, including one in 1832 and a more serious one in 1848–9,[13] causing a steep rise in the death rate and the need to find more space to bury the dead.

In consequence, the General Board of Health was set up in 1848 and their Report, published in early 1850, proposed a number of reforms, many of which were incorporated into the Metropolitan Interments Act 1850, enacted in August. The Board's Report had proposed that two large cemeteries be built for the metropolis (London and adjoining areas as defined in the 1850 Act) and that they should be accessible by river. As noted in Chapter 2, trains were already being used to transport coffins, though transport by steamboat was considered preferable. Indeed one of the two large cemeteries, the Great Eastern Metropolitan Cemetery, was proposed for a site on the east side of London, between Abbey Wood and Erith on the south bank of the River Thames. However, the practicalities of using the river to take the dead to this cemetery, with the slow speed of boats and the possible risk of decomposition during the corpses' retention in the house of reception and during the journey, do not seem to have been fully thought through. Perhaps not surprisingly, the proposal was never developed further.

The other large cemetery that was envisaged to the west of London, the Great Western Metropolitan Cemetery, was based on an expansion of Kensal Green cemetery. Although this is now located between two railway lines, the Great Western line to Bristol and the former London & Northern Western line to the north, it was never suggested that trains could be used to transport coffins to Kensal Green for burial. In fact the cemetery is adjacent to the Paddington arm of the Grand Union Canal and there was a proposal for an elaborate water gate to be built to allow coffins to be taken from canal barges directly into the cemetery. This had been included in the design by Henry Edward Kendall for the cemetery,[14] but it was not built. No evidence has been found that canals were ever significantly used as funeral transport, for the reasons stated above.

Part of Loudon's proposals was the suggestion that bodies were to be removed from a person's place of death to new 'houses of reception',

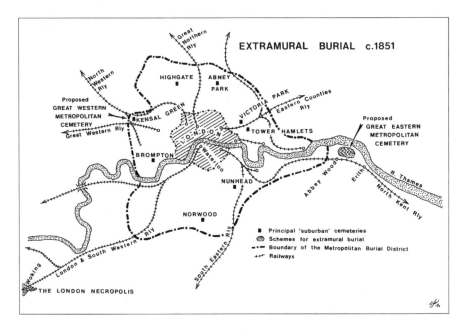

Map of cemeteries around London. (John M. Clarke Collection)

effectively local temporary mortuaries. Indeed, Section 2 of the 1850 Act set up the General Board of Health to implement its proposals and gave the Board specific powers, in Section 27, to set up houses of reception. However, these powers were only permissive and none were built under these legal powers.[15] After the repeal of the 1850 Act the permissive powers to provide houses of reception were bestowed on parish vestries, but few were provided until after 1889; even then it was well into the twentieth century before the dead were kept before burial separately from the living.[16] Arguably it was not the limited provision of houses of reception, increasingly called mortuaries after 1862, that facilitated this separation but the provision of chapels of rest by funeral directors, as part of their expanding range of services to the bereaved.

How often the bodies would be removed from any houses of reception to be taken on their final journey by boat to the proposed riverside cemetery in Kent or to the enlarged Kensal Green cemetery was never set out in any legislation. No doubt it was considered to be a matter of operational requirement. However, Section 29 of the 1850 Act also gave powers to the General Board of Health to enter into contracts with railway companies for carrying bodies together with their mourners. The actual wording reads:

> it shall be lawful for the board of health and the directors of any railway company, if they shall see fit, to contract for the carrying out of bodies in properly constructed carriages on the line of railway of such company to any burial ground provided under this Act, and for the carrying to and from such burial ground of the mourners and attendants of the bodies so carried, at such prices and charges, and for such term of years, as may be agreed.

Like Section 27, this power was permissive, i.e. the Board of Health was not obligated to enter into contracts with railway companies, but as an organisation created by statute the board could only carry out any functions for which it had been given statutory powers, under the legal doctrine of 'ultra vires'. What is particularly interesting about this Section of the 1850 Act is the wording further on in Section 29 which provides that:

> the charges agreed and contracted for with the said board shall not prejudice such railway company as to their charges for carrying any bodies other than the bodies to be removed to the burial grounds provided under this Act, or as to their charges for the general business of carrying ordinary passengers or things, any thing in any Act or special Act to the contrary notwithstanding.

The significance of this wording is the acknowledgment that railway companies could, and presumably already did, carry bodies to existing burial grounds that were not provided under the 1850 Act. No evidence has been found that any such contracts were entered into between the Board of Health and any railway companies, probably because the 1850 Act was repealed by the 1852 Act[17] almost before the Board could carry out any of its functions. It is also noteworthy that Section 29 envisaged that railways would carry the dead in 'properly constructed carriages' and indeed several railway companies eventually built their own specialist hearse vans. Sometimes these were called, in the language of the times, corpse vans and Chapter 9 provides more information on, and several photographs of, such vehicles.

The underlying intention behind the 1850 Act was, in effect, to nationalise the provision of funerals and burial grounds, but the Act was quickly repealed when it was found that its proposals were generally incapable of implementation. It was replaced by the Burial Act 1852, which prohibited any further burials in the metropolitan area and thus, perhaps inadvertently, gave a boost to Loudon's idea of using trains to take bodies to new out-of-town cemeteries. There were two cemeteries within the UK where such a service was provided and two others where plans were made which almost came to completion, as detailed below. There were also three cemeteries in Australia that became served by railways, the most famous of which was Rookwood Cemetery on the outskirts of Sydney.[18] That cemetery is still active but the railway service ceased in the 1940s.

Brookwood Necropolis Railway[19]

The railway funeral service within Britain that is well known, at least by many railway enthusiasts, is the one that ran from its own private station at Waterloo to Brookwood Cemetery near Woking, in Surrey. This ran from 1854 until April 1941, when the private station at Waterloo was bombed. The full story of this service, unique in the UK because it ran the funeral trains into a cemetery, has been told in detail by John Clarke in his book *The Brookwood Necropolis Railway*[20] and the author is grateful to him for allowing some extracts from that book to be used here. The author is also grateful to The Brookwood Cemetery Society[21] for allowing the use of some material from their publications about the railway.

It is worth noting that this was not, in fact, a railway company in its own right, but a railway service provided jointly between the London & South Western Railway company (L&SWR), which provided the motive power, and the company that operated the cemetery. This was originally called the London Necropolis and National Mausoleum Company but later became known just as the London Necropolis Company (LNC), by which name it is called in this chapter.

As recorded by Clarke, the plan for the cemetery at Brookwood was devised by Sir Richard Broun and Mr Richard Sprye at the end of 1849. This project was intended to solve the burials problem[22] in itself. The cemetery, to be situated beyond any future possible extension of London, at Woking in Surrey, could never endanger the public health of the capital, whilst its vast area would provide ample capacity for the anticipated volume of metropolitan dead for many years to come. The site could be reached cheaply and conveniently only by railway, hence the vital role of the L&SWR to the success of the enterprise, for the promoters were counting upon the cheapness of the land (hence the interments) and economy of transit to attract sufficient custom to the Necropolis. In effect, this scheme was more or less what Loudon had proposed in 1843 in his book *On the layout out, planting and management of cemeteries*, as set out above.

The LNC was created by an Act of Parliament in 1852 and bought about 2,000 acres of land from Lord Onlsow, 400 acres of which were laid out as a cemetery. A private station was built at Waterloo, next to the main terminus, with two stations being built within the cemetery, one for Anglicans, known as the South Station, and one for Non-Conformists and other denominations, known as the North Station. The cemetery was consecrated by the Bishop of Winchester on 7 November 1854 and opened to the public on 13 November 1854, when the trains began their sombre service. Clarke records that *The Spectator* reported the following day that:

> the novelty of the railway train is to have the newer novelty of the funeral train. Once a day the black line will leave the metropolis for Woking; the station will put on a funeral aspect, and death will take its turn amid the busiest traffic of life.

When the cemetery opened in 1854 it was not served by a station on the L&SWR line. Access to the cemetery, by relatives and friends of the deceased, or by other visitors, was limited to the daily funeral train, or by hiring suitable transport from Woking station (which had opened in 1838 as Woking Common and became Woking in 1843), about 2 miles away. The station at Brookwood, initially called 'Brookwood (Necropolis)' was opened in June 1864 and then was enlarged in 1890 before being virtually rebuilt in 1903 when the main line was quadrupled. The line into the cemetery came off the 'Down' line just to the south of the present station, forming a long siding, and the train was then propelled back into the cemetery. There was a run-round loop behind the station, which enabled the

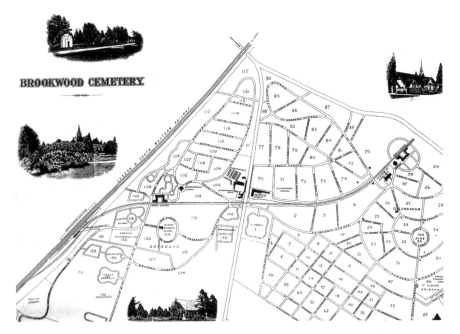

Brookwood Cemetery. Map showing layout of cemetery. (John M. Clarke Collection)

locomotive to re-couple to the front of the train for the return journey to London. Access to the 'Up' line for the return trip was by a series of cross-overs, controlled from the station by a signal box, which was also rebuilt in 1903.

Clarke also provides some information on how the service operated, noting that the funeral train was scheduled to run daily for the first few decades, being timetabled to leave at 11.35 a.m. on weekdays and 11.20 a.m. on Sundays. The LNC brochure claimed a journey time of forty minutes but this was rarely achieved until the 1920s. In reality the service was never as successful as had been envisaged, and the LNC only ever succeeded in drawing off a tiny proportion of the total metropolitan burials. For instance, during the first twenty years of the service operating (1854–74) the total number of burials in the cemetery never exceeded 4,100 in any one year, and only averaged 3,200 per annum in years when the average number of annual deaths in London was over 50,000. Indeed, from early on the regular service ran only on Tuesdays and Fridays, with other trains being provided as required, and the Sunday service was stopped from October 1900.

The train was hauled by a locomotive provided by the L&SWR, with no particular engines being dedicated to the service. From their introduction in 1897, an M7 0-4-4 tank engine[23] was usually in charge, operating in the livery of the time, i.e. L&SWR green until 1923 then in Southern Railway green until 1941 when the service terminated. Occasionally an additional carriage was added for mourners for the funeral of a special deceased. The train usually consisted of two parts, with a hearse van and two carriages for each part. One part was for Anglicans, the other for non-Anglicans, i.e. Non-Conformists, Roman Catholics and other denominations or religions. Over time the hearse vans and carriages were replaced by more modern vehicles, with the last hearse vans being built in 1899. The hearse vans were built by the L&SWR but owned by the LNC, whilst the carriage sets were owned by the L&SWR but dedicated to the funeral train service.

The usual method of operating the funeral trains in the cemetery was as follows: from the siding adjacent to the main line, the Necropolis Train was propelled through the cemetery to the North Station. Here the train was met by staff of the LNC who escorted the mourners to a private waiting room in the station, one of the chapels or the graveside, as appropriate. Meanwhile the hearse carriage was emptied of its relevant coffins (the last hearse vans built in 1899 could accommodated twenty-four each), which were placed on a special hand bier drawn by one of the LNC's staff. The LNC's Non-Conformist chaplain, and other ministers requested to officiate at the committal service, would also alight from the train. The funeral train would then proceed to the South Station where a similar procedure would take place.

After the funerals had taken place, mourners could enjoy light refreshments (and alcoholic beverages if desired) in the refreshment room attached to each of the cemetery stations. At about 2.13 p.m. the Necropolis Train left South Station for North, picking up those mourners who wished to travel to London directly; alternatively they could return to London by ordinary services departing from Brookwood station. Once at the run-round loop behind the station, the locomotive ran around the train and then propelled it into the siding adjacent to the main line. From there the train returned to Waterloo (Necropolis).

As Clarke notes in his Conclusions:[24]

when Brookwood Cemetery opened in 1854, it was the largest cemetery in the world, and the railway was the only available form of transport that could cheaply and conveniently transport coffins and mourners from London to Brookwood. This remained true for many years, and many thousands of Londoners – and others – were carried to their final resting place by this train. Yet despite the longevity of its railway funeral service, the LNC failed to attract the number of burials the cemetery was designed to accommodate. … even in its years of slow decline after World War I, (when it was derided as 'the dead meat train' or more coarsely as 'the stiff's express') still it represented a Victorian bid for more sanitary burial. Eventually the rise of motorised transport and more convenient methods of disposal succeeded in vanquishing this novel use of railway transport.

This conclusion ultimately applies generally to the functional transport of coffins by train, as will be discussed in Chapter 13. However, before that point is reached there are other cemeteries that either had a railway link or where a link was proposed but never built. An example of the former is the Great Northern London Cemetery in Southgate, whilst the City of London Cemetery in Ilford is an example of the latter. There was also a proposal, which almost came to be built, for a large cemetery on the outskirts of Birmingham, in an area now known as Dorridge. This would have been served by a railway line bringing coffins from a new station in Birmingham to be built by the Great Western Railway, and would possibly have been known as the Knowle Necropolis. It would have operated much like the railway service to Brookwood Cemetery and the reasons for it not being built have echoes of the comments of the Bishop of London, as mentioned above. These other actual or proposed links to cemeteries need examining in turn.

Great Northern London Cemetery

Apart from Brookwood, the only other cemetery in the UK that had a dedicated railway service was the Great Northern London Cemetery at Southgate. The full story of this little-known railway service was told by Martin Dawes, in his book *The End of the Line: The Story of the Railway Service to the Great Northern London Cemetery*. The book was published in 2003 by the Barnet Local History Society, to whom the author is grateful for being allowed to quote extracts. Before that book was produced very little published information about the service appears to have been in the public domain,[25] though a short article by R.G. Lucas appeared in the *Railway Magazine*, October 1954, pp.713–15, under the title 'Kings Cross Cemetery Station'. Now that historical issues of the *Railway Magazine* have been made available in their digital archive, it is possible to access this article more easily than finding a copy of the 1954 magazine.[26]

Plans were developed by the Great Northern London Cemetery Company (GLNC) in 1855 and authorised by an Act of Parliament passed on 23 July of that year. One hundred and thirty acres of land were purchased at Colney Hatch, next to the railway line northwards from Kings Cross station, run by Great Northern Railway (GNR), an unrelated company. The GNR station had been built in 1852 and in 1860 the GLNC built their funeral station, as previously agreed between the companies, on land belonging to the GNR just to the north of Gasworks tunnel on the eastern side of the main line. As recorded by Dawes:

> the building was a large, impressive affair built in the popular neo-gothic style with extensive use of different coloured brickwork. The station building was about 150 ft long and 25 ft wide, the tower with its strange wedge shaped spire adding another 20 ft in length to the northern end. It was a two-storey building which had a dual function in that as well as being a railway station with all the usual rooms and offices, it also provided extensive mortuary facilities.

Although this building was demolished in 1962, an accurate model of it was created and can be found on the well-known 00 scale model railway 'Gresley Beat'.

Kings Cross mortuary station, model on 'Gresley Beat' layout. (Photograph ©
Nicolas Wheatley)

At the northern end of the line a siding was provided between the western
part of the cemetery and the main line. The GNR station just to the south
of this location was originally called Colney Hatch but is now known as
New Southgate. Dawes tells us that:

> the platform at Colney Hatch Station was on the eastern side of the
> line and elaborate buildings were provided by the GLNC, again in
> the neo-gothic style so favoured in the latter half of the nineteenth
> century. In addition to waiting rooms, etc, a chapel was provided to the
> north of the main station building, which contained separate areas for
> varying denominations.

In that regard it was very similar to the provisions at Brookwood
Cemetery, which went one step further by having separate stations for the
different denominations.

The cemetery was consecrated on 10 July 1861 by the Bishop of Rochester, of whose diocese the parish of East Barnet was, at the time, a part. The first burial took place the next day, of a local child. The following day a burial took place of an elderly lady who had lived in Islington, north London, so she was probably the first person whose coffin was transported by train to the cemetery. The original plan was for the service to run daily, leaving Kings Cross funeral station at 11.00 a.m. and returning at 3.00 p.m., the seven-and-a-half mile journey taking roughly fifteen minutes each way.

Unlike the service to Brookwood Cemetery, however, the service to the Great Northern London Cemetery never caught on, with very low levels of usage, and it made financial losses from the start. In fact the service was so poorly used that the GLNC offered the use of the mortuary facilities at Kings Cross for free and the trains never ran a daily service as intended; indeed from the beginning of 1863 they only ran as required. As recorded by Dawes:

> 1863 saw a dramatic reduction in the service: in January there were only two trains, and in February, March and April one each, the March train being run on a Saturday. By 3rd April 1863, after less than two years of very unprofitable operation, the service ceased.

The service did apparently have a brief revival in 1866 during the last cholera outbreak in London, which was centred in the East End, causing the deaths of 5,000 people in and around the areas of Bethnal Green, Mile End, Stepney and Whitechapel. The GLNC had terminated its use of the funeral station the previous year, but it appears that some of the cholera victims made their final journey to the cemetery after being loaded onto trains at two sidings at Kings Cross goods yard, still known to railwaymen at Kings Cross as 'Cemetery Sidings' several generations later.[27]

Why did this service fail when Brookwood was more successful? The reasons given by Dawes are as follows:

1. The short distance from the city to the cemetery when compared to the only other rail-connected cemetery. (The Brookwood Necropolis).

2. The lower than expected level of initial interest in the cemetery as a place of burial for Londoners, and

3. The unexpectedly high proportion of paupers' burials.

The first factor meant that a smaller proportion of users than expected would use the train service; the other two affected severely the expected profitability of the undertaking and made the continued use of the railway an expensive luxury.

There was one other factor, noted by Dawes on page 32, which affected the demand for rail-based funeral transport, namely that 'there was considerable prejudice and opposition to be overcome'. It has been noted above that the Anglican hierarchy, for example in the form of the Bishop of London, was opposed to the transport of the dead by train, partly on account of its 'novelty' and partly because corpses of different classes and denominations might be carried by the same train. The first of these factors was, seemingly, fatal to the proposed scheme for the Knowle Necropolis near Birmingham, discussed below.

City of London Cemetery, Ilford

The City of London opened a cemetery at Ilford, to the east of London, in 1856. Prior to that, discussions had taken place between the City of London Commissioners (the Commissioners) and the board of the Eastern Counties Railway (ECR) for a railway service to deliver coffins to the cemetery. They would have been transported using the ECR's line from Bishopsgate to Romford that had opened in 1839, but ultimately the scheme was not implemented. Dr Brian Parsons has been kind enough to allow me to reproduce some text from an article he wrote about the service, which was published in the magazine of the Great Eastern Railway Society in April 2020.

As recorded by Parsons, based on the Commissioners' Minutes, the proposed working arrangements were as follows: a funeral train departs from the London terminus, halts just beyond the cemetery and reverses into the single-line bay platform. The coffins are then unloaded and deposited in the reception house (later referred to as a mortuary chamber) whilst the mourners gather in the waiting rooms. The funeral would then take place before the mourners returned by train to London. The cost of the siding and all necessary buildings within the cemetery were to be paid for by the Commissioners, who would also employ staff to load and unload the coffins at both destinations. Special trains would be provided, requiring two hearse carriages with a capacity of twenty-four coffins, along with two two–coffin-capacity hearse carriages, presumably for 'specials'. Parsons records the proposed charges as follows: artisans and paupers 5 shillings each; all higher classes 10 shillings each; special funerals 20 shillings. For mourners the charges were: First Class 3 shillings each, Second Class 2 shillings each.

Parsons notes that:

> by way of contrast, the London Necropolis Company's 1852 agreement with the London & South Western Railway (LSWR) was for the coffins containing paupers & artisans to be charged at 2 shillings and 6 pence and 5 shillings respectively. The ECR was driving a hard bargain which was probably based on the unclear level of potential traffic.

Indeed, it was this last issue which ultimately caused the proposal to founder. Parsons notes that:

> the Commissioners could not accurately predict the volume of traffic that would go by rail to the cemetery. Without this information the ECR were not prepared to invest in an exclusive funerary building and siding for the reception of coffins and to run a regular service to the cemetery.

The problem for the Commissioners was that the population of the City was falling rapidly, with figures quoted by Parsons showing that it fell by more than half between 1861 (112,063) and 1881 (51,405). In the following two decades it fell by half again, to 26,998 in 1900. This decline had started before 1861, from around 125,500 in 1849 shortly before the proposal was first considered. This caused a commensurate drop in the number of deaths and burials, as set out by Parsons. In addition, Parsons notes that not all deaths would have required the transportation of a coffin by train from London to the cemetery. The distance to the cemetery from the London terminus was only 7 miles, which was well within the capabilities of a horse-drawn hearse, as indeed occurred until the advent of motor hearses from around 1910.

As Parsons concludes:

transporting the dead by train to a cemetery appeared to be a rational and efficient use of the rail system. For the City Commissioners not only did the opening of their cemetery at Ilford demonstrate the importance of provision of sanitary burial space for their residents but also that they were willing to facilitate transport by using the most up to date means. The lack of evidence, however, to support the required investment literally derailed anything further than exploratory discussions. Had the scheme progressed it would have been a financial liability for both parties.

Indeed, as noted above, the failure of the railway service from Kings Cross to the Great Northern London Cemetery, a very similar distance and started only a few years later, only serves to reinforce this conclusion.

Knowle Necropolis, Birmingham

Another proposal in the 1850s for a cemetery to be served by a railway was made in Birmingham. Unlike the City of London scheme, the cemetery was never built but, like the Brookwood Necropolis Railway the proposal was for more or less all the dead of the nearby city (Birmingham rather than London) to be transported by train and buried in a very large cemetery beyond the built-up limits of the settlement. The author was first alerted to this proposed cemetery by a very brief mention in a book by Sarah Rutherford, *The Victorian Cemetery*,[28] which contains a cryptic reference to the scheme in just over one sentence on p.56. The story of the proposal is told in an article by the landscape architect and author J.M.L Lovie, in the *Warwickshire Gardens Trust Journal*, Autumn 2003, entitled 'The Next Train is for Knowle Necropolis Only'. The article is based on careful research in the Birmingham City archives, in particular the Minutes of the Corporation of Birmingham Burial Board and other relevant sources. The author is grateful to the Trust for supplying a copy of this article and to Jonathan Lovie for being allowed to quote extracts from it. This article, and the proposed scheme, certainly deserve to be better known.

Burials within churchyards had been prohibited in Birmingham in 1861, following an Order in Council granted in February 1858 under the provisions of the Burial Acts 1857. This was a few years after churchyard burials had been prohibited in London, but the two new cemeteries that had been provided in the city did not have sufficient capacity to meet the resultant demand. The first of these cemeteries was established by a commercial company formed predominately by Non-Conformists at Key Hill in the Jewellery Quarter and opened in 1839. The second was at Warstone Lane, also in the Jewellery Quarter, which had been established by the Birmingham Church of England Cemetery Company and opened in 1848.

The new Burial Board, also set up by the Order in Council, immediately set about finding a site for a new cemetery and reported to Birmingham Corporation in August 1858 that:

> your Committee have unanimously come to the conclusion that it will be advantageous in every respect … that one Cemetery only should be established for the Borough and that such a cemetery should be obtained if possible in a district exclusively rural or agricultural, and likely to continue so and thus at once remove the possibility of danger to health whether of the inhabitants of this Borough or of any other populous place in its vicinity …
>
> The land suitable for the purposes of a Cemetery should be accessible from a central part of the Borough by railways as a matter of obvious necessity, and in the opinion of your Committee that mode of conveyance, already extensively used in the interment of large numbers of the dead of the Metropolis will soon become the universal and only means by which the spirit of the Burial Acts can be satisfactorily complied with, by the Burial Boards of large Towns and their dead conveyed cheaply and decently to their last home, at such a distance from the habitations of the living as not to endanger the public health.

Though the Burial Board made no specific reference to Loudon's ideas about out-of-town cemeteries served by railways, the origin of the concept is obvious. Apparently the members of the Board had been authorised to visit the 'Woking Necropolis', as Brookwood Cemetery was then known, so they undoubtedly had that railway service in mind when proposing their own. The Board acknowledged that 'their propositions may be characterised (in the Midland District at least) as a novelty somewhat startling', but the City Corporation accepted their report and approved the Board taking forward the scheme for a single cemetery at a distance from the town served by rail. Eventually a site at Dorridge Farm, to the south-east of the town was identified, providing 135 acres to the north of the Great Western Railway (GWR)'s line, adjacent to Knowle station. A further 110 acres of undeveloped agricultural land to the south of the railway line was to be laid out as a cemetery.

Discussions with the GWR had been carried out regarding various aspects of the service, including the provision of a station in Birmingham, where four possible sites were identified. Interestingly, the GWR's existing Snow Hill station was not one of them, possibly because, although it had opened in 1852, it was considered to be a temporary facility and only became a permanent station when it was rebuilt in 1871. The GWR agreed to provide a locomotive, carriages and a guard for each train, while:

> all the requisite Station accommodation, Sidings, Turntables, &c are to be provided by the Birmingham Burial Board, in Birmingham and at Knowle, and their servants are to perform all the duties of loading and unloading the Funeral Vans and admitting Passengers into and out of the Carriages.[29]

Lovie records that discussions with the GWR had led to the following fares being initially agreed, though the rates for second- and third-class mourners were later reduced:

Pauper coffins (3rd Class) 2/- each.
Artisan coffins (2nd class) 4/- each.
All other coffins (1st class) 15/- each.
1st class mourners 2/6 each
2nd class mourners 1/9 each
3rd class mourners 1/3 each.

Special arrangements, at specially negotiated rates, could be made for the funerals of 'persons of rank' who happened to die in the borough. In reality, depending on their social and financial status, history shows that such people would often have been taken 'home' by train for burial there, as will be described in Chapter 8.

The Board presented the report detailing their scheme to the Corporation, which on 3 April 1859 rejected it, causing the Board to resign en masse two days later.[30] Lovie states that it is not entirely clear why the Corporation rejected the scheme, but he considers that it seems the Board were right when it commented in August 1858 that its proposal for a cemetery served by rail was a 'novelty somewhat startling' for the Midlands. Lovie also notes that a clue can be found in the first Report submitted to the Corporation by the new Burial Board on 18 May 1859:

> we were not long in arriving at the conclusion … that a Cemetery at a distance from the Borough, accessible only by Railway, rendering therefore that mode of transit, not optional, but compulsory, would not only be objectionable on the score of economy but would be a daily interference with the comfort, the convenience and the prejudices of a larger portion of the community.

It seems that the intended name of the proposed cemetery is not known, but the Burial Board Minutes consistently refer to the site as 'Knowle' rather than 'Dorridge'. Lovie expresses the view that 'necropolis might have been considered an old-fashioned term by the late 1850's but it was still applied to Woking or Brookwood, and is still useful for conveying the scale of the proposed scheme'. Although the scheme, if built, may have suffered from the same financial problems as the Great Northern London Cemetery service, and the same under-utilisation that affected the Brookwood Necropolis service, it is hard to disagree with Lovie's view that it is impossible not to regret that it fell victim to the 'prejudices of a larger proportion of the community'.

Although the failure of the Knowle scheme appears to be the last time a rail-served cemetery was proposed in the UK, the transportation of the dead by train certainly did not end there. Apart from the 'novelty' of the type of railway use, one of the factors that rendered railway services to cemeteries uneconomic was the cost of the infrastructure, i.e. the separate siding, stations and handling facilities that were needed. This all amounted to a considerable capital outlay, as the promoters of these schemes discovered, with only a limited amount of traffic from which to recoup the costs. Only the Brookwood Necropolis railway service ever generated enough traffic to cover its costs and even then the utilisation of the service was well below anticipated levels, as noted above.

However, the rail transportation of the dead on an individual basis suffered no such problems, as single coffins could be, and were, sent by timetabled trains. This obviously provided much greater flexibility, both in terms of times of departure and choice of destination. The coffins could be sent using existing railway carriages or vans, though several railway companies produced their own hearse vans, or corpse vans as they were called in the language of the time. Some railways had several corpse vans, such as the Midland Railway which built four in 1888 to replace some previous vehicles. There was clearly enough traffic to justify the construction of four specialist vehicles and Chapter 9 provides more information on these and other hearse vans that were utilised in coffin transport by rail.

Other than to Brookwood and the Great Northern London Cemetery, there is little evidence that coffins were transported by train direct to cemeteries, though many had (and still have) railway lines running close or even adjacent to them. For example, Brompton cemetery in West London is adjacent to a railway line that was constructed as the West London Extension Railway in 1863. Additionally, Kensal Green cemetery is located between two main-line railways, the Great Western to the south and the former London & North Western Railway to the north. However, no evidence has been found so far that coffins were transported by train directly to either of these cemeteries. The cemetery at West Norwood had a gateway, now blocked up, in the wall on its side facing the nearby railway station and it is believed that this gateway was sometimes used to deliver coffins from scheduled trains to the cemetery. More research is needed to ascertain the frequency of such use.

Aside from being used to transport coffins, railways played another important role within funerals, namely to transport mourners. The state funeral of the first Duke of Wellington, the 'Iron Duke' (1769–1852), in 1852 in London was a massive event, befitting the honour to which he was entitled as a soldier, Prime Minister and statesman. The Duke had died at Walmer Castle in Kent, where he was Lord Warden of the Cinque Ports, and his body was transported by train to London from the nearby station at Deal, in what was essentially a functional manner. His funeral itself, however, was a hugely ceremonial event, almost theatrically so, and reportedly over one million people travelled to London for it, many by train. This was the first time railways had been used on such a scale to facilitate mourners to attend a funeral.

A much more modest event took place in May 1879 in Cardiff involving the funeral of Frederick Marwood, Secretary of the Taff Vale Railway Company. He had died aged only 52 and was clearly held in high regard by his fellow company officials. As might be expected for such a prominent person, the report of his funeral is quite detailed and written in a typically florid style, beloved of Victorian local newspapers. Although his body was taken by horse-drawn hearse from his home to New Cemetery (now known as Cathays Cemetery, opened 1859), some of the mourners from the railway company had travelled by train to the 'Cathays crossing' at the cemetery. The exact location of this crossing is not clear, as the cemetery was then bounded by a railway line then operated by the Rhymney Railway on its eastern side, which still exists, and was bisected by another, now lost, line running from east to west, then operated by the Taff Vale Railway. There was, for a short period from 1906 to 1912, a siding off the south side of this latter line, adjacent to the cemetery, and there is some anecdotal evidence that coffins were delivered to this siding, but such use has not, so far, been established conclusively.

There was one railway station in Yorkshire which was actually called 'Cemetery' when it first opened. This is believed to be the only such-named station in the UK, apart from that used in the railway service to the Great Northern London cemetery. The station on the LSWR main line for Brookwood Cemetery was initially called 'Brookwood (Necropolis)', later becoming 'Brookwood', whilst the stations within the cemetery were known as 'North Station' and 'South Station'. The Yorkshire station named 'Cemetery' was located next to the eastern end of Hull General Cemetery (opened 1847) and was opened in 1853. It closed in 1854 due to a lack of passengers but was re-opened as 'Cemetery Gates' in September 1866. The station was renamed 'Botanic Gardens' in November 1881, and retained this name even after the closure in 1889 of the nearby botanic gardens from which it took its name. The station was at a road junction that was also served by trams, giving visitors a choice of rail-based transport to the cemetery, but there is no evidence that coffins were transported to the cemetery by either mode of transport. Sadly, the gates, the railway line, the station and the trams have all been swept away though the cemetery itself still survives.

No review of the links between railways and cemeteries would be complete without adding a little-known fact, that one cemetery in the UK is owned by a transport organisation. This is the Cross Bones Graveyard in Southwark, south London, on the corner Redcross Way and Union Street. This post-medieval burial ground is thought to contain 15,000 burials. It is famous for being the burial place of many people, mostly women and infants, who were outcasts from society. In particular, it is the unconsecrated burial place of women known as 'Winchester Geese', who were licensed as prostitutes by the Bishop of Winchester, within whose diocese that area was in ancient times.[31] The graveyard is now owned by Transport for London, operator of many railways in London, including the world-famous Underground. However, as the site was closed to burials in 1853, and served only a local population, there were no coffins transported by train to this historic location.

Rutherford has expressed the view[32] that 'although railways were embraced by Victorian society and industry wholeheartedly throughout the kingdom, surprisingly railway travel for funerals and mourners to cemeteries never became popular'. This is only partially true. It is correct that the development of rail-served cemeteries never occurred in the way that Loudon envisaged, apart from Brookwood and, to a limited extent, the Great Northern London cemetery, for the reasons discussed above. However, railways were used to transport individual coffins, and sometimes several coffins following major accidents, for nearly 150 years on the main line and have continued to be used for ceremonial transport until the present day on heritage railways. Mourners have also used railways to attend funerals, either of famous people, such as the Duke of Wellington, or to accompany the deceased on their final journey. To what extent this constitutes being 'popular' is debatable, but it certainly has been, and still is, an enduring and geographically widespread use of railways, as will be demonstrated in the following chapters.

4

TAKING THE FALLEN HEROES HOME: MILITARY REPATRIATIONS

Then, if you fight against God's enemy
God will in justice ward you as his soldiers;
If you do sweat to put a tyrant down,
You sleep in peace, the tyrant being slain.

Richmond, in Shakespeare's *Richard III*

Apart from in connection with the funerals of four monarchs and some high-profile individuals, some of the most notable uses of trains for funeral purposes have been related to military people. This chapter aims to provide information on a number of occurrences when trains were used to transport the coffins of military personnel, and in the repatriation of two high-profile individuals[1] who were not military but who were executed during the Great War (1914–18).[2] Such was the importance and fame of these two individuals at the time that the separate repatriations of their remains became major public events. One of them is still well remembered today, though the other is shamefully less well remembered outside his home town.

Dead and wounded soldiers of the 66th (2nd East Lancashire) Division being moved by light railway between Langemarck and Pilckem, during the Battle of Poelcappelle, on 10 October 1917. (Courtesy of IWM Q6043)

Trains were also used to transport the military victims of two major disasters involving airships, the R38/ZR-2[3] in 1921 and the R101 in 1930, but those events were sufficiently important to merit their own stories – see Chapter 5. The people covered in this chapter lost their lives in the service of their country, becoming heroes in the eyes of many people, and the natural desire of their surviving loved ones was to bring their bodies 'home' for burial. For these reasons this chapter has been titled 'Taking the Fallen Heroes Home'.

It is only very rarely that bodies are buried where a person dies. This most frequently occurred on a battlefield, as so often happened in the carnage of the Great War. Often during that conflict it was simply not practical in the heat of so many battles to transport the bodies to a place set aside for burial. There were some exceptions, however, as shown in this rare photo from the Imperial War Museum's collection.

However, after the Great War had finished, the remains of a great many military victims were exhumed from their place of immediate burial and reinterred in cemeteries created locally for that purpose.

As a notable exception, however, one casualty in particular was repatriated by train to the UK and given a special ceremonial funeral prior to reburial in a place of national importance. It is the centenary in November 2020 of the repatriation of the 'Unknown Warrior', as he became known, that gave rise to the production of this book, which aims to provide its own commemoration of that historic event.

Although in 1915 the government of the time stopped the repatriation of soldiers killed abroad in the Great War, there had been a few such repatriations before then, and there was one significant use of trains to return deceased soldiers 'home' within the UK during 1915 itself. There were several other documented cases[4] uncovered by research for this book of bodies of soldiers, sailors and airman who had died in the UK during the Great War being taken 'home' by train for burial.

The story of the use of trains in military repatriations starts before the Great War, as several cases have already been found and doubtless many more will be found in due course. The first three cases almost certainly required the use of trains to get the deceased home for burial, given the distance involved in the days before motor hearses were developed, though the details of the final journey itself have yet to be confirmed. Firstly, in 1890, Ernest Richard Hamilton (1869–1890) the soldier son of Thomas de Courcy Hamilton VC, died aged 21 in London, his death being registered in Kensington. He is buried in Bouncers Lane cemetery, Cheltenham, the family's home town. It should be noted that his parents are buried in the same grave, his father having died 1908, followed by his mother, who died 1913. Once their son had died it appears that his grieving parents brought him home for burial, arranging for themselves to be interred in the same plot in due course. Such family arrangements are, of course, very common.

Secondly, in 1901 Colonel Sir Henry Wilmot VC KCB (1831–1901), a soldier and MP who died in Bournemouth, was buried in St Mary's churchyard, Chaddesden, Derby, the town of his birth. His body would almost certainly have been taken by train to Derby and it will not be forgotten that the first recorded transport of a coffin by train was to Derby, from London, in 1840. In the third case in 1907 Henry Lysons VC, a soldier, died aged 49 in Marylebone, London and he is buried in Rodmarton, Gloucestershire. His connection with Gloucestershire awaits further research, however. His body was almost certainly taken by train, probably to Kemble station, on the Great Western Railway's line from Swindon to Gloucester.

The last pre-Great War case in this sequence does have a documented final journey by train. This was provided for a pioneer aviator named Lieutenant Edward Hotchkiss of the Royal Flying Corps, who died in September 1912, aged 29. Whilst flying a Bristol Coanda monoplane from an aerodrome on Port Meadow, to the north-west of Oxford, he was killed with another airman when the plane crashed. A memorial plaque to the two victims, incorporating a depiction of the plane, was placed close to the crash location on the former toll bridge over the River Thames on Godstow Road, Wolvercote, Oxford. His remains were taken home to Shropshire, as he was the first aviator from that county, where his coffin was unloaded at Craven Arms station. Edward Hotchkiss is buried in St John the Baptist church at nearby Stokesay, where a stained-glass window commemorates him.

Once the Great War started after the Declaration on 4 August 1914, it was not long before soldiers started to be killed, but the first known repatriation was of someone who died of a heart attack. Not surprisingly, this was not just an ordinary 'Tommy' but a senior officer whose family could no doubt afford to fulfil their desire to have his body returned home. Only a few days into the conflict, on 17 August, Sir James Moncrieff Grierson, Commanding Officer II Army Corps, General Staff died aged 55 on a train near Amiens, France, of an aneurism of the heart. He was very overweight and suffered from high blood pressure. His body was returned to UK and transported by train to Scotland, where he is buried in Glasgow Necropolis, in a grave he shares with his parents and sister.

Only two weeks later, on 1 September 1914, Lieutenant Norman Champion de Crespigny was killed at Nery, France. He was initially buried there but his aristocratic father, Sir Claude Champion de Crespigny, 4th Baronet (1847–1935), arranged for his remains to be exhumed and repatriated to the UK. They were taken by train from London to Maldon, Essex, and from there his remains were taken by horse-drawn hearse to the family estate at nearby Great Totham. Amid much military ceremony, as reported by the Essex County Chronicle on 13 November 1914, he was buried in the family mausoleum in the grounds of Champion Lodge, now known as Totham Lodge. This had been constructed to accommodate the remains of Sir Claude's first born son and heir, another Claude (1873–1910), who had sadly committed suicide in 1910 by shooting himself. The reasons for this are unclear but were thought to have been exacerbated as a result of influenza and a number of falls whilst playing polo.[5] He had previously seen active service in British East Africa and had been awarded the DSO. In 1935 the 4th Baronet was also laid to rest alongside his sons in the mausoleum. The mausoleum was an imposing structure but unfortunately has since been demolished and no parts above ground remain.[6] The Champion de Crespigny family were wealthy aristocrats owning land in south-east London, where there are streets named after them. No doubt the cost of repatriation of Norman's remains would have been considered well worthwhile, especially after the tragedy of the elder son's death.

During 1915 there were three known repatriations of military personnel killed abroad. The first was of William Glynne Charles Gladstone (1885–13 April 1915). He was the grandson of William Ewart Gladstone,[7] the famous Victorian politician who served four terms as Prime Minister. He had been elected as MP for Kilmarnock Burghs, Scotland, in 1911, and was still serving as an MP when he was killed by a sniper after only three weeks active service in France. Initially he was buried in France but was repatriated to Britain nine days after his death and reburied in St Deiniol's Church, Hawarden, North Wales. This village was the location of the Gladstone family's property, Hawarden Castle, which W.G.C. Gladstone had inherited, aged 7, on the death of his father in 1892. His repatriation was specially authorised by King George V and is said to be the last official repatriation of the Great War.[8] However, there were two further documented repatriations of fallen heroes later in 1915.

The first was of the body of Reginald Alexander John (known as 'Rex') Warneford VC (1891–17 June 1915). He was serving with the Royal Naval Air Service (RNAS) in Belgium flying a biplane, when he caused the German Army Zeppelin airship LZ37 to explode and crash by throwing a grenade on to it from above. The subsequent explosion turned his aircraft upside down and he had to land behind enemy lines to carry out some repairs. These were successfully completed within thirty-five minutes, after which he was able to take off again and return safely to his base in Ghent. For this act of heroism he was awarded the RNAS's first Victoria Cross,[9] and also the French award of the Légion d'honneur, which was presented to him on 17 June 1915. After a celebratory lunch he set off in another plane, which he was delivering to a different airbase, when that machine's right-hand wings collapsed, causing the aircraft to crash. A passenger in the plane was killed instantly and Warneford died on the way to hospital. His body was brought back to London, almost certainly by train. He was buried in Brompton Cemetery, west London, with thousands of people attending the event. An impressive monument was erected over his grave, paid for by public subscription, depicting in low relief the exploding airship and his plane above it.

The third in this trio of 1915 repatriations was of Captain (John) Aidan Liddell, VC MC. He was one of six children born into a prosperous family, his father being the director of an insurance company and also a Justice of the Peace (JP). He was born in Newcastle upon Tyne and the family eventually settled in Basingstoke, Hampshire. He served as a captain in the Argyll and Sutherland Highlanders in France, where he won the Military Cross (MC). He then trained as a pilot in the Royal Flying Corps. On 31 July 1915 he was flying reconnaissance over Belgium when his aircraft was attacked. Though severely wounded in the leg he managed to land the plane safely, saving the life of his observer. For this action he was awarded the VC, but sadly he died of his injuries a month later, on 31 August 1915. No doubt his influential father brought some pressure to secure Aidan's repatriation to the UK, almost certainly by train. He was buried in the Holy Ghost Cemetery in Basingstoke, close to the family's home since 1908.[10] His sister, Dorothy Liddell MBE, a nurse and pioneer female archaeologist, was later buried with him in 1938.

Another military repatriation also took place in 1915, but this was the aftermath of a major railway accident rather than of a single individual. On Saturday, 22 May of that year a troop train carrying over 200 soldiers from the 7th Royal Scots regiment heading south to Liverpool from Larbert, in central Scotland, collided at Quintinshill with a stationary northbound local train. There was no station at this location, a few miles north of Gretna, but there was a signal box to control two loop lines, one on either side of the

Soldier's coffin on gun carriage at unidentified rail-based location. Date unknown but believed to be early in the Great War, identity of deceased not known. (Courtesy of Brian Parsons)

north and south main lines. At the time of the accident, just before 7 a.m., freight trains were occupying each of the loop lines to allow passenger trains to go past. A northbound local passenger train was then shunted onto the southbound track to allow a late running northbound express train to overtake it. However, as a result of a signalling error the southbound troop train was allowed to approach the location at speed, whereupon it collided with the locomotive at the head of the northbound local passenger train. This first collision wrecked the troop train, the wooden carriages of which were old and disintegrated. There were undoubtedly many casualties from this first collision, including two dead in the local passenger train. Their bodies were later taken by train to Newcastle upon Tyne, their home town, for burial in Elswick cemetery.[11]

Worse was to follow, however, as shortly after the first collision the northbound express train ran into the wreckage, scattering it in all directions. An untold number of further casualties ensued, including the deaths of eight men and possibly one woman, whose complete remains were never fully recovered.[12] Five of the male victims in the express train were military

Quintinshill railway accident, May 1915. Part of the funeral procession in Edinburgh after coffins had been taken back there by train. (Courtesy of Brian Parsons)

people on leave and their remains were eventually taken, almost certainly by train, for burial in various locations.[13] However, the real tragedy of this accident was about to unfold. The wreckage of the wooden carriages in the troop train caught fire and burned for many hours. The remote location made efforts to extinguish the fire and rescue those injured difficult and eventually the death toll reached over 200, with some reports stating 215. The exact number will never be known as some soldiers were completely consumed by the fire and the regimental records were lost in the fire.

The full story of this appalling accident is beyond the scope of this book but is well told by Jack Richards and Adrian Searle in their excellent book *The Quintinshill Conspiracy*.[14] The relevance of the accident for this book is that many of the victims were returned by train to Edinburgh, though more than one train was required. As recorded in *The Quintinshill Conspiracy*, 'special trains [arrived] from Carlisle and Glasgow. Those trains, which must surely rank among the most sombre ever to be dispatched on a British railway line, eventually brought their coffins.'[15] On 24 May a funeral was held in Edinburgh involving a large procession. One hundred and one of the victims from the troop train were buried in Rosebank Cemetery, Leith, in a communal grave over which a large monument was later erected. This records the names of all the military victims from the troop train, but not the military personnel killed in the express train.[16]

A further railway accident occurred during the Great War that resulted in the military victims being transported by train, though in the UK it is largely forgotten outside the area where it happened.[17] On 24 September 1917 a train carrying troops from the New Zealand Expeditionary Force (who had recently arrived at Plymouth in Devon) was on its way to Exeter, its first scheduled stop. The troops were headed for a camp on Salisbury Plain and had not eaten since 6.00 a.m. They had been told that food would be available at the first stop but the train made an unscheduled stop about 3.50 p.m. at Bere Ferrers station, on the former London & South Western Railway line from Plymouth to Tavistock. Unfamiliar with the location, some soldiers disembarked from the train on the side opposite from the platform and found themselves in the path of an express train heading for Plymouth. Sadly this train was unable to stop in time and nine soldiers were killed at the station, with another dying later in hospital. It being too far to repatriate their remains to New Zealand, the soldiers' bodies were transported by train to Plymouth, where they were buried in Efford cemetery. Their graves are each marked with a headstone provided and maintained by the Commonwealth War Graves Commission, which lists the soldiers as 'New Zealand Reinforcements' on their website.[18] A brass plaque was erected in St Andrews Church in the village to commemorate the victims and another plaque was later erected at the station.[19]

There were many other cases of 'fallen heroes' being taken home by train during and immediately after the Great War. Space does not permit a full listing of all the ones known so far and this is an area where ongoing research is continuing to find more. However, some interesting examples are worth recording here. One of them is John Travers Cornwell (8 January 1900–16), known as 'Jack', who is the third youngest recipient of the Victoria Cross. He was a sailor, Boy (1st Class), in the British Navy and earned his posthumously awarded VC for actions carried out in the famous naval Battle of Jutland (31 May–1 June 1916). He sustained wounds which were being treated at a hospital in Grimsby, but sadly he died from them on 2 June 1916. His mother desired him to be buried close to her home in east London and his body was taken there by train at the Navy's expense. Initially he was buried in a communal grave in Manor Park Cemetery but, following a public campaign triggered by a report of the battle by the then Vice-Admiral[20] Sir David Beatty, Jack Cornwell was reburied in a private grave following a large funeral procession. His VC was awarded a few weeks later, being collected by his mother from Buckingham Palace in November 1916.[21]

These military repatriations were not limited to people who died in battle. For example, in the churchyard of Minster Lovell, near Witney in Oxfordshire, there can be found the grave of Harold Messenger. His headstone records that he served in the Royal Engineers and died aged 29 on 18 November 1918. This was after the Armistice of 11 November 1918 brought the fighting of the Great War to an end, so he probably died of wounds previously sustained or possibly during the pandemic of Spanish Flu. Research reveals that his death was recorded in Bristol, so it is highly likely that his remains were transported by train from Bristol to the nearest rail facility in Witney prior to his burial.

Another example of immediate post-war military repatriation is the case of William Douglas Henderson (1893–1918). He was a Flight Cadet and was thrown out of the cockpit of his aircraft whilst flying from Montrose airfield in Scotland. He was killed as a result of this incident on 28 November 1918, but his body was recovered and returned to his family in Gloucester. This was almost certainly by train given the distance involved, enabling him to be buried in Gloucester Cemetery a few days later.[22]

It was not only serving military personnel whose bodies were returned home by train. During the Great War, what is now popularly known as Dartmoor Prison was used as a place to detain conscientious objectors (COs).[23] It was then called 'H.M. Work Centre Princetown', and at least one person who died there had his body sent home by train. Henry William Firth died aged 30 on 6 February 1918 and his death certificate records his cause of death as 'diabetes arising from natural causes'. The quality of treatment (or lack of it) given to the conscientious objectors held at H.M. Work Centre, Princetown, contributed to his early death, as is clear from contemporary reports.[24] The certificate also records his occupation as 'formerly a shoemaker of 79 Sprowston Road, Norwich'.[25] The contemporary reports state that a male-voice choir led the procession of hundreds of men out of the prison gates down the mist-shrouded road to the station. His coffin was carried by a contingent of Norwich COs and his remains were sent by train from Princetown station, run by the Great Western Railway,[26] initially to Plymouth and then on to his home town of Norwich where he is buried in Earlham Cemetery.

Following the end of the Great War there were separate campaigns to repatriate the remains of three individuals who were each transported in the same railway van. These people were Nurse Edith Cavell and Captain Charles Fryatt, both repatriated in 1919, and the Unknown Warrior, repatriated in 1920. This happened over a period of eighteen months and the campaigns were not co-ordinated to bring about the use of the same van. The van itself had been built by the South Eastern & Chatham Railway (SECR) in early 1919, being given the number 132, and its use in the repatriation of Edith Cavell gave rise to it becoming known as 'The Cavell Van'. Remarkably, the van itself has survived and now exists in peaceful preservation in rural surroundings at Bodiam Station, East Sussex, on one of Britain's most attractive heritage railways, the Kent & East Sussex Railway (K&ESR).[27]

A summary of the stories of these individuals and their repatriations is told on a page[28] on the K&ESR's website and a fuller version of the stories is told in an excellent booklet *The Unknown Warrior and the Cavell Van* written by Brian Janes, curator of the Colonel Stephens Museum at Tenterden, the headquarters of the K&ESR. The booklet is available for purchase from that railway's online shop. The author is grateful to Brian Janes for allowing him to use some material from this booklet. However, this book would not be complete without at least a brief exposition of the stories, though the Introduction to this book starts with some information on the repatriation of the Unknown Warrior. Additionally, since the booklet was written in 2010 the interior of the van has been restored, as have the graves of both Edith Cavell and Captain Fryatt.

Nurse Edith Cavell was born on 4 December 1865 in Swardeston, a village near Norwich, in Norfolk. She was the eldest of four children and her father, Reverend Frederick Cavell, was the vicar of Swardeston for forty-five years. After a time as a governess to a family in Brussels, she returned home to care for her ill father. After his recovery she returned to Belgium and set up a school for nurses, eventually becoming matron of a hospital. During the early part of the Great War she used her links with the school of nursing to assist over 200 Allied soldiers escape from Belgium, which by then was occupied by the Germans. Following her arrest on 5 July 1915 she was subjected to a military trial, which found her guilty of harbouring enemy soldiers, contrary to German military law. She was sentenced to death and several efforts to secure her reprieve failed. The night before her execution on 12 October 1915 she was recorded as saying 'Patriotism is not enough, I must have no hatred or bitterness to anyone', words that are carved into a statue of her which was later erected in St Martin's Place, London.

Her execution caused a major international outcry and her death was regarded in Britain as martyrdom, though she did not regard herself as a martyr. Her memory was kept alive by two newspapers, *The Daily Telegraph* and the *Daily Mirror*, and after the end of the Great War arrangements were made for the repatriation of her remains. With great ceremony she was exhumed and full military honours were provided whilst she was brought back to England, landing in Dover. From there her body was transported by train to London in the newly built Van 132 provided by the SECR. Its roof was painted white, so that it could be easily identified by the many people who watched the train travel to London. In common with many other cases of coffin transport by train at the time, the mourners, including her sisters, were accommodated in a separate carriage which was also attached to a scheduled train, the 7.35 a.m. service to Victoria station on 15 May 1919. *The Times* reported that:

> at almost every station along the line and at windows near the railway line and by the bridges there were crowds of children quietly and reverently watching the passing. Schoolboys and schoolgirls in bright summer clothes had been brought by their teachers to the railside and stood three and four deep on the platforms. The boys saluted, the girls stood silently gazing[29]

A service was held in Westminster Abbey, after which the coffin was taken on a gun carriage as part of a large military procession to Liverpool Street Station, from where it was provided with a final journey by the Great Eastern Railway (GER) to Norwich. Edith Cavell was then taken from

Edith Cavell's coffin being carried to train at Liverpool Street station, May 1919. (*Great Eastern Railway Magazine*, Author's Collection)

Thorpe Station in Norwich, again with a military accompaniment, to the cathedral in that city, where she was buried in an area known as Life's Green, just outside the south-east corner of that magnificent building. During the journey from Liverpool Street Station the coffin was carried in the GER's hearse carriage, No. 512, a six-wheeled vehicle that had been converted from a carriage originally built in 1892. Like Van 132, it was draped on the inside, but it was a special train that was used for this part of Edith Cavell's final journey rather than the hearse van being attached to a scheduled train as on the SECR.

The loading of Edith Cavell's coffin into the GER train was depicted in that railway's magazine published the following month, Volume 9, No. 102, June 1919, p. 2.

Later in that issue, on p. 104, a poem about her last journey was included; this is reproduced here:

EDITH CAVELL'S LAST JOURNEY by Julian Kaye[30]

What greeting could we give, what homage pay
As home she passed, her foreign sojourn o'er?
No greeting like the sun that glorious day
That welcomed her at Dover to our shore,
And made those chalk cliffs shine in virgin white,
The men of Kent damp-eyed paid homage mute,
And sent her on her silent homeward flight,
Such was their greeting, such their last salute.

Nor could we with the Norman Abbey vie,
That was, one fleeting hour, her resting place
Contributing the funeral minstrelsy,
Great London's tribute, with befitting grace.
This, and the pomp of military bands,
The silent crowds that stood in patience long,
This was the tribute brought with willing hands,
This was the Empire's final passing song.

Here at the gateway into Essex, bowed,
The vanguard of East Anglian friends of hers,
We servants of the way of steel were proud
To her last journey to be ministers.
And eastwards through the leagues of countryside
The train was watched by thousands as it sped,
Who thought of her with humble thanks and pride
And lifted cap in honour of the dead.

Through Chelmsford, on through Roman Colchester
Who bowed in spirit as the cortege passed;
In sight of Harwich- Harwich thought of her,
And of another martyr.[31] Then at last
Through Suffolk, Ipswich - then to Norfolk, where
Her home had been in happy bygone time,
To Norwich – may she sleep in quiet there,
Her rest most restful, and her peace sublime.

On 14 May 1919, the day before Nurse Cavell's final journey, a service of remembrance had been held in St Paul's Cathedral,[32] attended by His Majesty King George V, 'in memory of the railwaymen of Great Britain and Ireland who have died in the service of their country during the war 1914–1918'. Also attending were about 4,000[33] railway people and their families. Over 186,475 railway workers from Great Britain and Ireland had fought in the war, on land, sea and in the air, and 18,957 names of those who died were recorded in the Order of Service. However, it is now known that more than 20,850 railwaymen were killed during the Great War.[34]

A few days before the service in London, similar services had been held on 10 May 1919 in honour of railwaymen from the North Eastern Railway who lost their lives in the service of their country. Services were held at York Minster, Newcastle Cathedral, Holy Trinity Church, Hull and St Mary's Church, Gateshead.[35] All of the services would have been significant events in the public consciousness and would no doubt have provided fertile ground for the later idea of repatriating a soldier whose identity was to be unknown. The repatriation of that soldier was also carried out in part in Van 132, which had quickly become known as 'the Cavell Van' following its use in part of Edith Cavell's final journey.

The repatriation of the Unknown Warrior in November 1920, together with the ceremonies which accompanied that event, such as the unveiling of the Cenotaph in Whitehall, can be seen as a significant contribution to the start of the commemorations held in remembrance of those who lost their lives in the Great War. It is remarkable that a humble railway van used three times as funeral transport in the space of only eighteen months can be regarded as having played its part in what has become over a century of remembrance. Surely no other railway van can claim such an important part in the country's history, and it all arose from the van's use for carrying the coffins of three individuals who are today remembered more for their untimely deaths rather than their important lives.

To fully understand the importance of the Cavell Van's place in history, it is necessary to also examine its role in the repatriations of Captain Fryatt in July 1919 and the Unknown Warrior in November 1920. Both of these were significant public events at the time and generated much publicity. Whilst the centenary of the repatriation of the Unknown Warrior in

November 2020 will no doubt generate many events of commemoration, the centenary of Captain Fryatt's repatriation in July 2019 was marked in more muted ways, though with an important series of events in Dovercourt, where he is buried, and in Harwich, within which Dovercourt is located.

The story of Captain Charles Algernon Fryatt is, today, rather shamefully little known outside his home area of Harwich in Essex. Apart from in Brian Janes' booklet, it has been told by Ben Carver, in his book *Captain Charles Fryatt: Courageous Mariner of the First World War*.[36] He was born on 2 December 1871 in Southampton, where some of the extended Fryatt family still live. Soon after 1881 his father, also named Charles, an officer in the merchant marine, took a position with the Great Eastern Railway's cross-Channel steamer service and moved to Harwich. In due course the younger Charles also joined the GER's steamer service and became captain of a succession of vessels. The GER endeavoured to maintain a service to the Netherlands, which remained neutral during the war. However, in February 1915 the Germans declared unrestricted submarine warfare in the seas around Britain. Enemy merchant ships would be sunk or captured wherever possible and the safety of neutral shipping would not be guaranteed. Sir Winston Churchill, as First Lord of the Admiralty, issued orders to the effect that, if threatened by a submarine, merchant ships should steer straight for it at maximum speed, forcing it to dive.

In an encounter with a German U-boat on 2 March 1915, Captain Fryatt, whilst in charge of the SS *Wrexham*, eventually managed to outrun the submarine and escape, sailing into his home port of Harwich to considerable public acclaim. For this bravery he was presented with a gold watch by the GER, inscribed with its appreciation for his courage and skilful seamanship.[37] Captain Fryatt and his crew were transferred to a larger vessel, the SS *Brussels*, but on 28 March 1915 they encountered another German submarine, *U-33*,[38] which signalled to Fryatt's ship to stop. Following the Admiralty's instructions, Captain Fryatt steered towards the submarine, causing it to dive. He managed to escape again, and reached the safety of Dutch waters. For this action he became a popular hero and was awarded gold watches and certificates of appreciation by both the Admiralty and the GER. The First Officer and the Chief Engineer also received gold watches from the admiralty for this action.

However, the Germans took exception to this action, considering it an act of war. Eventually, on the night of 22/23 June 1916, the SS *Brussels* was captured by a flotilla of German naval vessels and he was charged with being a '*franc-tireur*', i.e. a non-uniformed combatant or guerrilla, and for attempting to ram the submarine. A military trial followed on 27 July 1916, the fairness and legality of which were considerably in doubt, both at the time and ever since. Not surprisingly, Captain Fryatt was found guilty and sentenced to death; he was executed only two hours later. A public outcry and much international condemnation followed, with the Prime Minister of the time, Herbert Asquith, describing his execution as 'murder'. He was initially buried in a cemetery in Bruges, Belgium, though his grave was marked with a simple black cross inscribed in white with the words 'Here lies Captain Fryat [sic], Master of SS *Brussels* of glorious memory. RIP.'[39]

A few weeks after the repatriation of Nurse Edith Cavell, the remains of Captain Fryatt were exhumed and returned to England, amid much ceremony and with military involvement both in Belgium and on arrival in Dover during the afternoon of 4 July 1919. Much of the organisation was carried out by the Great Eastern Railway, and had many of the trappings of a state funeral. The coffin was placed in the Cavell Van, which had been draped inside with purple, and many wreaths were arranged on and around the catafalque. After being guarded overnight the van was attached to the 7.35 a.m. train to Victoria. It was detached at Chatham and coupled to a special train, which took it forward to Charing Cross Station, where it arrived at 11.00 a.m.

Following a funeral service at St Paul's Cathedral, attended by many senior officials from the GER, including its chairman, Lord Claud Hamilton, Captain Fryatt's coffin was taken through crowded streets to Liverpool Street Station. Here the coffin was placed in the GER's hearse van, No. 512, used only a few weeks previously for Edith Cavell's final journey. A special train, headed by former royal locomotive Claud Hamilton class (GER D56, LNER D15) number 1849, with suitable decoration, then took the coffin on its final journey towards Harwich, arriving at Dovercourt at 3.25 p.m. Captain Fryatt's coffin was taken on a gun carriage from the station to the cemetery of nearby All Saints Church, where he was buried, again amid much ceremony, in a grave now marked by a

IN MEMORY OF
CAPTAIN
CHARLES ALGERNON FRYATT
MASTER OF THE GREAT EASTERN
RAILWAY STEAMSHIP "BRUSSELS"

ILLEGALLY EXECUTED BY THE
GERMANS AT BRUGES ON THE
27ᵀᴴ JULY 1916

ERECTED BY THE COMPANY AS AN
EXPRESSION OF THEIR ADMIRATION
OF HIS GALLANTRY

PRO
PATRIA

ALSO
HIS BELOVED WIFE ETHEL, WHO DIED 30ᵀᴴ SEPᵀ 1956.

Captain Fryatt's grave, Dovercourt, as restored 2019, to commemorate the centenary of his repatriation. (Photograph © Nicolas Wheatley)

substantial memorial provided by the GER and unveiled by Lord Claud Hamilton in June 1920. Having fallen into a state of disrepair over several decades, Captain Fryatt's grave was restored in time for the centenary of his repatriation, as part of a series of events during July 2019 in Harwich and Dovercourt under the title 'Harwich Remembers'. The author was honoured to be able to participate in many of these events, particularly the church service and rededication of Captain Fryatt's grave, organised by Harwich Town Council and partly funded by the Railway Heritage Trust. Many thanks go to Councillor Garry Calver and Andy Savage of those respective organisations for their work to achieve these outcomes.

Given the respect with which Captain Fryatt was treated in his lifetime and following his death and repatriation, it is regrettable that his memory is now mostly maintained in the context of the Great War, importantly by his descendants and, appropriately, in Harwich. Hopefully this book, and especially its coverage of his repatriation in the Cavell Van, will bring him to a wider audience and go at least some way towards re-establishing his neglected reputation.

Following its use in Captain Fryatt's repatriation, the Cavell Van seems to have reverted to its normal use as a Passenger Luggage Van (PLV), carrying luggage for passengers using the cross-Channel ferries operated from Dover and Folkestone to France and Belgium. However, when it became time to repatriate the remains of the Unknown Warrior it was brought into service for that very special task. The story of the Unknown Warrior is outside the scope of this book, and several books and booklets cover the story, one of the best known being by Michael Gavaghan. No doubt more will be written in connection with the centenary of the repatriation about how the body was selected and the significance of the Unknown Warrior as a focus for grieving for those whose loved ones did not return from the Great War.

The relevance for this book comes in the use of the Cavell Van in the repatriation, starting with the arrival of the coffin in Dover on 10 November 1920. As before, the repatriation had been carried out with great ceremony provided by a range of military bodies, including the Royal Navy. The coffin had arrived in Dover Marine station in the mid afternoon and was placed in the van, the walls of which had been draped with purple cloth, garlanded with laurels, palms and lilies. The roof was painted white, as it had been for the previous repatriations, so that it could be seen more easily by

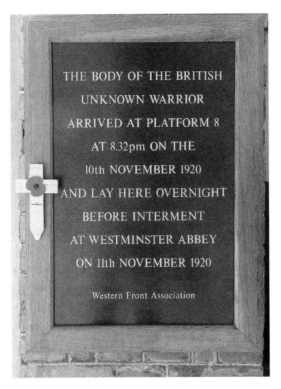

THE BODY OF THE BRITISH

UNKNOWN WARRIOR

ARRIVED AT PLATFORM 8

AT 8.32pm ON THE

10th NOVEMBER 1920

AND LAY HERE OVERNIGHT

BEFORE INTERMENT

AT WESTMINSTER ABBEY

ON 11th NOVEMBER 1920

Western Front Association

Unknown Warrior plaque commemorating the overnight stay of his remains (in the Cavell Van) at Victoria station in November 1920. (Photograph © Nicolas Wheatley)

the many people who stood by the lineside, and at the many stations the train passed through on its journey.

The coffin was placed under guard within the van, together with four enormous wreaths, and the original plan had been to keep the van overnight in Dover. However, concerns about delays on the journey to London and being late in arriving meant the van was attached to the 5.50 p.m. service train from Dover Marine station to the capital. The van was accompanied by a separate carriage in which travelled one officer and fifteen men guarding the coffin, together with Kirtley Nodes, the undertaker in charge of the coffin during its final journey. On arrival at Victoria, the van and accompanying carriage were moved from the SECR's side of the station to the separate but adjacent station operated by the London Brighton & South Coast Railway (LB&SCR). This was partly for security and partly for easier movement in the morning, 11 November. The van arrived at Platform 8, the LB&SCR's main arrival platform, and remained there under guard overnight.

It was not until 1998 that a plaque was installed close to the end of Platform 8 to commemorate the van's overnight stay, and fittingly the plaque was provided by the Western Front Association (WFA).

It took seventy-eight years for the plaque to be provided and the London Branch of the WFA has been holding short ceremonies to commemorate the arrival of the Unknown Warrior at Victoria Station during the evening of every 10 November since 1998 and continues to do so to this day. On 11 November 1920 the Unknown Warrior's coffin was removed from the Cavell Van at 9.20 a.m. and taken in a huge procession to Westminster Abbey, in what was effectively a state funeral. As the procession passed down Whitehall, King George V, who was leading the nation's mourning, stopped to unveil the newly built stone Cenotaph, which replaced a temporary wooden version built the previous year. The Unknown Warrior was buried near the entrance of Westminster Abbey and is the only grave within the Abbey on which it is forbidden to walk.

Having done its solemn duty in this third repatriation, the Cavell Van again returned to its proper role as a luggage van on continental boat trains. In the 1950s, when passengers stopped travelling around with as much luggage as previously, it was used to carry parcels and other miscellaneous goods, being redesignated as a PMV (parcels and miscellaneous van). It was eventually taken out of main-line service in 1946 and later used for a variety of internal uses within the south-east of England. The full story of its discovery, preservation and restoration is beyond the scope of this book but is covered in Brian Janes' booklet. Its survival is nothing short of miraculous and its future in the care of the Colonel Stephens Museum and the Kent & East Sussex Railway is assured, though it would be beneficial to its maintenance if some secure and weather-proof accommodation could be provided for it.

In the meantime the Van has enjoyed a sort of celebrity status in railway terms, having been displayed at various locations within England in connection with certain anniversaries. For two weeks in October 2015 it was displayed outside The Forum in Norwich as part of that city's commemorations of the centenary of the execution of Nurse Edith Cavell.

In July 2018 the Cavell Van was displayed at Arley Station on the Severn Valley Railway as part of their wartime weekends, though those events related more to the Second World War than the First. During October 2018 the Cavell Van made a shorter trip for a display on the Folkestone Harbour Arm, a tourist destination based on the former Folkestone Harbour station. This was in remembrance of the time on 8 November 1920 when it was used to transport a very special empty coffin to that port for its shipment to Boulogne in France, to be loaded with the remains of the Unknown Warrior.

The Van's most recent journey away from its home base was to Harwich, where it spent two weeks in July 2019 on display as part of the commemorations celebrating the repatriation of Captain Fryatt to that town. In its original role as funeral transport for Nurse Cavell and Captain Fryatt the Cavell Van had only been involved in their final journeys from Dover to London. However, it was fitting that the Van should be displayed in Norwich and Harwich, as the GER's hearse van No. 512, which had been used for the final part of the journeys to those places, had long since been scrapped. The interior of the Van has been used to create an exhibition of its use in the three famous repatriations and a visit to see this most important of railway funeral vehicles, and its exhibition, is well worth the effort from however far the visitor travels. Any role that the Cavell Van might play in the centenary commemorations of the repatriation of the Unknown Warrior remains uncertain at the time of writing, but will have become clear by the time this book is published.

Finally, it should be mentioned in the context of this chapter's title of 'Taking the Fallen Heroes Home' that the use of trains for funeral transport of military personnel was not limited to repatriations to the UK. In 1948 several wagons carrying the coffins of Free French soldiers who had died and been buried in the UK were taken back to France. In December of that year, 260 such coffins were transported in the steam ship *Shepperton Ferry*. This train ferry had been constructed in 1934 for the Southern Railway and ownership was transferred to the British Transport Commission when railways in the UK were nationalised in early 1948. The coffins had been exhumed from various cemeteries around the country and delivered to Dover Marine station by lorry. However, their final journey in a number of French (SNCF) railway wagons, albeit on board a ship, back to France qualifies them for an entry in this book.

Dover Marine station, December 1948. Repatriation of 260 coffins of exhumed Free French soldiers in SNCF wagon, soon to be loaded on ship *Shepperton Ferry* for repatriation to France, amid much ceremony. (Photograph (via Brian Parsons) courtesy of A. France & Son, funeral directors, who arranged the exhumations)

5

TWO AIRSHIP TRAGEDIES: R101 AND R38/ZR-2

'We're down, lads'

Of the two types of funeral trains, functional and ceremonial, most transported only one deceased person. However, there are some exceptions, usually trains that transported the victims of various accidents that involved numerous fatalities. Perhaps the most notable of these was the train that transported the victims of the R101 airship disaster in 1930 on their final journey to Bedfordshire, for burial at Cardington. This train transported no fewer than forty-eight corpses, who were given a communal burial in the extension graveyard on the opposite side of the road from St Mary's Church.

Large rigid airships had been developed by the Germans before the First World War, notably by Count Ferdinand Graf von Zeppelin (1838–1917), after whom the German versions were named. They were used during the war to drop bombs on various towns in England, but the first bombing raids attacked two towns on the east coast of Britain, Great Yarmouth and Kings Lynn in Norfolk, on the night of 19 January 1915,[1] causing four fatalities. Later, a raid on London in 1916[2] caused six fatalities, five of them to people on a tram, which led to a funeral that is featured in Chapter 10. The Norfolk bombings were arguably the first time in modern warfare

R101 airship accident. Composite photograph of airship and wreckage after crash near Beauvais, France. (Author's Collection)

that civilians in the UK nowhere near a battlefield had been deliberately killed by the dropping of bombs from powered aircraft as part of enemy action.[3] After the war had ended, the British government embarked on a programme to develop airships for civilian use, intending them to be capable of long-distance transport to service parts of the British Empire. At the time, heavier-than-air machines were incapable of covering great distances such as to India, Australia or Canada.

By 1929 two rigid airships had been constructed: the R101, built by the government's Royal Aircraft Works and the R100, which was government-funded but privately built. When completed at the giant hangars in Cardington, Bedfordshire, the R101 was the largest powered aircraft ever built, at 731ft (223m) long. Its size was not exceeded by another hydrogen filled airship until the German *Hindenburg* flew seven years later.[4]

After trial flights and subsequent modifications to increase lifting capacity, which included lengthening the ship by 46ft (14m) to add another gasbag, the R101 crashed on its first overseas voyage. Essentially it was too heavy and neither it, not the weather, were suitable for the flight it started but never completed. It was heading to India, setting off on Saturday, 4 October 1930. In the early hours of the next morning it went into two steep dives over France during a rainstorm, eventually crashing to the ground at 2.09 a.m. near Beauvais. Soon afterwards the wreckage caught fire, leaving the frame of the airship a tangled mess of metal, which was later sold as scrap. During the aircraft's final moments, the Chief Coxswain George W. Hunt (1888–1930) went to the crew's quarters to wake them, calling out 'we're down, lads.'[5] Sadly, his body was one of the many unidentified after the crash.

Tragically, forty-six of the fifty-four people on board were killed instantly and two died shortly afterwards. The dead included Lord Thompson, Secretary of State for Air; Sir Sefton Branker, Director of Civil Aviation; Major G.H. Scott, Assistant Director of Airship Development and the officer in command of the voyage; together with several other senior aviation figures and most of the crew. Before the flight Lord Thompson had said: 'R101 will, I hope, give me joy. To ride the storm has always been my ambition.' Fate decided otherwise, and although his determination to set off when the journey did has often been blamed as causing the tragedy, like many disasters there are many causal factors.

This was a major tragedy and it was arranged for the dead to be repatriated to the UK. At the crash scene it was found that many bodies could not be identified, because they had been badly burned or mutilated. Initially only five people were identified, mostly by their possessions or their uniforms. The crash happened early on a Sunday morning but by Tuesday the bodies had been loaded into a train which took them to Boulogne, from where they were carried across the English Channel to Dover by the destroyer *Tempest*. From there a special train left at 9.30 p.m. for Victoria, where it arrived at 1.25 a.m. on Wednesday morning. Despite the lateness of the hour, many people stood at wayside stations to pay their respects as the train passed by.

The Westminster Coroner carried out the necessary procedures, including identifying more bodies, reaching twenty-six in total. After this the coffins were allowed to lie in state in Westminster Hall in the Palace of Westminster, by special permission of His Majesty King George V, whilst a memorial service took place in St Paul's Cathedral, attended by the Prince of Wales (later King Edward VIII) and other dignitaries. Over

R101 airship accident, 1930. Double-headed train conveying forty-eight coffins of victims of the R101 airship accident from Euston to Bedford St John's station near Cardington, for communal burial. (Image courtesy of Kidderminster Railway Museum, Photo/ 103432)

90,000 people filed past the coffins in Westminster Hall and, although this was not a state funeral as such, it was clearly a significant occasion.

The following day, Saturday, 10 October, the coffins were all taken by road on twenty-four horse-drawn army wagons to Euston Station, where they were loaded on to a train, which was doubled-headed by two locomotives, both from the former LNWR 'Prince of Wales' class with a 4-6-0 wheel arrangement. The leading or pilot engine was number 5684, named *Arabic* (formerly LNWR loco 2092), carrying a wreath in a large wooden-framed glass box on the smokebox door, and the train engine was number 5685 *Persia* (formerly LNWR loco 2276). Both locomotives had entered service in April 1916, with the former being withdrawn in April 1936 whilst the latter survived until August 1936. Another locomotive from this class, LNWR number 2275 (later LMS number 5647) had been named *Edith Cavell* when it entered service in November 1915, in honour of Nurse Edith Cavell who had been executed by the Germans in October 1915.[6] No engines from this class have been preserved, but the nameplates from locomotive

R101 airship accident, 1930. Coffin of one of the victims being unloaded at Bedford St John's station before being taken by lorry to Cardington. (Courtesy of Brian Parsons)

2275 *Edith Cavell* still exist, forming part of the National Collection, and one is usually on display at the Colonel Stephens Museum in Tenterden.

The train left Euston at 12.30 p.m. and took the coffins to Bedford St John's station (no longer in existence), arriving at 2.30 p.m. From there the coffins were individually transported by forty-eight motor lorries provided by the army for the last 3 miles to Cardington for burial.

Only twenty-six of the bodies had been identified and although the coffins of these people carried name plaques, these were covered over with Union flags during the lying-in-state. As all the victims had died in the same accident, and so many had not been separately identified, it was felt proper to bury them all together in a communal grave. The coffins were placed in the grave in six rows of eight, each covered with a Union flag

R101 airship accident, 1930. Monument erected over communal grave in cemetery at Cardington. (Photograph © Nicolas Wheatley)

and four services were conducted by ministers from Anglican, Presbyterian, Wesleyan and Roman Catholic denominations, after which the blessing was given by the Bishop of St Albans.[7]

Later on, a large monument was erected over the grave, on which all the names of the victims are inscribed.

Although the R101 disaster was an event of national importance, until a few years ago there was no publicly accessible monument to commemorate it in the UK other than the grave memorial in Cardington itself. However, in France a monument had been erected in October 1933 at Allonne, close to the crash site, together with a memorial marker at the crash site itself. Within St Mary's Church in Cardington there is a small, wall-mounted plaque commemorating the event and also on display within the church is the tattered and charred RAF ensign that was carried on the tail of the airship.

It was not until November 2014 that a memorial plaque was placed in the floor of Westminster Hall to commemorate the lying-in-state of the forty-eight victims, following a campaign by Baroness Smith of Basildon working with the Airship Heritage Trust.[8] The ninetieth anniversary of the R101 disaster occurs in October 2020 and no doubt many commemorations will take place, much as they did after the eightieth anniversary in 2010, in Cardington, Bedford and elsewhere.

The immediate legacy of the accident was to bring about an end to the development of airships in the UK and the scrapping of airship R100, though some attempts have been made in the early twenty-first century to develop a new form of airship, which are outside the scope of this book. The importance of the tragedy for the story of funeral trains is that the final journey of the forty-eight coffins to Bedfordshire was the largest number of deceased people transported by a single train in peacetime in the UK. A larger number had been transported by train following the Quintinshill accident, in which over 200 soldiers were killed and taken back to Edinburgh. However, that had occurred in 1915 during the First World War and the military casualties may have been transported by more than one train. There were several civilians killed in that accident and two were returned by train to Newcastle for burial. Although the train from Euston to Bedford St John's station was essentially a functional transport of the many coffins, it was clearly carried out with a degree of ceremony, as witnessed by the wreath on the locomotive's smokebox door and the fact that the carriages carrying the coffins were draped with purple coverings, at least on the inside.[9]

The use of a train to repatriate the victims of the R101 disaster was not the only time a train had been used for this purpose following an airship accident. In August 1921 the R38 airship had broken in two and exploded over the Humber Estuary, killing forty-four people, many of them US Navy personnel whose bodies were then taken by train to Plymouth for repatriation by sea to the USA. The R38 had been commissioned during the First World War as one of four airships intended by the British government to patrol far out to sea, for days at a time, to look out for German submarines. Though not as big as the later R101 it was still massive, being 695ft (212m) long and 85ft (26m) high and it was the largest aircraft in the world when it was constructed.

Unfortunately for the government, the war came to an end before the aircraft was completed and an agreement was reached to sell it to the US Navy, which designated the aircraft ZR-2. The aircraft first flew on 23 June 1921 but during a test flight on 24 August 1921 with seventeen US Navy personnel on board, a sharp manoeuvre resulted in the airship breaking in two and crashing just off Victoria Pier in Hull. Thousands of spectators watched the tragedy unfold, which happened at 5.45 p.m. on a Saturday[10] and many people attempted to rescue the victims using small boats, as the crash site was close to the shore.[11] These rescue efforts involved considerable acts of bravery, as petrol had spilled from the fuel tanks for the engines and had caught fire, resulting in the surface of the Humber being in flames around the wreckage.[12]

Tragically all but one of the US Navy personnel were killed, along with twenty-eight British people, including Air Commodore Edward M. Maitland,[13] commanding Airship Base Howden, many other air-force personnel; two men from the National Physical Laboratory, who were conducting various tests; and Mr C.I.R. Campbell, who was Chief Designer and Superintendent of the construction of the R38 at Cardington. Also killed was Major J.E.M. Pritchard of the RAF, whose particular interest was developing new forms of engines using heavy oil for rigid airships, as he was 'of the opinion that the greatest danger to airships arose from the petrol fumes and not from the hydrogen'.[14] Whilst the greatest danger to airships was probably more the weather and the strength of their construction, the crashes and subsequent fires that befell the R38 and the R101 arguably demonstrated the correctness of Major Pritchard's opinion on fuel types for the engines.

As *Flight* magazine noted when reporting the R38 disaster:[15]

the calamity is the greater because of the number of valuable lives lost, counting among them many of the most capable and distinguished airship experts of this country and America … It now becomes our duty to see that the most searching enquiry is made as to the cause of the disaster and to incorporate the information this gained in improving airships. To think of abandoning airships would be treachery to those who have given their lives in the great cause, and would render their sacrifice in vain.

Sadly, the subsequent crash of the R101 showed that the development of airship technology probably had indeed been compromised by the loss of so many experts in the R38 crash. Certainly the development of airships never recovered from the loss of the second aircraft.

Almost setting a precedent for the funeral of the R101 victims, many of the British men killed in the R38 disaster were buried in a communal grave, whilst the US Navy victims were repatriated to the USA, using a train to transport their coffins on part of that final journey. The bodies of the sixteen American victims were all quickly recovered from the crash site and on 6 September 1921 at 6.30 p.m. a train left Hull for Devonport Dockyard, where it arrived at 10.00 a.m. the following day. No photos have, as yet, been found of this train, but any that exist would certainly be of interest in the context of this book.

At Devonport the coffins were loaded onto HMS *Dauntless*, a light cruiser that had been placed at the disposal of the American government by the Prime Minister. At almost the same time as the vessel left Devonport a memorial service was held at Westminster Abbey, starting at 12.30 p.m. on Wednesday, 7 September. A detailed report of the funeral and memorial service was printed in *Flight* magazine, Vol. XIII, No.36, September 1921, p.606.

On 2 September five British victims of the accident were buried in a communal grave in Hull Western Cemetery. At the time five other victims had still not been recovered from the crash site and some of the other victims were buried elsewhere, at their families' request. It is feasible that some of those were transported by train and further research is needed to clarify that possibility. The grave was constructed to be sufficiently large to accommodate more burials and a further four bodies were later interred there. In 1924 a large Portland stone memorial was erected over the grave, with separate plaques listing the names of all the British and American victims, noting which British people are buried there. The memorial became a listed structure in November 2002.[16] The bronze plaques originally installed were stolen sometime after 2005 and have never been recovered, so recently they have been replaced with stone ones.

A brass plaque commemorating the four US Navy officers who were killed was placed in 1928 on the interior wall of the St Mary the Virgin Church at Elloughton, a small village about 12 miles to the west of Hull,[17] though the reason for placing the plaque in this particular church is unclear.

R38/ZR-2 airship accident, 1921. The author standing by the monument erected over the communal grave for some British victims in Hull Western Cemetery. (Photograph © Nicolas Wheatley)

Like the train which transported the R101 victims, the train carrying the American R38 victims from Hull to Devonport was essentially a functional transport of coffins. Apart from the repatriations to Scotland after the Quintinshill accident in 1915, the R38 train carried, at the time, the largest number of coffins transported in one train in England originating from a single mass casualty event until the R101 disaster in 1930. On that basis both trains have their place in the history of coffin transport by train in the UK. Hopefully their inclusion in this book may help to revive the recollection of these two tragic events, both of which were important milestones in the ultimately unsuccessful development of British rigid airships.

6

ROYAL
FUNERAL TRAINS

There is one type of funeral train that has been fairly well documented and that is the various trains that have provided the ceremonial final journeys for a number of senior members of the royal family. These include four monarchs: Queen Victoria (1901), King Edward VII (1910), King George V (1936) and King George VI (1952). In fact, all but one of those people actually had their coffins transported by train twice, once for functional purposes to reach London and then again with more ceremony to travel from Paddington Station to Windsor for their burials. Queen Victoria died at her favourite home in Osborne House on the Isle of Wight, so her coffin had to be taken by sea to Gosport and from there by train to London, whilst King Edward VII died at Buckingham Palace. However, both King George V and King George VI died at the royal country house at Sandringham, Norfolk, and both needed to be transported to London for their ceremonial final journeys to Windsor.

These were not, however, the only members of the royal family whose final journey was made by train. Research for this book has identified at least nine other members of the extended royal family whose coffins were transported by train. These were (in date order):

1. 1844. HRH Princess Sophia Matilda of Gloucester[1] (b.1773). A first cousin of Queen Victoria, her coffin was transported by train from Paddington to Slough, as the branch line to Windsor was not opened until 1849.

2. 1857. HRH Princess Mary, Duchess of Gloucester and Edinburgh (b.1776). She was the fourth daughter of King George III and died in 'Gloucester House', though it is not clear whether this was in the family's home of that name in London or Weymouth (reports vary). She is buried in St George's Chapel, Windsor, so if she died in Weymouth she was almost certainly transported by train from there to London. If she died in London she was probably taken to Windsor by train.

3. 1884. HRH Prince Leopold, Duke of Albany (b.1853). Youngest son of Queen Victoria, he died in Cannes, France, and was taken by special train to Cherbourg, then by Royal Yacht to Portsmouth. From there he made his final journey by train to Windsor for burial.

4. 1892. HRH Prince Albert Victor ('Prince Eddy') (b.1864). He was the grandson of Queen Victoria, and was second in line to the throne after his father, the Prince of Wales (later King Edward VII). He died at Sandringham and his coffin was taken by train from Wolferton for eventual burial in Windsor. His younger brother married Princess Victoria Mary of Teck, known as 'May', to whom he had become engaged only six weeks before his death from influenza. The brother became King George V and the Princess became Queen Mary.

5. 1902. Prince Edward of Saxe-Weimar (b.1823). He was not royal by birth but was related to Queen Adelaide (1792–1849), consort and widow of King William IV (1765–1837). The Royal train conveyed the Prince of Wales from London to Chichester for the Prince's funeral and burial in Chichester Cathedral, in the crypt of his wife's family, the Dukes of Richmond and Lennox. It is almost certain that the Prince's body was also conveyed by same train.

6. 1925. HM Queen Alexandra (b.1844). Consort and widow of King Edward VII. She died at Sandringham, and her coffin was taken by train from Wolferton for burial in Windsor.

7. 1931. HRH Princess Louise, Princess Royal (b.1867). Daughter of King Edward VII, widow of Alexander Duff, 1st Duke of Fife (d.1912). She had died in London and was initially buried in Windsor but was later reburied in St Ninian's Chapel, Braemar, alongside husband. She was almost certainly taken to Scotland by train. (Her husband had died in Egypt and was initially buried in Windsor but was then taken in a special saloon by overnight train to Ballater, via Aberdeen, for reburial at Braemar.)

8. 1942. HRH Prince George, Duke of Kent (b.1902). Fourth son of King George V. He died in an air accident on active service in Scotland. His coffin was taken by train to London and then by a 'red painted commercial van' to Windsor for burial. This was during wartime and it may have been more convenient to transport the Prince's coffin to Windsor by motor vehicle. A photograph exists of the van arriving at Windsor and the transportation appears to have been carried out with hardly any of the ceremony that might be expected for the son of the King.

9. 1956. HH Princess Marie Louise (b.1872). She was a granddaughter of Queen Victoria and died in London. She is buried in Windsor and her coffin was taken there by train.[2]

The research has also identified a number of people (further research may well reveal more) who worked for the royal family who made their final journey by train. These include (in date order):

1. 1883. Queen Victoria's servant, John Brown (b.1826). Died at Windsor Castle, buried in Crathie Kirk, Aberdeenshire, close to his place of birth.

2. 1900. Lady Jane Spencer, Baroness Churchill (b.1826). She was the Lady of the Bedchamber to Queen Victoria from 1854 until her death overnight 24/25 December 1900, three weeks before the Queen died. Lady Churchill died at Osborne House, Isle of Wight, and was buried in Finstock, Oxfordshire on 29 December 1900.

3. 1924. Lady Elizabeth Dawson (b.1869). Lady in Waiting to HM Queen Mary. Daughter of 4th Earl of Clanwilliam, wife of the Honourable Edward Stanley Dawson (1843–1919), died in an

accident at Balmoral. Her coffin was taken by train from there (Ballater) to London, and onwards by motor transport to Bray, Berkshire, where she is buried with her husband.

It will be noted that all of the repatriations recorded above were ultimately cases where trains were used for functional purposes, to get a coffin to a place of burial. However, the trains transporting the monarchs on their final journey to Windsor were accompanied by much ceremony, as would be expected for such high-status individuals. The degree of ceremony attached to the final journeys of the other people listed is the subject of ongoing research and hopefully in due course a further book covering all royal funeral trains in the UK will be produced. It is intended that this will also include the final journeys by train within the UK of several members of royal families from other countries, of whom there are a surprisingly large number. The ones identified by research so far are listed in the Gazetteer, but there may be others as yet undiscovered. Indeed, there may be other members of the British royal family whose final journey was by train but where those journeys are not yet documented. In the meantime it is appropriate to set out a few details of the funeral trains of the monarchs mentioned above and also some details of the funeral train of a senior person related to the royal family who died in tragic circumstances.

When Queen Victoria died aged 81 in January 1901 she was not the first monarch to die in the railway age, which effectively had started in 1825 for freight and 1830 for passenger traffic, as King William IV had died in June 1837 at Windsor Castle. He did not need to be transported far for his burial but, as noted above, Queen Victoria died on the Isle of Wight, so her body did need transportation back to Windsor. The full story of how that was done is told in detail in the book by Peter J. Keat, *Goodbye to Victoria: The Last Queen Empress: The Story of Queen Victoria's Funeral Train*, published by Oakwood Press in 2001. This book is still available[3] from the website of Stenlake Publishing which has taken over Oakwood Press. In brief, her coffin was transported by train from Gosport in Hampshire in the GWR's Royal Saloon No. 229 marshalled within the royal train operated by the London Brighton & South Coast Railway (LB&SCR). From Gosport the train was hauled by a locomotive from the LSWR as far as Fareham, where it was changed for a locomotive from the LB&SCR. This locomotive, No. 54, was appropriately named *Empress* and is reported to have travelled at up to 80mph to make up lost time. The late Queen, who did not like travelling at more than 40mph in her lifetime, would not have been amused, but her grandson, the German Kaiser Wilhelm, was sufficiently impressed to congratulate the driver on arrival in London.

The late Queen's coffin was ceremonially taken across London on a gun carriage and then loaded onto the GWR's royal train at Paddington Station. The locomotive used for this part of the Queen's final journey was a 4-4-0 Atbara-class engine, which had been specially renamed *Royal Sovereign* for the occasion. The nameplates were later removed from the locomotive and one is on display at the National Railway Museum in York. In passing, it is worth noting that one of the two Class 67 diesel locomotives currently painted in Royal Claret and used to haul the present Royal Train is also named *Royal Sovereign*, carrying the number 67006. The train transporting Queen Victoria's coffin also carried a large number of mourners, including her son, the new King Edward VII; Kaiser Wilhelm; and many other royal and aristocratic people. In view of this and for security reasons, people were kept away from the route of the train and photographs of it during the journey are relatively rare and usually not of good quality. However, those that have been published often do show groups of people standing to watch the train pass, though not in as large numbers as stood by the lineside for the funeral trains of later monarchs or for Sir Winston Churchill.

The book by Keat is the only one published covering solely the funeral train of one monarch. However, other books on royal trains[4] usually have a chapter, or at least some information, on royal funeral trains, and a book about the Windsor branch line[5] has a complete chapter on the use of Windsor station for the funeral trains of the four monarchs taken there by train. In view of the information available from these other sources, this book will not seek to duplicate what is already published. However, a book about funeral trains in the UK would not be complete without at least some photographs of, and images related to, the ceremonial funeral trains for the four monarchs, which have been included, together with some relevant information.

The first image is not of Queen Victoria's train itself but of the arrangement of the GWR train from Paddington. It shows not only the various parts of the train, starting with the locomotive, but also which people were

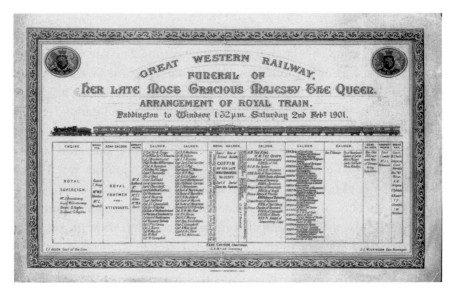

Queen Victoria. Document showing formation of Queen Victoria's GWR funeral train from Paddington to Windsor, February 1901. (Author's Collection)

supposed to be in the various carriages. These included many mourners who were related to the late Queen, including several Kings, Crown Princes and Dukes, together with numerous military people as well as various other dignitaries. These included the Chairman of the GWR, Earl Cawdor, in whose name the document was issued.

The next image is a photo of the funeral train of King Edward VII at Ealing in May 1910. The locomotive was GWR 4-6-0 Star class 4021, appropriately named *King Edward*. It had carried this name from when it was built in 1909, and is the only locomotive that has hauled a monarch's funeral train where the name of the locomotive matches the name of the monarch. The *King Edward* nameplates were removed in 1927 and one is on display at the National Railway Museum in York. The locomotive was renamed twice in 1927, becoming firstly *The British Monarch* and then finally *British Monarch*, before being withdrawn and scrapped in 1952.[6] The fate of the later nameplates remains unknown.

The funeral transportation of the body of the late King George V, who died aged 70 at Sandringham House on 20 January 1936, started at Wolferton in Norfolk. Initially LNER (London and North Eastern Railway) B12 class 4-6-0 locomotive No. 8520 took the LNER's Royal

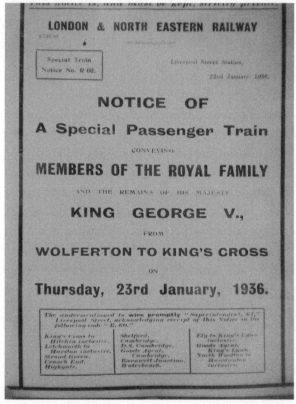

Edward VII. Star Class locomotive 4021 *King Edward* with funeral train passing Ealing on its way to Windsor, May 1910. (Author's Collection)

King George V. Special train notice, LNER. (Author's Collection)

King George V. Funeral train hauled by Sandringham-class locomotive 2847 *Helmingham Hall* passing through Cambridgeshire, January 1936. (Photograph courtesy of Brian Hall/B17 SLT)

Train from there to Kings Lynn, where it had to reverse due to the layout of the track. A new locomotive was then coupled to the other end of the train to take it forward to King's Cross in London. This locomotive was from a design originated by Sir Nigel Gresley, one of the B17 class locomotives which were known as the Sandringham class.[7] This followed the naming of the first locomotive, No. 2800, as *Sandringham* with the King's permission when it was delivered into traffic in December 1928. This particular locomotive would have been the obvious choice to haul the late King's funeral train, but unfortunately it had just gone into Stratford works for some repairs when the King died and they could not be completed in time. Another locomotive from the same class that was the most recently introduced into service (in August 1935) was therefore chosen to carry out the sombre duty and this was No. 2847 *Helmingham Hall*. The funeral train is seen here crossing Stretham Fen in Cambridgeshire, a few miles south of Ely.[8]

Like many other classes of steam locomotives, all the B17s were scrapped during the 1950s and '60s, although a project is underway to build a new B17 which will be called *Spirit of Sandringham*. This will carry what would have been the next number allocated by British Railways to the class, 61673. Details of the project, run by the B17 Steam Locomotive Trust (B17 SLT)[9] can be found on their website, www.b17steamloco.com. Though the locomotive that hauled King George V's funeral train was scrapped, its nameplates were preserved and one is owned by the B17 SLT. Helmingham Hall, near Needham Market, Suffolk, is owned and occupied by the Tollemache family.

Sadly, both the engine driver and the fireman from this royal funeral train suffered tragic and premature deaths. The driver was Frederick Collis, a Cambridge-based regular driver of the Royal Train, and the fireman was Eric Foister, also from the Royal Link based at Cambridge. Only a month after driving the Royal funeral train, Driver Collis, on 29 February 1936, had a sudden collapse whilst at Cambridge station, dying on the spot aged only 55. Following an inquest the coroner concluded that he died of 'angina pectoris' and influenza. He is buried in the cemetery at Trumpington, Cambridge, and a project to restore his grave memorial is being developed.

Fireman Eric Foister rose through the ranks to become a driver but tragically was killed in an accident at Ely station on 12 September 1951 whilst preparing his engine for its next duty. The locomotive had been watered and turned, and was being driven in reverse by the fireman, whilst Driver Foister walked alongside on his way to inform the signalman that they were ready to couple up to their train. Whilst the exact circumstances were never established, it appears that Driver Foister was struck by the locomotive and suffered a serious head injury from which he died instantly, aged only 51. His tragic death only five months before the premature death of King George VI meant that Driver Foister was no longer available to drive the funeral train for the son of King George V. Though not certain, it is likely that he would have been considered a favourite to drive the funeral train for King George VI.[10]

Once in London the late King's remains had a period of lying-in-state in Westminster Hall before being transported on his final journey from Paddington to Windsor. This used the same LNER royal train that had brought his coffin to London, but from Paddington the train was hauled by GWR 4-6-0 Castle-class locomotive 4082 *Windsor Castle*. This locomotive was specially chosen because, in 1924, during a visit to Swindon Works, the

PRIVATE.—For the use of the Company's Servants only.   NOTICE No. 20.

GREAT WESTERN RAILWAY

TIME TABLE
OF
ROYAL TRAIN
FROM
PADDINGTON
TO
WINDSOR & ETON
AND BACK

In connection with the Funeral of
HIS LATE MAJESTY
KING GEORGE V
ON
TUESDAY, JANUARY 28th, 1936

THE L. & N.E. COMPANY'S ROYAL TRAIN WILL BE USED.

☞   This Notice, which will be distributed by the
     Divisional Superintendent, Paddington, to
     all Staff affected in the London Division,
     must be acknowledged immediately on receipt
     by *Telegram* as follows : " ARNO TWENTY."

King George V. Special train notice, GWR, January 1936. (Author's Collection)

King and Queen Mary had been treated to a ride in the cab of the locomotive and indeed the King had driven the then brand-new locomotive, under supervision, from the works to Swindon station. Afterwards a plaque was fitted to the cab side recording the event. When the time came for the King's funeral train it was deemed appropriate that this locomotive should perform the solemn duty of hauling it to Windsor.

It was only sixteen years later that another monarch needed a funeral train when King George VI died aged only 56. As before, initially his coffin had to be brought from Wolferton station after his death on 6 February 1952 at Sandringham House. The first part of the journey was a short trip to Kings Lynn hauled by ex-LNER 4-6-0 No. 61617 *Ford Castle*. This locomotive had started life as a B17 Sandringham-class machine in 1930 but had been rebuilt, with only two cylinders instead of three, as a B2-class engine in 1946. It had kept its name when rebuilt and was the standby royal engine at Kings Lynn, so it fell to this locomotive to haul the royal funeral train for its first 6 miles to that town from Wolferton.

From there it might have been expected that another Sandringham-class locomotive would have been used for the journey to London. This would

King George VI. Funeral from King's Lynn hauled by 70000 *Britannia* at Harringay, north London, February 1952. (P. Ransome-Wallis Collection, courtesy of SSPL)

have been No. 61671, built as 2871 in 1930 and initially named *Manchester City*. It was renamed *Royal Sovereign* in 1946, which then became the usual engine for royal trains on the route to or from Wolferton. However, British Railways had not long taken delivery, in late 1951, of the first of a new Standard class of 4-6-2 locomotives, an express passenger type which became known after the first engine, which was named *Britannia*, and numbered 70000. In view of the prestige attached to this new locomotive it was prepared for its special duty, having its cab roof painted white, and was coupled to the royal funeral train at King's Lynn before hauling it to King's Cross on 11 February 1952.

As before for the funeral train of King George V, the ex-LNER's royal train stock was used, with the late King's coffin being transported in first-class saloon No. 46. The internal fixtures had been removed to allow the King's coffin to be placed within it. The exterior was painted black, hatchments of the King's Coat of Arms were mounted centrally on each side of the carriage and the roof was painted white. On arrival at King's Cross station, the King's coffin was removed amid great ceremony, watched by his widow, HM Queen Elizabeth the Queen Mother, his daughters

HM Queen Elizabeth and HRH Princess Margaret, and by many other dignitaries. The late King's mother, HM Queen Mary (1867–1953) was too ill to attend and indeed she died only a year later in March at the age of 85.

The King's coffin was taken to Westminster Hall for a lying-in-state until 15 February, when it was taken amid great ceremony to Platform 8 of Paddington station. Although this was normally used as the arrivals platform, it was adjacent to the former roadway through the station linking Praed Street and Bishopsbridge Road. This provided a wide space for the various ceremonial activities that took place during the arrival of the late King's coffin, its loading onto the hearse carriage No. 46 and the train's eventual departure for Windsor.

The locomotive used to haul King George VI's funeral train from Paddington appears to be ex-GWR 4-6-0 Castle class 4082 *Windsor Castle* but appearances are deceptive. It had been intended to use this locomotive, the same one that had hauled the funeral train from Paddington for the late King George V. However, this particular engine was in Swindon Works at the time undergoing some repairs, so the most recently overhauled Castle-class locomotive was substituted. This was 7013 *Bristol Castle*, built in 1948. The name and number plates were exchanged with those of 4082 *Windsor Castle* and were never changed back after the event. The plaque recording that King George V had driven the locomotive at Swindon in 1924 was also transferred to 7013 *Bristol Castle* to complete the illusion of being the same locomotive, though this caused some controversy and the plaque was, it is believed, later reattached to the genuine 4082 *Windsor Castle*. After the locomotive had performed its solemn duty with the late King's funeral train it reverted to its normal duties and was withdrawn in 1965. The real *Windsor Castle* had been withdrawn the previous year and both were scrapped. Happily, seven locomotives from the 171-built Castle class have been preserved, in varying states of repair or operation, including the doyen of the class, 4073 *Caerphilly Castle*, which is on display at the excellent STEAM Museum in Swindon.[11]

The last final journey in this chapter is that of a senior British statesman who, though not a member of the royal family by birth, was the uncle of HRH Prince Philip, consort of HM Queen Elizabeth II. He was thus a member of the extended royal family, with many close personal links to it.

King George VI's coffin being placed on the train at Paddington station, 15 February 1952. (Image courtesy of Colin Marsden)

Born in 1900 at Frogmore House on the Windsor estate as Prince Louis of Battenberg, he is better known to history as Lord Louis Mountbatten, 1st Earl Mountbatten of Burma. He had a distinguished career in the Royal Navy, becoming First Sea Lord from 1954 to '59 and being Admiral of the Fleet. In 1947 he had been the last Viceroy of India and was that country's first Governor General from 1947 to '48. He had been created Viscount Mountbatten of Burma in June 1946 and then elevated to become Earl Mountbatten of Burma in August 1947. His illustrious life is beyond the scope of this book, as are the details of his assassination at the hands of the Irish Republican Army (IRA) whilst on holiday in Ireland, when his boat was blown up by an explosion that killed not only him but three other people. This took place on August Bank Holiday, 27 August 1979, causing much outrage internationally.

In view of his status, both on his own account and being related to the royal family, he was accorded a full ceremonial funeral in Westminster

King George VI's funeral train at Paddington station, headed by 4082 *Windsor Castle* (in reality 7013 *Bristol Castle* with name and number plates swapped over). (Author's Collection)

Abbey on Wednesday, 5 September, after which his remains were transported by a special funeral train from Waterloo station to Romsey in Hampshire. From there his coffin was taken by motor hearse the short distance to Romsey Abbey, where he is buried. The nearby country house, Broadlands, had been Earl Mountbatten's home and remains the family home of his grandson, the 3rd Earl Mountbatten of Burma.

The desire to have the 1st Earl's remains buried close to the family home reflects a human wish that underlies most of the cases where trains have been used to transport coffins 'home' for the burial of the deceased in a place of importance to them or their relatives. This book is full of examples where that has happened. The significance of the repatriation of Lord Louis Mountbatten's remains is that it was the last time a private funeral train has operated on the UK main line. It is also the only time that such a funeral train was hauled by a diesel locomotive, as the return journey of Sir Winston Churchill's funeral train, hauled by a diesel locomotive, was no longer carrying his coffin.

In fact, Lord Mountbatten's funeral train was hauled by two diesel-electric locomotives, both from a class of ninety-eight engines built by the Birmingham Railway Carriage & Wagon Company between 1960 and

Earl Mountbatten. Funeral train leaving Waterloo station for Romsey, 5 September 1979. (Photograph taken from Waterloo Signal Box by Jim Oatway, now in Collection of Alan Sainty)

1962. They were initially numbered from D6500 upwards but were later designated Class 33. The class is sometimes given the nickname 'Crompton' after the name of the company that manufactured the electrical equipment fitted to them. This class of locomotive was built especially for the Southern Region of British Railways and, apart from the diesels used on the Waterloo–Exeter services in the 1960s and early 1970s, were the main type of diesels used on the Southern Region. The locomotives selected for hauling Lord Mountbatten's funeral train were numbers 33027 and 33056, formerly D6545 and D6574 respectively.

As can be seen from this photo, the train did not carry any decorations, unlike the royal funeral trains, though the locomotives are immaculately turned out, including the front buffers of the leading engine being painted silver. The train itself was not the royal train, a new set of carriages having been created for this in 1977. The leading coach, however, did come from the royal train, being saloon number 2906 in claret livery. This was occupied by several police officers and two members of the Royal Staff. The rest of the train comprised four first-class carriages; a restaurant buffet car; a corridor composite brake; and a full brake (a BG in railway parlance) M80867, appropriately decorated inside, which transported the coffin. These were all in the then standard British Rail livery of blue and light grey. According to Hoey,[12] this was considered to be less obvious than the Royal Train for security reasons.

Apart from members of Lord Mountbatten's family, the train also conveyed several senior members of the Royal Family, including HM The Queen, HRH Prince Philip, HRH Prince Charles, HRH Princess Anne and her then husband, Captain Mark Phillips. Possibly because of the security concerns, very real during the time of the Troubles in Northern Ireland, which occasionally led to bombings in the UK mainland, there seem to be very few photographs of the train during the Earl's final journey. The photograph on page 129 (which may never have been previously published) shows the train heading south just past Wallers Ash Loop, between Micheldever and Winchester.

It can be said for certain that this was the last private funeral train run on the UK main line[13] and it would require some very exceptional circumstances for another to be operated. However, plans had been made in 1977 for a funeral train for HM The Queen, under the code name 'Operation London Bridge'. This was at a time when she was travelling around the country a great deal, often by Royal Train, as part of her Silver Jubilee celebrations.

These plans were held at The National Archives, under file reference AN156 976, and were closed until 2008. The file includes a letter dated 13 January 1977 from the General Manager, Paddington, Mr L. Lloyd, to various senior railway managers. The letter includes references to various changing circumstances, including the introduction of HST (High Speed Train) sets, the replacement of the Royal Train with new stock in May 1977 and the need to relay some track at Windsor station to provide access to the second platform. The letter also records that 'if the Sovereign died at Balmoral or Sandringham the Earl Marshall requests that the body is conveyed by train to London'. The BR file, reference X92-54A, is clear that the arrangements made had been developed in liaison with the Earl Marshall, who is the hereditary office holder in charge of arrangements for royal events, including funerals.

Whether Her Majesty Queen Elizabeth II will have a royal funeral train, given the changes to the railway network and its operation since 1977,

Lord Mountbatten's funeral train heading south past Wallers Ash Loop between Micheldever and Winchester, 5 September 1979. (© Colin Marsden)

is uncertain. It will be remembered that following the deaths of HRH Princess Margaret and HM Queen Elizabeth The Queen Mother, both in early 2002, their final journeys were made by motor hearse rather than by train, so whether the Sovereign has a royal funeral train when her time comes remains to be seen. It will also be recalled that Diana, Princess of Wales (1961–1997), did not make her final journey on a royal funeral train, although the Royal Train was used on 6 September 1997 to convey HRH The Prince of Wales, HRH Prince William and HRH Prince Harry and Earl Spencer from London Euston to Long Buckby for her private inter-ment at the Spencer family estate in Althorp.

It is no secret that plans for royal funerals are made well before they are needed and, indeed, the people involved engage in developing and review-ing those plans on a regular basis. Hoey[14] states that 'precedent is everything in preparing for a Royal duty and often, macabre as it may sound, the principals involved will concern themselves with the most tiny detail of their own funeral'. There has not been a funeral train for a monarch since 1952 and hopefully, if there is to be another one, it will not be needed for a long time.

7

SIR WINSTON CHURCHILL AND HIS EXTENDED FAMILY

I am prepared to meet my Maker.
Whether my Maker is prepared for the great ordeal
of meeting me is another matter.

Sir Winston Churchill

Perhaps the most famous funeral train in living memory was the one that carried the mortal remains of Sir Winston Churchill KG (1874–1965) from Waterloo Station in London to 'Handborough for Blenheim' station[1] in Oxfordshire. The fiftieth anniversary, on 30 January 2015, of the occasion of Sir Winston Churchill's funeral generated many TV programmes, reports, articles and even some books about the event. The only state funeral of a commoner in the twentieth century was remembered for many reasons, not least the unequalled contribution that Churchill made to British history including, famously, his leadership during the Second World War.

However, the part of the event that took place on 30 January 1965, which is relevant to this book, is the train that transported his coffin and the family mourners from London, following the funeral in St Paul's

Cathedral, to Handborough. This is the nearest station to his burial plot in the churchyard of St Martin's Church, Bladon, close to his birthplace at Blenheim Palace. Churchill was the grandson of the 7th Duke of Marlborough (1822–1883), though as the elder son of the Duke's third son, Lord[2] Randolph Churchill (1849–1895), he was not in line to inherit the title. He had, however, requested during his lifetime that he be buried in the family plot at Bladon, and had also been closely involved in the planning of his funeral, including the use of a train to convey his coffin.

As noted elsewhere in this book, whilst the transport of coffins by train was relatively common in the nineteenth and first half of the twentieth centuries, the practice was diminishing by the early 1960s, though it did not cease on the main line until 1988. However, in honour of Churchill's national status, a ceremonial funeral train was arranged, this being the last occasion when a steam locomotive hauled one on the main line. The use of steam locomotives on the UK main line stopped in August 1968, so the later ceremonial funeral train in 1979 for Earl Mountbatten was diesel hauled by a pair of Class 33 locomotives.[3] This train carried his coffin from Waterloo to Romsey for burial at Romsey Abbey, close to his family seat at Broadlands.

Churchill had suffered a series of strokes in the 1950s, when his health declined significantly, so planning for his funeral began at the end of 1959, under the code name 'Operation Hope Not'. He broke his hip in a fall in Monte Carlo in 1962, by which time he was already 87. In anticipation of running the funeral train, British Railways selected and set aside an ex-Southern Region bogie luggage van, S2464S, which was specially painted in Pullman umber and cream livery in 1962. However, Churchill recovered, so the van was kept in secure storage until it was required. Sadly, Churchill suffered a major stroke in early January 1965, dying several days later on 24 January, coincidentally on the same date that his father had died in 1895. The van was then repainted ready for use in the funeral train on Saturday, 30 January.

The train itself consisted of this van, used as a hearse van with a catafalque added in the centre of the vehicle on which the coffin was placed at Waterloo Station.

The rest of the train comprised five Pullman cars in umber and cream livery, marshalled in the following order for the outbound trip: *Car 208*

Funeral of Sir Winston Churchill, 30 January 1965, coffin being loaded into hearse van at Waterloo Station. (Press Association 1235708)

(second-class brake, with brake leading); S2464S luggage (hearse) van; *Carina* (first-class kitchen, with kitchen trailing); *Lydia* (first-class kitchen, with kitchen trailing); *Perseus* (first-class parlour, with large saloon leading); *Isle of Thanet* (first-class brake, with brake trailing).

The locomotive selected to haul this very special, though private, train was a Bulleid Battle of Britain class 4-6-2 locomotive, number 34051,[4] appropriately named *Winston Churchill* (it was never renamed 'Sir Winston Churchill' after he was knighted in 1953). Churchill had been invited to perform the naming ceremony in September 1947 but had declined, saying in effect that he was 'too busy', even though the war had finished and he was no longer Prime Minister. This 1946-built loco was based at

Funeral train of Sir Winston Churchill passing through Barnes station in south-west London, 30 January 1965. (Author's Collection)

Salisbury locomotive shed (70E) from June 1951, where it had spent some time in semi-retirement before being used for the most famous working of its existence. It had previously been shedded at Nine Elms from February 1950 until April 1951 and so for the occasion of the funeral train was refitted with a 70A shed plate appropriate for that shed.

The funeral itself, the carrying of the coffin on a barge up the River Thames to Waterloo station and the train journey to Hanborough were broadcast live on television and millions of people all around the world watched. Many photos have been published of the train during its trip to Oxfordshire, and many were republished to commemorate the fiftieth anniversary. However, it has been possible to find two photographs of the train during Churchill's final journey that are perhaps less well known. One is of the train passing Barnes, in south-west London. The number of people on the tracks would certainly not be tolerated today!

Another image that is perhaps less well known shows the train passing slowly through Oxford station. The footplate crew had been requested to

Funeral train of Sir Winston Churchill passing slowly through Oxford station, 30 January 1965, hauled by Battle of Britain class locomotive 34051 *Winston Churchill*. (Photograph by Alan Maund, in Collection of Michael Clemens)

pass through at only 20mph and the tolling of church bells could clearly be heard by them[5] and by the mourners on the train if the windows were open.

However, what are less well recorded are the backup arrangements, the return trip to London and the subsequent fate of the vehicles used in the train. Though in the event it was not needed, a standby loco had been positioned at Staines Central, this being another Bulleid Pacific, 34064 *Fighter Command*, now sadly scrapped. The loco used to return the train to London, Paddington Station rather than Waterloo, was the relatively new Western-class diesel hydraulic D1015, *Western Champion*, in its original and unique 'golden ochre' livery.

Happily, this loco has been preserved and restored privately, and is certified to run on Network Rail, which it does hauling excursion trains to various parts of the country. For the return trip, another standby loco, Western-class diesel, D1028, *Western Hussar*, was based at Reading, though again it was not needed, and it too has since been scrapped. The star loco 34051 was not initially scheduled for preservation and even saw some

Funeral train of Sir Winston Churchill waiting to leave Handborough station for return to London, 30 January 1965, hauled by Western-Class locomotive D1015, *Western Champion*, in unique 'Golden Ochre' livery. (Photograph courtesy of Colin J Marsden)

service after the funeral before withdrawal in September 1965, but happily it was eventually saved for posterity by its addition to the National Collection and was on display at the National Railway Museum in York for many years.

Following the funeral, the hearse van was put up for sale by BR and was eventually sold to a businessman in the USA. It was exported via London's Royal Victoria Dock in October 1965 and spent many years at the City of Industry in Los Angeles. For a time it was part of a display recreating a British-style station, but ended up as the store for a golf club on the site. Two of the cars used in the funeral train, *Isle of Thanet* and *Lydia*, which had formed part of a train used during the Second World War by General (later President) Eisenhower, were donated by the British Government to the American; they were formally handed over during a ceremony at Kensington Olympia. Both cars were shipped to the USA in 1969 as part of the promotional train run by Alan Pegler, hauled by his privately preserved loco LNER A3 Pacific 4472, *Flying Scotsman*[6] and Pullman Observation Car 14 was also part of this train. One car, *Isle of Thanet*, was dropped off at the American National Railroad Museum in Green Bay, Wisconsin, where it was displayed with two ex-LNER carriages, whilst *Lydia* stayed with the Scotsman train.[7] Although the first trip was a commercial success, a second trip in 1970 (the train stayed in America) became financially ruinous, bankrupting Pegler and leaving the loco and Pullman cars stranded in San Francisco, California.

Happily, in November 2000, the two Pullman cars *Isle of Thanet* and *Lydia* were repatriated to Britain at the instigation of a supporter of the Swanage Railway, who had bought them and who wished to remain anonymous. The intention had been to run them on that railway as part of a dining train, but they remain at Carnforth until covered storage can be provided for them at the railway. The story of the repatriation of these Pullman cars deserves telling, but is outside the scope of this book.

Meanwhile, back in California, the hearse van's fate became intertwined with that of Car 14, and both were repatriated through the project management of a senior figure then associated with the Swanage Railway. The project to repatriate Car 14 had been started in 2005 and eventually this project expanded to include repatriation of the hearse van too. It had become surplus to requirements from its use as a store for the café on the golf course. The van's owners were happy to have the van taken away, but the cost of transport proved a barrier. Happily, the City of Industry stepped in and agreed to pay for the van's shipment back to Britain. This was done in recognition of the historical importance of the van and its place in British railway history. The shipping back to Britain was carried out by a roll-on roll-off ferry that conveniently sailed regularly from Long Beach, California to Southampton Docks. Car 14 was also repatriated by the same route and can now be seen running on the Swanage Railway.

After cosmetic restoration and repainting at Cranmore, by the East Somerset Railway, the hearse van was taken to Dorset and spent some time based at Corfe Castle station on the Swanage Railway. An application for a grant to develop the interior of the van as a museum telling the story of the railways during the Second World War was, unfortunately, turned down by the Heritage Lottery Fund, and the van became a store for tools used in the restoration of other carriages.

Hearse van S2464 from the Churchill funeral train after repainting at Cranmore, East Somerset Railway, March 2010. (Photograph © Nicolas Wheatley)

The Churchill funeral train was a unique event, being the only private ceremonial funeral train on the main line using solely Pullman cars, apart from the hearse van painted into Pullman-style livery. It also became the only funeral train to be the subject of an exhibition celebrating its own anniversary. From 30 January 2015 parts of the train, including the hearse van, were displayed in the Great Hall at the National Railway Museum (NRM) in York as part of an exhibition commemorating the fiftieth anniversary of the running of the funeral train. Originally the exhibition was only scheduled to last until early May 2015 but due to its popularity it was extended until the end of that month. The hearse van was featured along with loco 34051 *Winston Churchill*, which was cosmetically restored at Ropley on the Mid Hants Railway, with financial support from the Friends of the NRM.

One other vehicle from the funeral train also formed part of the display, this being first-class kitchen car *Lydia*, which had been substantially restored to its original condition, both externally and in its interior. Following the end of the exhibition as such, *Lydia* reverted to its private owner's possession and is once again in storage at Carnforth.[8] The locomotive and hearse van continued to be displayed at the museum in York for some time, before being transferred for display at 'Locomotion', the museum's branch in Shildon, County Durham. The locomotive is still there,[9] though the hearse van, still in the ownership of the Swanage Railway Trust, was moved in September 2019 to a private storage facility in Margate, Kent, part of the old Hornby factory warehouse, where it is no longer on display to the public. However, the owners of the facility hope to open it as a museum to the public in due course.

What of the other vehicles used in the train? Happily they all still exist, with *Perseus* in regular use as part of the Belmond (formerly VSOE) British Pullman train, and *Car 208* can be found in Galway, Ireland, where it is used as part of a restaurant at the 5★ luxury Glenlo Abbey Hotel.[10] *Isle of Thanet* is still stored at Carnforth awaiting completion of its restoration, and *Carina* is awaiting a major restoration on the Bluebell Railway.

Although the Churchill funeral train was a major event, and is the only time a Pullman train has been privately chartered to carry a coffin for transportation to a burial, it was still subject to the potential hazards of railway operation, and the mourners on the train were there because of a sad event within the Churchill family. Two small incidents illustrate these points. Apparently, when the time came for the coffin to be unloaded, it was found that the weight of the guardsmen acting as pallbearers, who had travelled in *Car 208*, had caused the outwards-opening doors of the hearse van to jam against the ramp down to the platform. Fortunately six platelayers had been retained on standby and they moved the ramp to allow the doors to be opened, before replacing it so that the ceremony could continue. This potentially embarrassing incident is recounted by retired railwayman Bill Sidwell (b.1927) in the book *Tales of the Old Railwaymen*.[11] No doubt this incident did occur, though he also mentions there being television cameras present, which in fact was not the case for the unloading at Handborough and the burial at Bladon.

The private nature of the funeral train was captured by Emma Soames, one of Churchill's granddaughters, aged 14 at the time of the funeral, in a BBC interview in 2014. She poignantly said that the loading of the coffin onto the train marked the point when the very public funeral became a private event,

Funeral train of Sir Winston Churchill during return journey to London Paddington, 30 January 1965. (Photographer unknown, Author's Collection)

'when grandpapa was given back to the family'. In accordance with the wishes of Churchill's widow, Lady Clementine, film and TV cameras were banned from Handborough and the burial at Bladon, and only a few still photographs exist of the train at the station, where the light was fading at nearly 3.30 p.m. on that cold January afternoon. Remarkably, however, a colour photograph has emerged (reproduced above in black & white) of the funeral train on its return to London, at an unidentified location almost certainly in Oxfordshire. Darkness had fallen by the time of the train's arrival at Paddington at 5.35 p.m. and no photos of that occasion have been discovered so far.

The funeral train for Sir Winston was very much a ceremonial event, though it also had the functional purpose of delivering his coffin to Handborough for burial at Bladon. Other members of the Churchill family have also had their coffins transported by train to a station close to their places of burial. In fact, this has happened to no fewer than seven other members of the extended Churchill family, so, although Sir Winston's funeral train was the most famous, it was also the last of several.

For a family as aristocratic as the Churchills, the place of burial was significant and the cost of transporting the body of a family member who had died away from that place was not a financial problem. Indeed, John Churchill, the 1st Duke of Marlborough (1650–1722), was initially buried in Westminster Abbey but, in accordance with instructions given by his widow Sarah, his remains were relocated to the chapel at Blenheim Palace, to lie side by side with her, after her death in 1744. This set a precedent for the burial of subsequent Dukes of Marlborough, including the 5th and 6th Dukes, who died after railways had started to transport coffins. They had died in 1840 and 1857, respectively, but both had died at Blenheim Palace, so there was no need to repatriate them. However, the 7th Duke, Sir Winston Churchill's grandfather, was the first to die away from Blenheim Palace. He died suddenly in London aged 61 in July 1883 and his remains were transported by train to Oxfordshire for his burial in the private chapel at Blenheim Palace.

Twelve years later Lord Randolph Churchill, Sir Winston's father, died aged only 45 in London, on 24 January 1895. Though he did not qualify for burial in the chapel at Blenheim Palace, he was buried in the churchyard of St Martin's Church, Bladon, within sight of Blenheim Palace.[12] On Monday, 28 January the London funeral director firm of J.H. Kenyon arranged for his coffin to be taken to Paddington station and it was despatched on the 10.20 a.m. train. He was buried at Bladon the same day, at 1.30 p.m.,[13] and Sir Winston is now buried in close proximity.

The next member of the Churchill family to have their coffin transported by train was Sir Winston's aunt, Lady Georgiana Elizabeth Spencer-Churchill (1860–1906), the fifth daughter and tenth of the 7th Duke's eleven children. In 1883 she had married Richard George Penn Curzon, (1861–1929), who at the time was styled Viscount Curzon, though he became 4th Earl Howe on the death of his father in 1900. Lady Georgiana thus became Countess Howe and was a noted society hostess, entertaining King George V and Queen Mary at her homes both in London and at the family's country estate, Gopshall Hall, Leicestershire. Sadly she died on 9 February 1906 at the family's London home, Curzon House, Mayfair, at the early age of only 45,[14] having never fully recovered from a 'paralytic seizure' (probably a stroke) three years previously.

Her husband arranged for her to be buried in the church in the village of Congerstone, near to the family estate at Gopshall. This was close to

Coffin of Countess Howe (aunt of Sir Winston Churchill) at Shackerstone station, Leicestershire, having been unloaded from the train. February 1906. (Photograph courtesy of Brian Parsons)

Shackerstone station, built in 1877 by the Midland Railway on land sold by the 3rd Earl Howe. The station has survived and is now the headquarters and northern terminus of the heritage railway known as The Battlefield Line.[15] The Countess's coffin was transported in one of three saloons added to the 11.00 a.m. train from Euston to Nuneaton on 14 February. From there, the three carriages were taken as a special train to Shackerstone station, arriving at 1.20 p.m. The coffin was then transferred to a horse-drawn hearse for the short remainder of the Countess's final journey to St Mary's church in nearby Congerstone.

The funeral was reported in depth, with photographs by *The Hinckley Times*, and on 7 March 1991 the newspaper reprinted its coverage of the report under a 'Nostalgia' feature and a copy of this reprint is on display at Shackerstone station. In 1916 a large and elaborate memorial was erected in the church, which is still there. However, in 1919 the Howe family sold Gopshall Hall, which was demolished by 1952, leaving no trace, and it is believed that the Countess's remains were exhumed and reburied closer to the present home of the Howe family at Penn, near Amersham, in Buckinghamshire. There is no trace of her former burial site in the churchyard at Congerstone.

The second of Sir Winston's parents died in 1921. His mother, known as Lady Randolph Churchill (born in the USA as Jennie Jerome, 1854–1921), had married Lord Randolph in 1874 when she was only 20. After his death she married twice more, but reverted to the name Lady Randolph Churchill by deed poll. She died aged 67 at her home in London following complications arising from a fall. Once again J.H. Kenyon arranged her funeral, including sending her coffin on a final journey by train to Oxfordshire, where she is buried next to her first husband in the churchyard at Bladon.

Lord Randolph Churchill's older brother, George, had become the 8th Duke of Marlborough in 1883 on the death of their father, but sadly George died aged only 48 in 1892. He died at Blenheim so he did not need to be repatriated there for burial in the family chapel. However, the 9th Duke of Marlborough, Charles Spencer-Churchill (1871–1934) died in London on 30 June 1934 and his body was transported by train back to Oxfordshire for his burial at Blenheim. He was a first cousin and lifelong close friend of Sir Winston, being only three years older than him.

A more distant cousin, Victor Albert Francis Charles Spencer (1864–1934) succeeded to his father's title as 3rd Baron Churchill in 1886 and was created 1st Viscount Churchill in June 1902. He was a director or chairman of various transport companies, including the Great Western Railway, of which he was chairman from 1908 until his death in January 1934, becoming its longest-serving chairman. Following his death, the GWR facilitated his final journey to Finstock in Oxfordshire, a village close to Cornbury Park, which had been the family's estate since the 2nd Baron Churchill had become lord of the manor in 1857. The station for this village, on what is now known as the North Cotswolds Line, was originally named Finstock Hall but was opened by the GWR only in April 1934. In consequence, the Viscount's coffin was probably unloaded at the next station along the line, Charlbury, which had been opened in 1853 by the line's original developers, the Oxford, Worcester and Wolverhampton Railway.

It is not known where Viscount Churchill's father had died, but his mother died at Osborne House on the Isle of Wight, where she had been a member of Queen Victoria's household. Lady Jane Spencer, Baroness Churchill (1826–1900) had been one of the Queen's close friends and advisers, serving in her role as Lady of the Bedchamber since her appointment in 1854, making her the longest serving of the Queen's personal household. She died during the night on 24 December 1900 and was found the next morning, Christmas Day. Initially there was some reluctance to inform the ailing Queen of Lady Jane Churchill's death, and indeed the Queen was distressed to learn the news. On 28 December 1900 Lady Jane's body was taken back to the mainland, where she was buried in Finstock the following day. The details of her final journey have yet to be established but would have required transportation by train, as motor hearses had not yet been developed. It is noteworthy just how quickly this funeral, and the transport it required, was arranged given the time of year, though in those days trains ran on both Christmas Day and Boxing Day.

The Queen herself died less than four weeks later, on 22 January 1901, and became the first UK monarch to have a final journey by train. In fact she had two, one a functional trip taking her remains to London, then a more ceremonial journey from Paddington to Windsor for burial in the royal mausoleum at Frogmore. This is covered in Chapter 6 but the full details are contained in the book by Peter J. Keat, *Goodbye to Victoria: The Last Queen Empress: The Story of Queen Victoria's Funeral Train.*[16]

That eight members of the extended Churchill family had their final journeys by train is unusual in its scale, and possibly unique, apart from members of the royal family. However, the Churchill family had many members in public service and were able to afford the costs of repatriating deceased members to the family's chosen place of burial. Although Sir Winston Churchill's state funeral was paid for by public funds, the cost of hiring the train, by then not part of the state funeral, was recharged to his family. However, as the cost of hiring each Pullman car was charged at only 15 guineas,[17] it is unlikely that anywhere near the full cost was recovered by British Railways. However, in view of Sir Winston's stature, the cost to the public of subsidising this final journey has never been questioned.

8

OTHER KNOWN (AND UNKNOWN) PEOPLE

Paradoxically for a chapter on other known people who had their coffins transported by train, this is the place where the author feels it is appropriate to mention the thousands of corpses transported by train whose identities have not been recorded. In due course, research may identify some of the individuals whose final journey was by train. However, it is unlikely that the remains involved in some of the mass exhumations from central London churchyards who were relocated to Brookwood Cemetery will ever be identified. For example, in his book on the Brookwood Necropolis Railway, Clarke mentions[1] the case of the exhumations from the burial ground of Cure's College, in London, which was required for the building of the South Eastern Railway in 1862. At least 8,000 bodies were relocated from this site to Brookwood Cemetery, using special trains that ran at night, carrying the bodies in 220 'very large cases, each containing 26 human bodies besides children', rather than in the regular hearse vans.

There is another category of deceased who will probably never be identified, but whose final journeys took them to places where they made important, though unrecognised, contributions to medical science. These were the corpses which were taken by train to various schools of anatomy, where they were dissected for the purposes of medical education and training. Often these were people living, or at least dying, in poverty, sometimes in Victorian workhouses. Instead of being given a proper burial, their corpses were sold to medical schools and transported by train to the towns or cities where those schools were based. More research is needed to confirm the total scale of this traffic, but the information that has been published so far indicates that scores, probably hundreds, of corpses were involved over many decades. One of the leading schools of anatomy was based in Aberdeen, Scotland, where the cost of transporting corpses from England, at 1 shilling per mile, was the cause of comment and complaint by those in charge of the medical schools. This is the subject of ongoing research by Dr Dee Hoole from the University of Aberdeen, to whom the author is grateful for sharing some of her findings.

Other medical schools that used corpses that were brought in by train were in Oxford and, notably, in Cambridge. This has been the subject of research published in 2012 by Elizabeth Hurren in her book *Dying for Victorian Medicine: English Anatomy and its Trade in the Dead Poor c.1834-1929*.[2] One of her main findings was:

> the reliance of the anatomy trade on the railway system in Victorian England. On a daily basis, where there was a fast train, there was a corpse for anatomy being transported in a rear carriage in a dead box.[3] Smaller towns in East Anglia or surrounding Oxford supplied a disproportionate number of dead bodies because they were ideally located on the railway line to do so.[4]

Earlier in her book[5] she had established that corpses were transported by train to Cambridge up to three times a week from the north of England, Doncaster being mentioned as a particular place where these corpses would start their final journey.

The transportation of these corpses would have been carried out in a functional manner, as defined in Chapter 2, and, perhaps not surprisingly, no photographs are known to exist of this traffic. They remain the 'unknown dead' and their unwitting contribution to the advancement of medical knowledge goes largely unappreciated. The role of trains to transport their corpses is only slowly being recognised but this part of this book will, hopefully, shine a small beam of light into one of the darker corners of the use of trains to transport the dead.

More broadly, research for this book has identified a significant number of individuals whose coffins are known to have been transported by train and some of them have already been mentioned. Others will have their stories told in later chapters. It would require a book as least as big again to tell everyone's story but the Gazetteer at the end of this book contains some brief details of the many people identified as having their final journey by train. Within the space available it is possible to highlight only a few of them.

The first of these was George Peabody (1795–1869). He was born in Massachusetts in the USA and had a career as a financier. Having previously visited England on several occasions, in 1837 he settled in London and started a banking business from which several other banking organisations can trace their origins, including J.P. Morgan. Having become extremely wealthy but with no family, he became a philanthropist. In London this took the form of providing housing of a decent quality for the 'artisans and labouring poor'. The organisation he founded still operates as the Peabody Trust, providing social housing in London.

After his death in London in November 1869 he was initially and temporarily buried in Westminster Abbey, but his will provided for him to be buried in the town of his birth. Prime Minister William Gladstone arranged for a ship from the Royal Navy to take his body back to the USA, where it arrived at Portland, Maine. From there it was transported by a decorated train to Salem, Massachusetts, where he was buried in February 1870, with hundreds of people attending. The reason for including this funeral train in this book is that the image below is the earliest depiction so far found of a ceremonial funeral train transporting the body of someone who, though not British, nevertheless had close associations with the UK. It will be noted that the decorations on the train include both the American and UK flags on the front of the locomotive. The van behind the locomotive carrying his coffin is not decorated on the outside but was appropriately draped inside, and it will be noted that the first carriage is also decorated.

The first funeral train in the UK for which an image of the train has been found relates to William Ewart Gladstone (1809–98). He was four

Funeral train in the USA for George Peabody, 1870. He was an American-born financier who turned philanthropist, providing social housing in London, where he died. His body was repatriated to the USA and is buried in Massachusetts. Note the US and UK flags on the locomotive. (Author's Collection)

times Liberal Prime Minister during the reign of Queen Victoria, though apparently she did not particularly like him. However, when he died in May 1898 she gave her consent to his body being buried in Westminster Abbey, and his family were persuaded to agree, though their initial desire was that he be buried in Hawarden. As he had died at the family's estate at Hawarden Castle, Flintshire, in north-east Wales, a final journey was required to take his body to London. A special train was organised by the London & North Western Railway (LNWR), with five carriages, one of which was used to carry the coffin. This was either a brake van or a postal sorting tender[6] which was painted black, decorated internally with black drapes and marshalled in the centre of the train. The LNWR arranged for an appropriately named locomotive, a Hardwicke-class 2-4-0 engine No. 1521 *Gladstone*[7] to be painted black, with grey lining, to haul the train.

Although there was (and still is) a station at Hawarden, the line through it does not lead towards London. Accordingly, Gladstone's coffin was taken

Broughton Hall station, near Hawarden, north-east Wales, May 1898. The coffin of Prime Minister William Ewart Gladstone is loaded into a special train to London, where he was buried in Westminster Abbey. (*Illustrated London News* via Mary Evans Picture Library, 13048075)

the short distance to Broughton Hall station[8] (since closed, though the up-platform buildings shown in the image above still exist), where it was placed into the train, as depicted in this contemporary image from the *Illustrated London News*.

The train set off at 7.52 p.m. on 28 May and made its way via Chester non-stop to Willesden Junction, where the locomotive was changed. A four-coupled tank engine, No. 788, was attached, which had condensing gear fitted for operating on the Underground. The train proceeded via the West London Extension Railway and Earls Court to Westminster Bridge[9] station, where it arrived at 1.02 a.m., and the coffin was taken straight to Westminster Hall. The reason for running the train at that time of day was to avoid the crowds of people that would have been present to pay their respects, as the family wanted the transportation to be carried out with more privacy than ceremony. This funeral train is the only one to have run over the rails of the London Underground system. Two years later, in June 1900, Gladstone's wife, Catherine (1812–1900), died at Hawarden and she is buried next to him. It is certain that her coffin was transported by train to London, but the details of her final journey are yet to be researched.

William Gladstone's final journey started with a degree of ceremony but was essentially a functional trip to get his coffin to London for burial. A few years later another famous person had a final journey where the ceremony was displayed at his destination rather than at the point of departure. This was the case of the Honourable Charles Stewart Rolls (1877–1910), third son of John Rolls, who progressed upwards through Victorian society, becoming the 1st Baron Llangattock, a village near Monmouth, in south Wales.

As he was not in line to succeed his father to the peerage or the family estates, Charles sought his fame and fortune in other fields. After graduating from Cambridge University he became a premium apprentice, training with the London & North Western Railway in Crewe. However, in due course he met with Henry (later Sir Henry) Royce (1863–1933) and between them they formed the Rolls-Royce motor manufacturing company. Although the company went from strength to strength, Charles Rolls' direct involvement diminished as he had less and less direct engagement in its activities and turned his interests to the fledgling world of aviation. He became only the second person in Britain to be granted a pilot's licence and sadly he became the first person in Britain to die in an accident involving a powered aircraft. Taking off from an airfield at Hengistbury, near Bournemouth, on 12 July 1910, his aircraft, a Wright Flyer, crashed during a flying display after part of its tail broke off, killing Charles Rolls instantly. He was only 32 years old but had already earned his place in history.

His family wished that he be buried in the family plot at St Cadoc's church at Llangattock-Vibek-Avel, the nearest church to the family home at The Hendre, near Monmouth. For his final journey his coffin was taken by train from Bournemouth to Monmouth (Troy) station, the nearest one to the Rolls' family home. The 'homecoming' of such an important local hero was a matter of considerable local interest and he was greeted by the attendance of a great many people and appropriate funereal ceremony. The photos opposite show the crowds that had gathered to welcome home the coffin of one of Monmouth's most famous sons, an honour he shares with King Henry V, who was born in the town in 1387.

Coffin of Charles Rolls (of Rolls-Royce fame) after being unloaded from the train at Monmouth (Troy) station, 1910. The station building was later dismantled and is now Winchcombe station on the Gloucestershire Warwickshire Steam Railway. (Author's Collection)

Coffin of Charles Rolls in a horse-drawn hearse soon to leave forecourt of Monmouth (Troy) station, 1910. (Lens of Sutton Association)

Coffin of Sir William Grantham, barrister, MP and later High Court judge, being unloaded at Barcombe station, near Lewes, close to his Sussex estate, after his death in London, 1911. (Photograph courtesy of Roger T. Price, Bluebell Railway archive)

After being unloaded from the train, his coffin was placed onto a horse-drawn hearse and taken the last few miles to the church at Llangattock-Vibek-Avel, where Charles Rolls was buried and now rests next to other members of his family. Following the total closure of the railway through Monmouth (Troy) station in 1964, the building was, in the late 1980s, dismantled stone-by-stone by volunteers from the nascent Gloucestershire Warwickshire Steam Railway (GWSR). It was eventually re-erected as Winchcombe station, though in truth it is located nearly a mile from the town whose name it bears.

Just over a year later the unloading of another high-status person's coffin was recorded in a photograph. William (later Sir William) Grantham (1835–1911) pursued a career as a barrister before being elected as a Member of Parliament in 1874. He resigned from Parliament when he was appointed as a High Court judge in 1886, having been knighted the previous year. In 1911 he was severely rebuked by the Prime Minister, H.H. Asquith, after making an indiscreet speech in court and he died later that year, on 30 November in London. His family estate was at Barcombe Place, near Lewes in Sussex, and he made a final journey there by train. The photograph to the left shows his coffin being unloaded from the train at Barcombe station, which was closed in 1955. Part of the former line, from East Grinstead to Lewes, was reopened as the Bluebell Railway in 1960, though stopping at Sheffield Park, several miles to the north of Barcombe.

Unfortunately there are not as many recorded cases of women having their coffins transported by train as there are men, so the next two photographs have a degree of rarity value. Lady Christina Anne Jessica Sykes (1856–1912) was the wife of Sir Tatton Sykes (1826–1913), 5th Baronet, who was thirty years older than her, though it was not a happy marriage and he disclaimed her debts after they had separated. She was a renowned society hostess, and apparently was described as 'the most prominent woman in England', but she died aged only 56 in London on 3 June 1912. The Sykes family estate is at Sledmere, near Malton in East Yorkshire, and she made her final journey there four days later. As recorded by Parsons:[10]

> her coffin was taken to Kings Cross station for a train departing at 6.30 am. Stopping at York to pick up additional mourners, the train then made its way to Sledmere & Fimber station.[11] The photograph shows a group of Roman Catholic clergy leading the coffin which is being shouldered from the platform before being placed on a farm waggon for the final journey to Sledmere.

Perhaps better remembered these days than Lady Sykes is Emily Wilding Davison (1872–1913). She was a prominent suffragette, being a member of the Women's Social and Political Union (WSPU). Her many activities whilst a member of the WSPU are outside the scope of this book but of relevance is her well-known death at the Epsom Derby in June 1913. She was knocked down in a collision with King George V's horse, Anmer, on 8 June and died in hospital four days later. This resulted in her coffin being transported by train not just once but twice.

Two days after her death, her coffin was transported by train from Epsom to Victoria station in London, where it spent a short time under the

Coffin of Lady Sykes on Sledmere & Fimber station, Yorkshire, accompanied by several Catholic priests, June 1912. She had died aged 56 in London. (Photograph courtesy of Brian Parsons)

Emily Wilding Davison, 1913. Her coffin is under guard by fellow suffragettes at Victoria station. Her coffin had been brought by train from Epsom for her funeral in London and was later taken by train to Newcastle for burial in Morpeth. (TopFoto)

watchful guard of several members of the WSPU, as shown in the photograph bottom left. The coffin was then taken in a procession to King's Cross station, stopping on the way at St George's, Bloomsbury, for a short service. The procession comprised about 5,000 women with hundreds of men following on behind. From King's Cross the coffin was taken by a timetabled train to Newcastle upon Tyne, with a guard of honour during this final journey provided by several suffragettes. After an overnight stay at Central station in Newcastle, the coffin was taken by train to Morpeth, Northumberland, where Emily Davison was buried in the family plot in the churchyard of St Mary the Virgin Church. Although she had been born in Greenwich, London, both of her parents came from Morpeth, her father having died in 1893. A small photograph of her procession leaving Morpeth station appears on the website of St Mary the Virgin Church.[12] Although the transport of her coffin on the two trains was done for functional purposes, to get it to Morpeth for burial, the processions in London and Morpeth were clearly large ceremonial events.

Another famous woman who had her final journey by train was the social reformer and founder of modern nursing Florence Nightingale (1820–1910), who became known as 'the lady with the lamp'. The story of her life and her contribution to the improvements to medical practice, especially for soldiers injured or taken ill during the Crimean War during the 1850s, are beyond the scope of this book. However, at the end of her long life, her body was taken from her home in London, where she died on 13 August 1910, to Hampshire for burial. Although she was born in Florence, Italy, her family owned property at Embley Park, near East Wellow, so her coffin was taken by special train probably to Romsey, the closest station to East Wellow. Details of this final journey are still being researched, but it is typical of the use of trains to take a person 'home' after their death for burial in a place with a familial connection. She is buried in the graveyard of St Mary's Church in East Wellow, her family having turned down the offer of having her buried in Westminster Abbey.

It was not just famous people who had their bodies returned home for burial. One of the more poignant stories discovered in research for this book concerns the death of Edward Booth, who was killed aged 25 in a train crash in 1906. The accident occurred at Ulleskelf, south of York, when the North Eastern Railway (NER) train on which Edward Booth was

Edward Booth's headstone in Hull Western Cemetery. He was the fireman on a locomotive which crashed at Ulleskelf, south of York in 1905. His body was taken by train for burial in his home town and the headstone is now Grade II listed. (Photograph © Nicolas Wheatley)

fireman ran into the rear of another train after having passed signals at danger. Sadly the driver was also killed, though his subsequent fate is largely lost to history. However, Edward Booth's mother, Ann, arranged for his remains to be returned by train to their home town of Hull, where he is buried in Hull Western Cemetery.

His mother commissioned a headstone that depicts very accurately, even down to its correct number, the locomotive on which Edward Booth lost his life. The headstone also tells the story of how her son lost his life in the accident, also noting sadly, 'I do not know what awaits me, God kindly veils mine eyes'. In 2017 the headstone was restored and granted a Grade II listing.[13] The historical significance of the accident was that afterwards there was a greater impetus for the implementation of safety devices to warn train drivers of passing signals at danger, so as to prevent future accidents.

As mentioned in Chapter 1, railway workers were frequently the victims of fatal accidents on the railways, and even today those killed on the railway tend to be suicides, trespassers, people killed on crossings, or railway workers. At the time of writing, the last time a passenger was killed during a train crash was as long ago as 23 February 2007, when one person was killed in a derailment of a Virgin Train at Grayrigg, Cumbria. One hundred years earlier, an accident took place in Salisbury that resulted in the coffins of two railway workers being transported by train. A photograph of their coffins at Salisbury station is the only known photograph showing the coffins of railway workers who were killed in an accident being carried to a train.

The circumstances were as follows. In the early hours of Sunday, 1 July 1906 the boat train from Plymouth Friary, operated by the London & South Western Railway (LSWR), travelled through Salisbury station at an excessive speed, for reasons that have never been fully established.[14] The ensuing derailment caused the deaths of twenty-eight people, including the driver and fireman of the boat train, two other railway workers and twenty-four passengers, most of whom were American. Many of the passengers were embalmed and repatriated to America, with five making a final journey by train to Liverpool and then on the Cunard steam ship *Carmania,* which took them to New York, arriving on 24 July. These bodies were accompanied by a senior staff member of the undertakers, J.H. Kenyon, which had carried out the embalming.[15] The train crew were based at the LSWR's depot at Nine Elms in south London, near where they lived, and

The coffins of Driver Robbins and Fireman Gadd being loaded onto a special train at Salisbury, Tuesday, 3 July 1906. (E.W. Fry Collection, courtesy *Daily Mirror*)

their bodies were taken back there by train. On 8 July 1906 they had a joint funeral at All Saints Church, Devonshire Road, South Lambeth, before being interred side by side in Tooting Cemetery.[16] As might be expected, the funerals were accompanied by much ceremony, with many railway workers attending, both from the LSWR and other companies. This photograph, admittedly of very poor quality, shows the coffins of Driver Robbins and Fireman Gadd being carried to the train for their final journey.

Space now only permits the inclusion of two more people known to have had a final journey by train and both were remarkable, though for different reasons. There are no photographs of their respective funeral trains, though an internet search will bring up facial images of them both. Unfortunately neither image is of reproducible quality for this book.

The first person to mention was born as William Darby in Norwich. There is some uncertainty as to his date of birth, being either 1796, which would accord with the dates on his grave marker, or 1810. This latter date is the year stated on the Blue Plaque affixed to the John Lewis store that now stands on or near the supposed site of his home in Norwich. In any event he died in 1871, but had led a remarkable life. He was an accomplished equestrian and was the first person of colour (some reports state he was of mixed race) to become a circus proprietor in the UK, adopting the stage name Pablo Fanque. His show was hugely famous during mid-Victorian times, touring many parts of the country, including putting on several benefit shows for various people, one of which was in Rochdale on 14 February 1843.

Unfortunately, during a show in Leeds in 1848 part of the temporary wooden stadium collapsed and the only fatality was his wife, Susannah Darby, aged 47. She was buried in Leeds, in the then Woodhouse Lane Cemetery, which has since largely been cleared of headstones and is now known as St George's Field. Pablo Fanque remarried and carried on touring, but he died in Stockport, near Manchester in 1871. His body was taken by train to Leeds so that he could be buried next to his first wife. The procession of the hearse transporting Pablo Fanque's coffin from the station was accompanied by a band and his favourite horse led four carriages carrying the mourners.

Apart from his extraordinary contribution to Victorian entertainment, which is largely sadly forgotten, his enduring claim to fame is that he is commemorated in the words of a Beatles song, 'Being for the Benefit of Mr Kite'. This song appears on the *Sgt Pepper's Lonely Hearts Club Band* album, released in 1967. The lyrics include the line 'the Hendersons will all be there, late of Pablo Fanque's fair, what a scene!' and this is a direct reference to the famous circus proprietor. This wording has been incorporated into the Blue Plaque in Norwich. Apparently John Lennon saw an old copy of the poster for the benefit show in Rochdale staged in February 1843 for sale at an antique shop in Sevenoaks, Kent. Having bought it, Lennon proceeded to write a song, the lyrics of which actually follow the wording of the poster quite noticeably,[17] including the title, 'Being for the Benefit of Mr Kite', which is taken verbatim from the poster. Being immortalised in a Beatles song was not in the least related to Pablo Fanque's final journey, but he is certainly the only person whose coffin was transported by train who has achieved posthumous fame in this way.

The last person to mention in this brief survey of people known to have made a final journey by train is another person who was well known in his lifetime but is now almost completely forgotten. His name, most appropriately for this book, was Walter Coffin. He was born in Bridgend, in South Wales, in 1784 and is acknowledged as being the first person to exploit the coal fields in the Rhondda valley on a commercial scale. He rose through the ranks of Welsh society, becoming Mayor of Cardiff in

Pablo Fanque. Blue Plaque in Norwich recording that he is named in the Beatles song 'Being for the benefit of Mr Kite'. (Photograph © Nicolas Wheatley)

1848. He was elected to Parliament as MP for Cardiff and served from 1852 to 1857, though he never spoke in the House once during all that time. His connections with railways included becoming a deputy chairman of the Taff Vale Railway in 1848 and its chairman in 1855. After moving to England permanently in 1857 to be near his family, he eventually died in London on 15 February 1867. Like many of the cases in this book, his family desired that he be buried back in the town of his birth and his coffin was taken to Bridgend for burial. In 1972 the trustees of the Unitarian Church in Park Street removed his headstone and covered his grave with tarmac. Sadly, neither he nor his siblings had any children to perpetuate this unusual name, but apparently there are still other people with the same family name in Cardiff, concentrated in the Rhiwbina area of the city.[18] It is perhaps fitting that this short review of people who had their coffins transported by train should end with someone who experienced that final journey whilst being named 'Coffin'.

9

RAILWAY TECHNOLOGY: VEHICLES AND EQUIPMENT

Because I could not stop for Death
He kindly stopped for me
The Carriage held but just Ourselves–
And Immortality

'Because I could not stop for Death', Emily Dickinson (1830–86)[1]

The transportation of coffins by train was initially carried out by placing them in the guard's compartment of passenger trains. This was a new type of freight and the railway companies had not thought there might be a need for any type of specialist vehicle in which to carry coffins. However, in due course several railway companies did develop such vehicles, most notably the hearse vans built by the London & South Western Railway (LSWR) for use on the railway service to Brookwood Cemetery. This service was provided by LSWR for the London Necropolis Company (LNC), which owned and operated the cemetery but, as was noted in Chapter 3, the LNC owned the hearse vans and the train carriages were provided by the LSWR, being dedicated to the necropolis service. As was also noted

Midland Railway corpse van, 1888. (SSPL Image 1997-7397-DY-6476)

in Chapter 3, there was never a 'Necropolis Railway Company', either in Brookwood or London.

The hearse vans built for the Brookwood necropolis service were required because of the anticipated level of traffic though, as noted in Chapter 3, demand for the service never reached such levels. However, the nature of the operation was that the coffins were transported separately from the mourners, who travelled in carriages attached to the same train. Reflecting Victorian social and class distinctions, provision was made for first-, second- and third-class travellers, both alive and dead. Starting from 1854, the vehicles used in the Brookwood service were replaced and modernised from time to time, as recorded in Clarke's book.[2] However, the last hearse vans to be built were constructed in 1899, so they were already becoming old when the service was terminated as a result of the LNC's private station at Waterloo being bombed in April 1941.

From the first coffin that was transported by train from London to Derby in 1840, traffic must have grown steadily as other railway companies started to develop their own hearse vans, or corpse vans as they were often known at the time. In January 1888 the Midland Railway ordered no fewer than four new corpse vans.

These were replacements for earlier vehicles, one of which was built in 1869 with another in 1872. There was clearly sufficient traffic to justify building four replacement vans, and four vehicles survived the Grouping, being renumbered 1840–1843 by the LMS in 1923. Although the exact dates of withdrawal are not known, they had all gone by 1933.[3] From its Derby base near the centre of England, and with its lines running over large parts of the country, the Midland Railway would have been able to use its vans to transport coffins across large parts of the country using its own trains. However, the evidence of coffin transport discovered by research for this book also shows that vans were often detached from trains that were not going to the coffin's final destination. In those cases the vans were then coupled to other trains, sometimes from different railway companies, and taken forward to a station nearer to the intended burial place. One such example mentioned in Chapter 7 is the train transporting the coffin of Countess Georgiana Howe, aunt of Sir Winston Churchill, which had a break of journey at Nuneaton in 1906, before the coffin was taken forward to Shackerstone station by special train.

North of the border, the Glasgow & South Western Railway (GSWR) also had its own corpse vans and these were very similar in appearance to the Midland Railway versions, being built around the same time. In the days before refrigeration or embalming,[4] both types of corpse van were provided with more ventilation than was needed for ordinary goods vans of the time. Indeed they were based on other types of van used at the time to transport perishable products such as meat or butter. Like the Midland Railway's corpse vans, these vans would have been run in passenger trains and so they were painted and lined in the same manner as passenger coaches of the time. The Midland's corpse vans would have also been painted in the passenger carriage livery of the time, i.e. crimson lake.

The Caledonian Railway, which merged into the London Midland & Scottish Railway in 1923, also had its own corpse van but details of its use are still being researched. Staying with railways in Scotland, the North British Railway (NBR) also had four corpse vans. The NBR corpse vans are reported to have travelled far beyond the railway's own network, having been seen in both Lancashire and Yorkshire as well as in the north

Glasgow & South Western Railway corpse van. (Photograph courtesy of Ian Middleditch, G&SWR Association)

of Scotland. I am grateful to John Clarke for allowing me to use some material from an article, as yet unpublished at the date of completion of this book, covering these and other hearse vans. Clarke writes that:

The NBR built a very distinctive style of hearse vehicle quite unlike those of any other railway company. They were similar to GWR shunters' trucks and the superstructure, which did not extend the full length of the chassis, had two large roof doors. These were hinged, and the sides folded down to provide access to the inside of the vehicle. The side and end framing was raised two inches above the sheeting and two ventilators were arranged at each end. The chassis included coach axle guards connected by a truss bar. Mansell wheels, vacuum and Westinghouse brakes were provided, allowing the vehicles to be operated across other companies' lines as required. Officially known as 'corpse vans' they were a common sight attached to the rear of passenger trains arriving at Edinburgh where the coffin would be lifted out of the van and then placed in a waiting hearse. The mourners, who had travelled in the same train, would form up and the cortege would depart. In NBR days the vehicles would have been painted in coach lake, [a shade of crimson also used by the Midland Railway], with black ironwork and with light yellow lettering, shaded vermillion and white. The Mansell wheels were finished in brown with black ironwork and white tyres. A total of six vans were built and numbered 159-162 and 203-204, suggesting they may have been supplied in two batches. These vehicles survived into LNER ownership and some were known to be running in post-Grouping livery before being withdrawn. The vehicles were renumbered 9159-9162 and 9203-9204.[5]

It has been noted in Chapter 4 that the Great Eastern Railway (GER) also had its own hearse carriages, one of which, No. 512, was used in the final journeys from Liverpool Street for Nurse Edith Cavell and Captain Charles Fryatt, both in 1919. An article by John Watling in the *Great Eastern Journal* in 1981 (No. 28, October) provides some useful details about and two photographs of the GER's hearse carriages. Initially one van was constructed in 1879, being numbered 226 (after a different number at first) for most of its existence. Its double doors to the coffin compartment were discreetly marked 'Private Carriage'.

In May 1908 two further hearse carriages were constructed by the GER, Nos 512 and 513, both being converted from six-wheeled passenger vehicles built in 1892, and by the end of 1909 carriage 226 had been withdrawn. These carriages were of composite construction, with a passenger section and a separate section that could accommodate four coffins. It is not known if they ever carried more than one coffin at a time, but it would be unusual in funeral terms for two separate parties of mourners to travel together. In January 1921 four more vehicles were converted to hearse carriages, and numbered 508–511. No. 508 was withdrawn in June 1927, possibly after an accident, and 509 survived until 1947, when it was photographed by H.C. Casserley at Wentworth, his photograph being one of the two used to illustrate the article in the *Great Eastern Journal*.

The others were all withdrawn and scrapped between December 1938 and April 1940, by which time six-wheeled passenger carriages on the main line were becoming a rarity. These vans were unique in providing accommodation for both mourners and coffins and no other railway hearses were designed in this way. Indeed, even motor hearses in the UK do not provide accommodation for mourners. The survival of these hearse carriages until the late 1930s suggests that there must have been sufficient use for them to justify their retention, though records of the scale of that use have not been found.

Apart from the hearse vans noted above, there are only four other railway vehicles believed to have been used on more than one occasion as funeral transport. The first is the Cavell Van, the three uses of which have already been covered in Chapter 4. The second is Queen Victoria's Diamond Jubilee Saloon No. 2[6] from the Great Western Railway's Royal Train, which was used to convey Queen Victoria's coffin from Paddington to Windsor in 1901. The furniture was removed from the interior to allow the catafalque to be located in the centre of the saloon and a similar arrangement was used in 1910 when the saloon was used again for the final journey of King Edward VII from Paddington to Windsor. On that occasion, as no doubt previously, the walls were decorated with purple and white.[7]

The third multiple use was again in the context of royal funerals. This time one of the semi-royal carriages, No. 46, from the London & North Eastern Railway's (LNER) royal train, was used to transport the coffin of Queen Alexandra (1844–1925), consort and widow of King Edward VII, to London, from Wolferton. This was the station nearest to Sandringham in Norfolk, where she had died on 19 November 1925. It is likely that this saloon vehicle was also used to transport the late Queen on her final journey from Paddington to Windsor for burial. On the death of her son King George V at Sandringham in 1936, the same carriage was again brought into service and used to transport his late majesty to London's King's Cross station. From there, the LNER royal train was worked around to Paddington station, from where the train transported the late king, again in the semi-royal carriage No. 46, on his final journey to Windsor for burial.[8] Carriage No. 46 was also used again in the train that transported the mortal remains of King George VI to London's King's Cross station from Wolferton in 1952. As with the funeral train for King George V, the LNER's royal train, including carriage No. 46, was then taken round to Paddington station,[9] from where his late majesty was taken on a final journey to Windsor for burial. Since that event, semi-royal carriage No. 46 has been scrapped, though exactly when is not known.

The fourth vehicle known to have been used more than once as railway funeral transport is an altogether different type of van. This is the Ffestiniog Railway's (FR) hearse van, which was converted from a Mark 2 Quarrymen's carriage in 1885–1886. It was principally used to transport the corpses of any workmen who died working in the quarries at Blaenau Ffestiniog back to their homes further down the line towards Porthmadog. The extent of its use to transport coffins on such occasions has not been documented and it has not carried a coffin during the FR's period of operation since its reopening in 1954. Its last functional use before closure of the FR in 1946 was to transport the coffin of a Mr Evans from Dduallt to Blaenau Ffestiniog. However, it has been used in ceremonial funeral service to transport the ashes of respected volunteer Maggie Warner in 1991 and also the ashes of Michael Seymour, an important volunteer on the FR, in 1999. Its last use in funeral service appears to have been in October 2017, during the FR's Victorian weekend, when it carried the ashes of an unnamed volunteer.[10]

The hearse van was restored in the early 1990s and for many years was on display at the Welsh Highland Heritage Railway's museum at Gelert's Farm Works near Porthmadog, where it was photographed in 2016.

Note that it is painted black, with four small urn-type decorations on its roof, one in each corner. It has also been fitted with an empty coffin, resting on the rollers which make it easier to load and unload, to show its functional use.

There are two unique aspects of the FR hearse van, one being that its doors are at its ends, rather than on its sides. Its small dimensions mean that the coffin has to be carried length-wise, but that requires the van to be separated from any other vehicle to enable its doors to be opened. The other unique aspect is that it is also the only known hearse van built or converted for use on a narrow-gauge railway in the UK. The Welsh narrow-gauge Talyllyn Railway (TR) has twice operated funeral trains carrying a coffin, once in 1902 and again in 1989, but on both occasions TR's Guard Van No. 5 was used. On the latter occasion the funeral train was for Hugh Jones, who had been born in 1904 to a former platelayer on the TR in the days before it closed. After it had reopened in 1951 as the UK's first preserved railway, he rose through its organisation to become vice president. Only four days after his death on 18 September 1989, the TR was able to fulfil

Ffestiniog Railway hearse van, running in train during Victorian Weekend, 2017. (Photograph © Tim Maynard)

Ffestiniog Railway hearse van. External view. (Photograph © Nicolas Wheatley)

Ffestiniog Railway hearse van. Internal view. (Photograph © Nicolas Wheatley)

his wish to have his final journey on the line. His coffin was transported from his house at Rhydyronen to Pendre, where the coffin was taken off the train.[11] The fireman on the funeral train was his grandson, so clearly working on the TR ran in the family.

The FR hearse van is also one of only three known surviving vans used as funeral transport from before the practice was stopped by BR in 1988, the others being the Cavell Van and the hearse van used in the funeral train for Sir Winston Churchill. It is possible that one other railway van used as funeral transport has survived on a heritage railway, but this is not confirmed. On 5 September 1979 the last private funeral train on the main-line network took place, to transport the remains of Earl Mountbatten from Waterloo station to Romsey, in Hampshire. From there his coffin was taken to Romsey Abbey for burial, this location being close to his family home at Broadlands. The coffin was carried in its own van, a BR Mark 1 brake vehicle known in railway terms as a BG. This was in the then standard BR livery of blue and grey, and was numbered as M80867. The coffin was accompanied in this van by Mr M. Kenyon,[12] from the funeral director firm of J.H. Kenyon, which provided the motor hearse to take the coffin from the station to Romsey Abbey. The fate of van M80867 after its use in Lord Mountbatten's funeral train requires further research.

There is one remaining railway van that was used in a funeral train that must be mentioned. This was a DVT (Driving Van Trailer) of a type used on services on the West Coast Main Line between London and Scotland. Typically they were used at the London end of the train, which was powered by a Class 87 electric locomotive at the other end. On 20 August 2001, DVT 82142 was used to transport the coffin of Jimmy Knapp from Euston to Glasgow. At the time of his death from cancer, aged 60, he was the leader of the RMT (Rail & Maritime Union), having previously been General Secretary of the NUR (National Union of Railwaymen). In that capacity he was one of the leaders of railway unions to whom a letter had been sent by BR in March 1988 notifying them that BR was withdrawing a concessionary rate for the union members to have their coffins transported by train because BR was stopping that service. This is covered in Chapter 13, where a copy of the letter is reproduced.

Despite coffin transport being officially ended on the main line, an exception was made to transport Jimmy Knapp's coffin to Scotland, in view of his important role in the railway industry. The coffin was loaded into DVT 82142 at Euston station, which had been specially draped internally, where it formed part of the 1830 Virgin Trains departure for Glasgow on 20 August 2001. An extra First Class carriage had been added to the train for the accompanying family and mourners, in the same way that this had been done in the nineteenth and twentieth century (until 1988) on countless occasions when coffins were transported by train. Jimmy Knapp's final journey by train took him to Glasgow, from where his coffin was taken by road to his home town of Kilmarnock, where he was buried. This unique final journey, essentially a functional trip though carried out with a degree of ceremony, was the last time a coffin was transported by train on the UK main line and the only recorded occasion when an electric locomotive (Class 87 No. 87033 *Thane of Fife*) provided the motive power. The fate of DVT 82142 is not known but loco-hauled trains using DVTs on the West Coast Main Line have now largely been replaced.

Apart from specialist vans within which to transport coffins, the railway network also had some specialist equipment to handle those coffins at stations. Coffin carriers were essentially large wooden cases on wheels used to hide coffins between their delivery to the outside of a station by the undertakers and when they were placed onto a train. This was required particularly at larger stations (e.g. London termini) where a greater number of coffins would be transported and the distances between road access and the trackside would be greater. The coffin carriers were used to provide some privacy to the coffin (or at least to the relatives of the deceased) if it was being transported for functional purposes, and also to avoid causing potential distress to other travellers at the station. In passing, it can be noted that in the 1961 film *Terminus*, directed by John Schlesinger, there is a scene in which a coffin is wheeled across Waterloo station by the funeral directors in plain sight of the surrounding travellers. The authenticity of this manner of operation is doubtful, but at least it illustrates one aspect of an activity at a large railway station that is now lost to history.

Another way privacy was achieved was by the erection of screens whilst the coffin was being loaded, as recalled by Chris Turner and John Copsey in their recollections of working at Leamington Station during the 1950s.[13] They recorded that 'the local undertaker loaded corpses into the guard's brake van and a special screen was provided for the purpose. We raised

Coffin carriers. LNER coffin carrier on display at National Railway Museum, York. (Photograph © Nicolas Wheatley)

charges on a mileage basis.' However, if the coffin being transported was that of someone important and being done with a high degree of ceremony, for example Sir Winston Churchill, then the loading of the coffin was part of the ceremonial activity and needed to be visible.

Some of these pieces of specialist coffin-handling equipment still exist and are on display at various locations, though some are unmarked and are 'hidden in plain sight', with people visiting those locations often not realising what they are. A particular case in point is the LNER's coffin carrier in the National Railway Museum on York. This item is one of the very few, if not the only, small exhibits on display on the platform of the former goods shed part of the museum that does not have a label attached explaining what it is. However, a check of the records using its accession reference number (1975-7080) confirms its identity, though it does not record where it was previously in use.

Another coffin carrier whose past history is unknown can be found on the Bluebell Railway, where it can normally be found at Horsted Keynes station. In 1990 it was featured on a postcard produced by the railway which sadly is long out of print. It shows a recreated scene of a coffin being

GWR coffin carrier from Paddington station, at Didcot Railway Centre. (Photograph courtesy of Ann Middleton, GWS)

loaded into the luggage section of a passenger carriage, a scene similar to many that would have occurred in past times. The coffin carrier is understood to be privately owned and the oval windows were cut into the sides of the carrier during its preservation days. Although the roundels showing 'SR' (Southern Railway) are probably authentic, the wording 'Coffin Carrier' would not have appeared on the side on the carrier during the time of its original use. It is not known at which station this coffin carrier was previously used.

Another coffin carrier exists, the history of which is known. The GWR used this particular carrier at Paddington Station, as is clearly recorded on its side. It was kept under the ramp leading to Platform 8, which formerly provided road access directly to that platform, enabling funeral directors to deliver coffins close to whichever train was being used to transport the coffin away from London. Fortunately this coffin carrier was saved once its use by BR ceased and it now exists in preservation at the Didcot Railway Centre in Oxfordshire. Its exact location there has changed over time and it has been repainted since the photo above was taken.

It is known that the Midland Railway also had a coffin carrier, and a photo exists of it in use at St Pancras Station, during the 1920s or 1930s. The picture shows it being pulled by a horse together with trollies

Bier, possibly from Derby station, at Midland Railway Centre, Butterley.
(Photograph © Nicolas Wheatley)

carrying other types of freight no longer transported by train, including milk churns. Unfortunately it has not been possible to reproduce this image to a sufficient quality for its inclusion in this book.

Going down in size from vans and coffin carriers, the next type of equipment used by railways to handle coffins was a bier. These would have been used at smaller stations, probably once passengers had disembarked from the train and the coffin could be unloaded discreetly. It is believed that many smaller stations would have had such a piece of equipment, but sadly few have survived. The author was told by a former local resident of Dymock in Gloucestershire that once the station in that village was closed (to passengers in 1959 and to freight in 1964) the station bier was given to the local church, though its subsequent fate is not known.

However, two former station biers are known to still exist. One, which is believed to have been used at Derby Station, is now an unlabelled exhibit within the museum at the Midland Railway Centre, Butterley, Derbyshire.

Another bier that is also unlabelled and hiding in plain sight can be seen at Oakworth Station on the long-established Keighley & Worth Valley Railway in Yorkshire. This bier originally came from the station at Hellifield on the Settle to Carlisle line, further to the north-west in Yorkshire. That

Bier from Hellifield station on platform at Oakworth station, Keighley & Worth Valley Railway. (Photograph © Nicolas Wheatley)

junction station was more important in past times, especially in the days when it was part of the Midland Railway's route from London to Scotland. It may well have been the place at which coffins were transferred from main-line express trains between those places to more local stations within Yorkshire, though more research would be needed to establish the extent of such activity.

As noted earlier in this chapter, many coffins were transported in a functional manner in the guard's or luggage compartments of carriages on scheduled passenger trains. Sometimes coffins were placed in separate vans attached to passenger trains, and when this occurred the vans were known in railway terms, especially if the train needed to be given priority by signallers, as a 'VANCO', i.e. van containing a coffin or a corpse.

It is worth noting that using some types of ordinary vans to transport coffins by train sometimes caused problems. As early as 1910 there was criticism from some undertakers about what they considered to be inappropriate vans being used. In an article in *The Undertaker's Journal* in January 1910, one of the strongest reasons being put forward for the adoption of the then new motor hearse was 'to do away with the great inconvenience connected with railway transit, as well as the objection of having the bodies conveyed in milk, fruit and other vans, used by railway companies for this purpose'.[14] It appears that this criticism was sometimes justified, for in October 1913 the South Eastern & Chatham Railway (SECR) published a notice about various operational matters, part of which related to 'the Provision of Vans for Corpse Traffic'. This section of the notice reads:

An instance has just been brought to notice of a Van which had previously been used for the conveyance of fish being provided for the conveyance of a Corpse. All concerned are hereby warned that Vans free from fish or other obnoxious odour must be selected for this Traffic and, when necessary, must be disinfected as long as possible prior to use. If a Van of good inside appearance cannot be provided, then the station forming the Vehicle in the Train must procure a supply of sawdust with which to well sprinkle the floor.

This notice also has a section headed 'Transfer of Corpse Traffic at Victoria to LB&SCR Company'. It will be recalled that the two railway companies had separate but adjacent stations at Victoria, and the division between them can still be seen, though access between the two is now much easier. The section about the transfer of corpse traffic reads:

in order to avoid any delay to this Traffic at Victoria special covered trolleys are provided for conveyance between the SECR and LB&SCR stations and in future all such Traffic will be so transferred. Any station loading a corpse for transfer to the LB&SCR Station at Victoria must notify Victoria by wire as long in advance as possible, so that a van may be procured by the LB&SCR for the reception and forwarding of the Traffic.[15]

The 'special covered trolleys' mentioned in this section are almost certainly similar to the coffin carriers described above and depicted in the photo of the coffin being loaded onto the train on the Bluebell Railway.

309

STATION INSTRUCTIONS.

COACHES REQUIRING TO BE DISINFECTED—*Continued.*

When application is made to convey the body of a person who has died from an infectious disease, the authority of the Superintendent of the Line must be obtained. No such application must, however, be entertained until the Medical Officer of Health certifies that the body may be removed, and if necessary the vehicle used must be subsequently sent to Swindon to be disinfected.

Bodies of persons who have died from Spotted Fever must not be accepted unless coffins are hermetically sealed and a certificate is received from the Local Medical Officer of Health certifying that there is no danger in handling and conveyance by rail. The vans used must, in all cases, be disinfected

The following are the charges agreed generally by Railway Companies for the disinfection of coaching vehicles :—

	s.	d.
Saloon or corridor carriage or compartments in corridor carriage or complete non-corridor carriage	30	0
Compartment in non-corridor carriage	10	0
Guard's van conveying corpse	20	0

The charge to be credited to the Company performing the disinfection.

It is imperative that all carriages used for the conveyance of FOREIGN Emigrants should be thoroughly disinfected immediately after the journey is completed, and before the vehicles are utilised for other traffic.

This applies not only to Foreign Emigrants travelling in large numbers, but also to small parties for whom one or more compartments are reserved. In the latter case it is essential that any small number should not be allowed to mix with ordinary passengers.

To ensure all carriages, or odd compartments in carriages, being thoroughly disinfected, it will be necessary for the forwarding station to advise the receiving station so that the latter can make the necessary arrangements. The compartments should be plainly labelled to assist the staff at intermediate and terminating points.

Great Western Railway 1930 Rule Book, Appendices. Extract regarding disinfecting of carriages used for conveying corpses. (Author's Collection)

The SECR was not the only railway company concerned about disinfecting railway vehicles that had been used to transport coffins. No record has been found of the GWR having any purpose-built hearse vans, so coffins were transported by the GWR in the guard's compartment of passenger carriages or occasionally in separate vans. If these needed disinfecting they would have to be taken out of service whilst that was carried out, and a charge was payable. An Appendix to the 1930 Rule Book sets out, on pages 308–309, the requirement for disinfection and an extract is shown here.

With regards to the costs of transporting coffins, in 1859 an organisation called the 'Railway Clearing House' set these at one shilling per mile and this rate seems to have stayed the same for several decades. Certainly it is the rate shown in the attached list of charges which was found in the front of a book of records held in the archives of a firm of London undertakers.[16] Although undated, the list is thought to be from the early 1900s, certainly from before the Grouping in 1923 when some of the railway companies

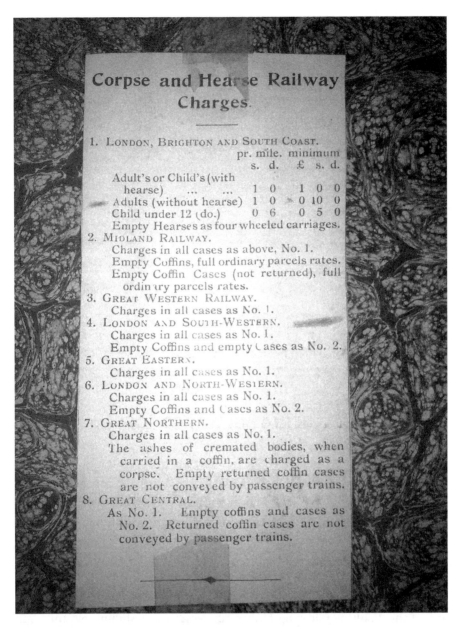

List of railway charges for carrying coffins and coffin carriers. (Courtesy of Brian Parsons)

Advertisement for coffin factory run by Ingall, Parsons, Clive & Co. in Harrow, north London. (Image courtesy of Brian Parsons)

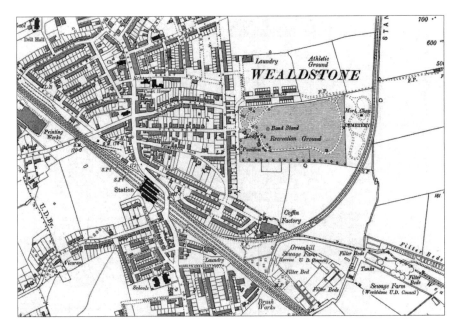

Harrow & Wealdstone: location map for coffin factory. (Ordnance Survey, Middlesex Sheet X NE published 1916. Original Scale Six Inches to the Mile/880 Feet to One Inch. Crown Copyright has expired)

listed were formed into larger companies. It will be noted that charges are listed for sending empty coffins as well as empty coffin cases, and that both the Great Northern Railway and the Great Central Railway stipulate that 'empty returned coffin cases are not conveyed by passenger trains'.

Clearly, empty coffins were being sent by train as well as corpses encased in them. An example of this happening as late as the 1970s is recorded in Chapter 12. In earlier times, however, many coffins were made by the firm of Ingall, Parsons, Clive & Co., in their rail-connected factory near Harrow in north-west London. The photo shown[17] is an advertisement for their business and the map shows that their factory was connected to a branch line that ran from Harrow & Wealdstone station (location of the 1952 tragedy) to Stanmore. The rail connection to this branch would have enabled empty coffins to be sent by train to wherever they were destined. The most famous coffin made in this factory was the one for the Unknown Warrior in 1920, whose repatriation is covered in Chapter 4.

PRIVATE AND NOT
FOR PUBLICATION

BRITISH RAILWAYS
(WESTERN REGION)

NOTICE NO. 62
(SIX TWO)

District Operating Superintendent's Office,
Paddington Station.

12th February, 1952.

WEDNESDAY FEBRUARY 13th.

With reference to Weekly Notice No.7:-

7.50am SPECIAL TRAIN OF EMPTY KITCHEN CARS ETC., OLD OAK COMMON TO
PADDINGTON
With reference to Manuscript Notice No.21, formation now to be:-

Saloon	9004
Kitchen Car	9633
Kitchen Car	9670
Kitchen Car	9666
Kitchen Car	9668
Diner	9558
Diner	9561
Diner	9537
Kitchen Car	9669
Kitchen Car	9663
Kitchen Saloon	9117
Kitchen Saloon	9118
Saloon	9005

7.55am (Parcels) PADDINGTON
Van extra Slough.

8.15am EMPTY VANS OLD OAK COMMON TO KENSINGTON
"K" CCT (50') extra Kensington.
"K" for loading scenery to connect 6.10pm Kensington Parcels same day.

1.0pm PADDINGTON
To be formed with two "Q" sets on this date.

4.10pm PADDINGTON
PADDINGTON to reserve two Third Class Compartments in leading
Wolverhampton Van Third for Signal Department workmen joining at
Bicester North for Birmingham.

5.35pm PADDINGTON
Third extra Didcot (front)
(Vehicle works up on 12.37pm Didcot same day as shewn on Manuscript
Notice No.281.)

10.40pm (Parcels) PADDINGTON
"G" LBV extra Bath Spa.
"G" To convey corpse as per small order.

11.50pm PADDINGTON
"J" Vestibule Third extra Bristol.
"J" To be formed next engine and reserved for MRS. GRIFFIN'S PARTY
as per small order.

1.0night PADDINGTON
"Q" First Class Sleeping Car 9087 extra Carmarthen.
"Q" To be formed next First Class end of regular Sleeping Compo.

SEE SHEET TWO

BR (Western Region) Traffic Notice, 12 February 1952. Refers to corpse being
transported in LBV to Bath. (Image courtesy of Great Western Trust, Didcot)

Finally, in this review of the technology of coffin transport, it can be noted that when a coffin was to be transported by train this information was often included in the daily notices issued by the management of railway companies. These would give the locomotive crew and guards (and others) of the trains involved details about any special requirements that might apply to a particular service. These documents are ephemeral, with relatively few having any lasting value after the day of their validity has passed, but one relevant to this book has survived and is reproduced here. This notice,[18] issued on 12 February 1952, records that on the following day an extra van, an 'LBV' (understood to be a luggage bogie van) was being attached to the 10.40 p.m. parcels service from Paddington to Bath Spa to convey a corpse. Although this was not a passenger-carrying train, it would have run at passenger-train speeds, rather than at the much slower speed of goods trains, thereby enabling the coffin to reach its destination in good time, probably for a funeral service the next morning. The identity of the person making this final journey has not been established.

10

TRAMS USED AS FUNERAL TRANSPORT

One of the less well-known aspects of the transport of the dead by rail-based vehicles is that trams were also used for this purpose and, indeed, continue to be used on some rare occasions in the UK. All around the world there were tram systems used to transport the dead to cemeteries located outside towns or cities. These systems have been the subject of a book entitled *Last Rides: Funeral Trams Around the World*[1] by the well-known tram expert and writer David Voice.[2] This profusely illustrated book should be in the collection of anyone with an interest in funeral transport generally or trams in particular, though copies are difficult obtain as only 200 were printed.

Despite there being tram systems in many UK cities and towns in the late nineteenth and early twentieth century, only one system in Britain was used on a regular basis to take coffins to a cemetery. That system was the Great Orme Tramway near Llandudno in North Wales, Britain's only cable-hauled tramway, which is still operating today. The system operates in two parts, with passengers having to change trams at Halfway Station in the middle of the route. The tramway was used to transport coffins from the town to Halfway Station, for onward carrying to the graveyard surrounding St Tudno's church on the Great Orme. The local council had

Jockey Car on Great Orme Tramway, early 1900s. It was one of three which were used, in part, to carry coffins to St Tudno's Church graveyard. (Author's Collection)

extended the graveyard beyond the original one associated with the church and the 1898 Act of Parliament that authorised the building of the tramway required the company to carry corpses to St Tudno's cemetery 'at a reasonable fixed charge and in a decent and seemly manner'.[3] The tramway was opened in 1902 and carried coffins in special vehicles known as 'Jockey Cars' rather than in the trams themselves.

These were either propelled by the trams or could be attached directly to the cable that hauled the vehicles up the hill. It is not known how many coffins in total were transported before the practice stopped, in about 1910 or 1911, when a new cemetery was built by the local council on the edge of the town. The fare for transporting the coffins was 2 shillings and sixpence (2/6), which was one eighth of a pound. The mourners were charged the regular fare of sixpence for a single journey or nine pence return. The current fare is £8.10 for adults and £5.60 for children.[4]

The Great Orme Tramway was the only known tram system in the UK that transported coffins for functional transport, as defined in Chapter 2.

However, there have been several instances of trams being used in the UK to transport coffins for ceremonial purposes, both in the original days when trams were used for passenger transport and, more recently, at the tram museum at Crich Tramway Village in Derbyshire. There have been no instances found by research for this book of modern-day tram systems, e.g. in south London, Manchester, Sheffield, Birmingham, Nottingham or Edinburgh, being used to transport coffins, even for ceremonial purposes.

The first known case of ceremonial coffin transport on a UK tramway occurred in 1901, when Martin Cadman's coffin was given this honour by the Dudley, Stourbridge & District Electric Traction Company. As David Voice records in his book:

On the afternoon and evening of 4th February 1901 there was a severe snowstorm over the Black Country. Conditions for the tram drivers were particularly harsh, as all the tramcars were open fronted giving the motormen no protection from the elements. Tram driver Martin Cadman was driving on the Cradley line and had a great struggle getting his tramcar back to the Hart's Hill Depot. Finishing his shift he then had a walk back to his home near the centre of Dudley in the early hours of the morning. He suffered from heart problems[5] and on arriving home he collapsed and died. The tramway wanted to honour his devotion to duty and arranged a tramway funeral for him.

An old four wheel flat wagon, left over from the steam tram days, was given a canopy and plinth, all draped in black and purple material, to become the hearse. It was placed between two single deck tramcars carrying the mourners. The mourners were both tramway staff and the deceased's family. The cortege procession began at his house in Dudley and travelled past the Hart's Hill Depot, through Brierley Hill and Amblecote to Woolaston. The final section was over the new Kinver Light Railway lines, which were not due to open to the public until 5th April, making the cortege the first passenger carrying journey over that part of the line.[6] In Dudley there were around 2,000 people present to see the procession start. All along the route the pavements were lined with people. The funeral service and burial were carried out at St James Church, Woolaston.[7]

Coffin of tram driver Martin Cadman on specially built hearse wagon, Dudley, Stourbridge & District Electric Traction Company, February 1901. (Rare photograph courtesy of Dr Paul Collins/History of Wollaston Group)

The Kinver Light Railway, to the west of Stourbridge, was itself the subject of a ceremonial tramway funeral on 28 January 1915, to honour the Reverend Ernest Hexall. As David Voice records:

The Rev Hexall was Pastor at the Providence Mission, Churchbridge, Oldbury, also known as 'the Wooden Church'. He worked to relieve the suffering of the poor of Oldbury, particularly children. He founded the 'Midland Counties Crippled Children's Guild' in 1906, where small groups of disabled children were sent to Mr Martindale of Kinver. He took exclusive use of 'Eden View Cottage' and very quickly 'Hyde House', a forty room building. This was renamed 'Bethany House' and was paid for by street collections and an appeal for one million pennies. They were successful and the children taken in were cared for and taught a trade. The Kinver Light Railway Depot was located nearby and Rev Hexall became interested in the welfare of the light railway staff and worked closely with the management to improve the welfare of workers.

Coffin of Reverend Ernest Hexall on hearse wagon, Kinver Light Railway, 1915.
(Photograph courtesy of History of Wollaston Group)

His work with disabled children relied on his fund raising. This included taking a brass band made up of children in his care in the Guild's charabanc to local events to raise money. Unfortunately this led to his demise. On one fundraising occasion he fell from the charabanc and died from his injuries. The tramway men wanted to honour him and the management arranged for a tramway funeral. The hearse used for Mr Cadman's funeral some fourteen years previously was still available. A cortege, similar to that used in 1901, was made up with the hearse in the middle of two single deck tramcars. The Guild charabanc accompanied the parade. The procession started at 'Bethany House', The Hyde, and travelled through Amblecote, Brierley Hill Dudley to Oldbury, where he was laid to rest.

It will be noted that this cortege travelled in the opposite direction to Martin Cadman's, but in addition to being ceremonial processions they each had the functional purpose of delivering their respective coffin to a place of burial. These were not the only times when trams had been used for the ceremonial transport of the coffins of people killed in tram accidents. There are two other known cases, one following the Pye Nest accident in Yorkshire in October 1907 and another case in 1912,

Pye Nest, Halifax, 1907. Coffin of Conductor Walter Robinson being loaded into tram. (Photograph courtesy of Tramway Museum Society archives)

following an accident within a tram depot in Blackpool, which remains the only town in Britain to have kept its original tram system.

In relation to the Pye Nest accident, David Voice records that:

Halifax and its surrounding town and cities have large numbers of steep hills that sometimes caused difficulties to their various tramways. On the Halifax tramway tramcar number 6 suffered a loss of electricity whilst climbing Pye Nest Road. The tramcar started to roll backwards. The driver applied the brakes, without noticeable effect. The conductor, Walter Robinson, had been collecting fares on the open upper deck. He realised the problem and ran downstairs to apply the handbrake at his end of the tramcar. However, the tramcar continued to career down the hill. The conductor shouted at passengers to sit and hold tight, while yelling at pedestrians to get off the tracks. The tramcar jumped the rails, mounted the pavement and crashed into the front of a shop before falling over, tearing the top deck off.

Conductor Robinson and two passengers were killed instantly and two other passengers lost their lives in hospital. An enquiry determined that different emergency braking arrangements at each end of the tramcar contributed to the accident. Survivors of the accident praised Conductor Robinson for trying to save the situation and warn others. The local papers acclaimed him as a hero and postcards were printed with poems about the accident. The Tramway decided to give him a special funeral. The funeral cortege consisted of a line of two double deck cars for the mourners, a demi-car[8] for the coffin, and another double deck car for more mourners. Large crowds watched the event and a memorial stone was erected, paid by public subscription, to recognise his actions.

The use of a tram to carry a coffin in Blackpool in 1912 did not arise from such tragic circumstances as in Halifax but nonetheless involved a respected employee of the tramway company. Once again David Voice provides the story:

In December 1911 Alexander Hollas, a Blackpool Tramway Inspector, was killed on duty. Mr Hollas was born in 1865 in Halifax and moved to Blackpool with his parents. When he reached working age he joined the tramway, advancing his career to Inspector. In December 1911 he was working in the Blundell Street Depot when he was involved in a fatal accident. The tramway management wanted to give him a special honour and arranged for him to have a tramway funeral, the only one in the whole history of Blackpool Tramways. The funeral took place on 5th January 1912. Six uniformed tramway employees went to Mr Hollas' home at 45 Kent Street, a short walk from Rigby Road tram depot. They placed the coffin on a bier and pushed it to the depot. Tram number 5 was waiting. The tramcar had been decorated in black drapes. A lower saloon window had been removed to enable the coffin to be placed into the lower saloon. The tram hearse was followed by tramcar number 6, also decorated with black drapes. The immediate family and friends were carried in this tramcar. Two further tramcars, for around 50 tramway employees, completed the funeral cortege. The parade left the depot and drove along Princes Street, The Promenade, Talbot Square, New Road and Talbot Road. There were large crowds at the depot and at Layton Cemetery and many people stopped to watch the procession. At the cemetery the coffin was removed through the window space and carried between an avenue of tramway employees to the graveside.

Blackpool Tramways 1912. Coffin of Inspector Alexander Hollas being removed from tramcar. (Photograph courtesy of David Voice)

Blackpool Tramways, 1912. Funeral procession of Inspector Alexander Hollas. (Photograph courtesy of Tramway Museum Society archives)

Research for this book has uncovered another photograph relating to this funeral, which is believed to be previously unpublished. It shows the procession for Alexander Hollas' funeral on its way to the cemetery.

Once again it will be noted that this funeral cortege, whilst carried out with considerable ceremony, was also functional in its nature, having an end purpose of delivering the coffin to the cemetery. The more recent uses of trams within funerals at the Crich Tramway Village have been purely ceremonial, with a motor hearse being used to deliver the coffin to the cemetery, as will be described below.

The biggest city in the UK, London, does not appear ever to have used trams as hearses, though there are some links between trams and funerals in the capital. The London United Tramways (LUT) company in 1902 had a demi-car known as a 'social saloon' which could be 'engaged by parties visiting theatres, concerts, balls and other social festivities', including use by mourners for funerals. However, it is not known how much use it had for funerals and any information on this aspect would be gratefully received. The hire charge was 7 shillings and sixpence (7s 6d) return for every penny of the ordinary fare.

This vehicle, numbered 175, a conversion from a 'W' class tram but fitted with luxury seating, was often to be seen in a private siding at Garrick Villa, the Hampton Court home of the LUT Managing Director, Sir James Clifton Robinson, in south-west London. He had been involved in the construction and management of tramways in Britain and abroad, including in the USA. It was whilst he was in New York in November 1910, returning on a tramcar to his hotel with his wife, that he became seriously ill and collapsed unconscious. He died by the time medical assistance arrived and it is perhaps fitting that he should have died on a tramcar, as David Voice tells us he was known as 'the Tramway King'.[9]

A further use of trams in London in connection with a funeral occurred during the First World War. As reported by David Voice:[10]

In September 1916 a bomb dropped by a Zeppelin fell close to Streatham Hill railway station. The blast hit a London County Council tramcar, killing the driver, conductor and two passengers. In October a funeral was held for the tram crew at Streatham Cemetery (actually in Tooting) that was attended by a large number of tramway staff. Six tramcars were used

Exterior view of London United Tramways 'Social Saloon', 1902. (Author's Collection)

Interior view of London United Tramways 'Social Saloon', 1902. (Author's Collection)

Edith Cavell's grave in October 2015 with flowers left to commemorate the centenary of her execution. (Photograph © Nicolas Wheatley)

Cavell Van interior as set up with an exhibition telling the stories of Edith Cavell, Captain Fryatt and the Unknown Warrior. (Photograph © Nicolas Wheatley)

Cavell Van on display outside The Forum, Norwich, October 2015, during the centenary commemorations of her execution. The re-enactors turned up unannounced, posed for a few minutes and left. Their identities were not established. (Photograph © Nicolas Wheatley)

Jimmy Knapp's coffin being carried onto a timetabled Virgin Train at Euston station, August 2001. His coffin was transported to Glasgow then taken to Kilmarnock for burial. (Photograph courtesy of Press Association, 1467956)

Bluebell Railway, 1990. Re-enactment of coffin being loaded onto train at Horsted Keynes station. Postcard produced by Bluebell Railway. (Author's Collection)

Velocipede named Morticia with Phil Naylor in charge. Taken at Goathland station, North Yorkshire Moors Railway, 2014. (Photograph © Jacqui and Kevin Thomas)

Coffin decorated with GWR train. (Photograph © Colourful Coffins)

Keighley & Worth Valley Railway (KWVR). On 15 September 2003 the coffin of Jack Rowell is loaded onto a special train at Oxenhope station. (Photograph © Gerard Binks)

South Devon Railway, 2011. Coffin of Brian Cocks being carried to train at Buckfastleigh station. (Photograph © Sarah Harvey)

South Devon Railway, 2018. Coffin of David Knowling under guard on train at Totnes Riverside. (Photograph Ron Smallpage)

Coffin of John Bunting on train at Hood Bridge. South Devon Railway, 2019. (Photograph © Colin Wallace)

Dean Forest Railway, Gloucestershire, 2012. Coffin of Richard Eagle at Norchard Low Level station. (Photograph © *Gloucester Citizen*)

Lavendon NGR – Lavendon Narrow Gauge Railway, 2006. A private miniature railway in Buckinghamshire. Its creator, Brian Collins, is given a final journey, with his son and other family members following on foot. (Photograph courtesy Alamy, BRHGKY)

Audley End Railway, June 2017. Coffin of Lord Braybrooke being carried on a train on the miniature railway he created at Audley End House, near Saffron Walden, Essex. (Photograph © Ron Greensitt)

Isle of Man, 2009. The funeral train carrying the coffin of Tony Beard, Chairman of IoM Steam Railway Supporters Association. (Photograph courtesy of Richard Dodge)

Fawley Hill railway, March 2018. Coffin of Sir William McAlpine being carried on a train in his private estate. (Photograph © Andy Savage)

Romney Hythe & Dymchurch Railway, Kent, January 2020. Funeral train carrying coffin of driver Richard Batten for a final journey, at Dungeness, being driven by his son Simon Batten. (Photograph © Steve Town)

Streatham, London, 1916. Mourners walking from tramcars to Streatham Cemetery (actually in Tooting) for funeral of tram crew killed in Zeppelin bombing raid. (Image courtesy of Brian Parsons)

to carry the mourners to the cemetery. It is not known if the two coffins were also carried by the tramcars or if they travelled in dedicated hearses.

Apart from the system in Blackpool all the tramway networks in Britain were closed down by the end of the 1960s, often many decades before. However, a group of enthusiasts set up a working tram museum in an old quarry at Crich, near Matlock, Derbyshire, starting in 1959. Although it is not generally permitted to transport coffins on the trams, there have been three exceptions to this, when people who made significant contributions to the Tramway Museum Society that runs the site were given a ceremonial final journey along all or part of the tramway line.

The first was in 1985 for Richard Fairbairn, who had been born in 1895 at the Worcester Tramway Depot, where his father was the manager. After his retirement in the mid 1960s, he moved to live on the site at Crich as Resident Security Officer, a post he held for eighteen years. In 1981 he became the first person to hold the one-year appointment as President of

Crich Tramway Museum, September 1985. Glasgow 166 carrying coffin of
Richard Fairbairn. (Photograph © David Frodsham)

the Society and on his 90th birthday he was made vice president. Once
again, David Voice provides the details of his funeral that took place at the
tramway museum in September 1985, which:

> started in the museum grounds with the coffin being carried on
> Blackpool toastrack tramcar number 166. The tramcar had been modified
> by removing two seat backs to allow the coffin to rest on the seats. The
> car had been draped in black and a black pennant hung from the trolley
> pole. Four bearers were carried at the rear of the car. The mourners were
> carried in tramcars Glasgow 812 and Paisley 68. A group of members,
> employees and villagers paid their respects as the tram drove from the
> depot to the main gate. Here the coffin was transferred to a motor
> hearse and the mourners made their way to St Mary's church [nearby in
> Crich]. Given that Richard Fairbairn had started life in a tramway depot
> it was entirely fitting that his final journey took place on a tram at the
> tramway museum.

Crich Tramway Museum, December 2008. Sheffield 330 towing a
hearse wagon carrying the coffin of Winstan Bond, OBE. (Photograph
© Malcolm Wright)

Crich Tramway Museum, May 2019. Blackpool 166 carrying the coffin of Robert
(Bob) Hall. (Photograph © Malcolm Rush)

The second time was in December 2008 for Winstan Bond OBE (1936–2008). He had joined the Tramway Museum Society two years after its formation and had been an active volunteer at Crich since its start in 1959. He served in various capacities in the management of the Society and donated his personal collection of 11,000 books and documents relating to tramway history to the Society. He died after a short illness on 5 December 2008 and his funeral was on 15 December. As David Voice records:

> the museum committee wanted to recognise his significant contribution and as part of his funeral procession his coffin was placed on a black draped flat trailer and drawn along the museum site by Sheffield works car 330. There were nearly 200 mourners. At the terminus the coffin was transferred to a motor hearse for the final part of the journey to St Mary's Church in Crich.

He is buried in the extension graveyard to the church, with a headstone giving his full name as Alan Winstan Bond OBE noting, amongst other things, that he was 'a pillar and guiding light of the Tramway Museum Society'.

A third occasion when a tram at Crich was used in a funeral occurred in May 2019, when Robert Cubin Hall's coffin was transported on a tram as part of his funeral. Bob Hall had been born in Bath in 1938 and eventually found employment in Derby with Rolls-Royce. After being made redundant by them in 1971 when the aero-engine company collapsed, he became the first paid employee of the Tramway Museum Society (TMS), remaining a full-time employee in a variety of important posts until his retirement in 1998. He was also involved with fire protection at the museum and through that role had links with the local fire service. During his retirement he maintained his links with the museum and so it was fitting that he should have been given a ceremonial final journey, using Blackpool 166, the same tram used to carry Richard Fairbairn's coffin back in 1985. On the last part of his final journey his hearse was led out from the museum village at Crich by a fire engine on its way to the crematorium, witnessed by a large number of people paying their last respects to a person who had made a considerable contribution to the TMS.

It is not only in Wales and England that trams have been used in funerals. On the Isle of Man in October 1999 Mike Goodwyn's coffin was taken for

Isle of Man, Manx Electric Railway, 1999. Coffin of Mike Goodwyn being removed from Trailer 37 at Ramsey. (Photograph courtesy of Richard Dodge)

Isle of Man, Manx Electric Railway, 1999. Winter Saloon 20 towing Trailer 37 at Derby Castle. Funeral of Mike Goodwyn. (Photograph courtesy of Richard Dodge)

a final journey on the Manx Electric Railway (MER). Although technically a railway, the MER operates vehicles which resemble trams both in appearance and the way in which they are driven. Mike Goodwyn had been the chairman of the Manx Electric Railway Society (MERS), so he was given the honour of a final journey on the MER. His coffin was taken, together with the mourners, from Derby Castle, the Douglas terminus of the MER, to Ramsey station, from where it was taken to a nearby church and then on to Peel for his burial. The vehicles used were Winter Saloon 20 for the mourners and Bulkhead trailer 37 for the coffin, which was strapped to the seats of the trailer. Both vehicles were draped with black sashes.[11]

There is another funeral that involved a tram enthusiast which must be mentioned, though the gentleman involved did not have a final journey on a tram. However, he was enclosed in a coffin decorated to resemble a tram. This was Eric Thornton, who had been keenly interested in trams throughout his long life and he was the joint author of the definitive history of Halifax Corporation Tramways. When he died aged 89 in 2007, his family arranged for him to have a special coffin[12] decorated with a printed representation of a single-deck Halifax Corporation tramcar, number 105, with the destination board appropriately showing 'Terminus'.

Apart from these recorded instances of trams used in, or connected with, funerals, there were a number of tram routes that terminated at cemeteries, or at least passed nearby, thereby enabling mourners to visit their buried loved ones with reasonable ease. At the tramway museum at Crich, the Sheffield 74 tram sometimes shows its destination blind as 'Cemetery Gates'.

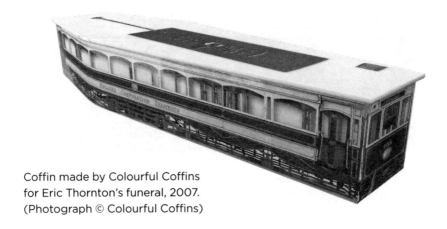

Coffin made by Colourful Coffins for Eric Thornton's funeral, 2007. (Photograph © Colourful Coffins)

The map of the former Derby tram network in the reconstructed Derby Assembly Rooms building at Crich shows that one of the routes terminated at a cemetery. Additionally, Route 1 on the Worcester tram network terminated at Astwood Cemetery[13] and in Hull a tram route passed the entrance of the General Cemetery, which was opened in 1849 on the western side of the city. In fact, there was a railway station across the road from the entrance to this cemetery, the station initially being named 'Cemetery', later becoming 'Cemetery Gates' before becoming 'Botanic Gardens' in 1881. It retained this name even after the nearby Botanical Gardens themselves closed in 1889 until the station was closed in 1964.[14]

One final link between trams and cemeteries for this chapter is to be found in north-east Manchester, where a stop on the modern tram network is called 'Cemetery Road', as the eponymous road leads to the nearby Droylsden Cemetery.

Sheffield 74 at Crich, showing destination 'Cemetery Gates'. (Photograph © Nicolas Wheatley)

11

MODELS AND DRAWINGS

It might be thought that models of hearse or corpse vans would be few and far between, especially as the prototypes ceases to exist long ago, with no private funeral train having run on the main line since the one for Earl Mountbatten in 1979. Indeed, in that train his coffin was carried not in a specially converted hearse van, like the one for Sir Winston Churchill, but in an ordinary Mark 1 full brake van, number M80867 in the then current BR standard blue and grey livery.[1] That van was, however, specially decorated inside for the occasion, as was only fitting for such a special use.

Given the historical importance of the Cavell Van, the former SE&CR Van 132, it might have been thought that a Ready to Run (RTR) model would have been made of this vehicle. Sadly no such models of this significant van have been made, though Bachmann have made a 00-scale model of a very similar vehicle. The prototype Cavell Van was built without ventilators protected by metal hoods on its sides, underneath the windows, but the production versions did have such ventilators and were designated as Parcels and Miscellaneous Vans (PMVs), in later days of operation by British Railways. Once the need for separate vans specifically for passengers' luggage had diminished, the vans were reclassified as PMVs, Parcels and Miscellaneous Vans. The models made by Bachmann are Southern

Railway olive-green livery PLVs (39-525, van number 2186), or British Railways green livery PMVs (39-530). The author has tried to persuade Bachmann to make an exact RTR model of the Cavell Van itself, but apparently changing the PLV/PMV tooling to omit the side ventilators was considered 'not worthwhile'.

The prototype Cavell Van 132 carried a livery of umber with yellow lettering, as did the subsequent forty-five production vans, although other liveries of the basic SE&CR PLV vans could be produced to broaden the van's appeal, but Bachmann's decision was no doubt based on commercial considerations. However, under their 'Parkside Models' range, Peco have introduced a 00-scale kit version (PC36) of the original SE&CR version of the PLV, i.e. without the additional side ventilators. Although the kit body is moulded in green plastic, it could be painted umber and finished as Van 132, the Cavell Van. Indeed, the author has such a model kindly assembled and painted for him by a friend.

There is also an 0-scale kit version of the SE&CR PMVs available from Slaters (7C020), costing £79, which is modelled without the side ventilators. A fellow member of the LMS-Patriot Project has made one of these kits and painted it umber with yellow lettering, as the Cavell Van. A photo appears on page 57 in the August 2018 issue of *The Warrior*, the newsletter of the project. It is regrettable, however, that such a historically significant railway vehicle does not exist in RTR model form, in either 00 or 0 scales. This is especially so as 2020 sees the centenary of the repatriation of the Unknown Warrior, which will no doubt involve significant events of national commemoration. Many railway modellers might wish to mark these events by buying models of the Cavell Van, but some will be deterred by their lack of skills to make and paint the kits currently available.

Several models of other hearse/corpse vans are or have been available, though some are now not easy to find. In the author's personal collection there are models of five different vans, some in more than one scale, making a combination of eight distinct models altogether. A kind person who knew of the author's interest in these things gave him an uncompleted 00-scale kit of the Glasgow & South Western Railway (G&SWR) corpse van, as made about three decades ago by Ian Middleditch of the Scottish-based Model Wagon Company. Though Mr Middleditch is still with us, and is Chairman of the G&SWR Association, the kits are no longer in production. However, an exchange of emails with him did lead the author to learn that a 7mm 0-gauge model of the G&SWR corpse van had also previously been available in kit form.

A model of the corpse van from the North British Railway (NBR) is been introduced in kit form in 00 scale, in a joint venture between the North British Railway Study Group and NBR 4mm Developments. Retailing at £34, this kit will be available at a reduced price to members of the North British Railway Study Group, but it is not clear when the model will actually become available. A photo of the unpainted prototype of the kit appears on the North British Railway Study Group website.[2] Chapter 9 contains some more information about the use of the NBR corpse vans.

The Midland Railway corpse van has been the subject of kits in both 00 scale and 0 scale, both fortunately still available to the public. These are etched brass kits made by Mercian Models, from Stourport in the West Midlands, a company run by Trevor Cousens. The company often has its trade stand at model-railway exhibitions in the West Midlands, for example the Warley Show at the NEC, Birmingham, and the 7mm NGA annual show in Burton in June. The 00-scale kit is £33 and the larger-scale version is £90, but a degree of expertise is needed to assemble the kits, and a considerable degree of skill to paint and line them attractively. Fortunately the author was honoured to have his 0-scale kit assembled and painted by a senior member of the 0 Gauge Guild.

Previously, the Midland Corpse Van kit had been made by two other companies, one of them being Oldbury Models, whose 00-scale kit was reference 4001, though the reference for the 0-scale version is not known. The 0-scale version was at one time marketed by SM Models. The Midland Corpse van was also previously made by Midland Carriage Works, item J103, Diagram 424, but it is not clear if that company is still going.

The 1899 version of the London Necropolis Company's (LNC) hearse van was the subject of etched brass kits by Blacksmith Models, from Surrey, in both 00 and 3mm scale, though neither version is currently available. The company has closed down, but is has not been possible to trace if their product range has been taken on by anyone else. The Blacksmith's Models kit originated as a Mallard Models kit in its 'Connoisseur Models' range, the 00-scale version of which were limited to 300 numbered kits. The kits were produced in both 0 and 00 scales and occasionally the 00-scale versions appear on eBay, though they now seem to be sold as collector's items rather than being bought to be constructed. The 0-scale versions seem to be particularly rare.[3]

Hornby have produced a model of the Drummond M7 locomotives of the type that hauled the funeral trains to Brookwood cemetery. The author's version of this model is in L&SWR livery, a special edition by Hornby (R2678) of the locomotive as preserved at the National Railway Museum. The real locomotives used on the special trains to Brookwood were normally in the livery of the period, as were the hearse vans and passenger carriages,[4] i.e. L&SWR green until the formation of the Southern Railway, when engines in SR green provided the motive power. An illustration on the front cover of John Clarke's book *The Brookwood Necropolis Railway* (4th edition) shows a loco in Southern Railway green livery. There are several known black-and-white photographs of the necropolis train either en route or within Brookwood cemetery but, as yet, no colour photographs have been found. The necropolis train would never have been hauled by a locomotive in BR black livery, as the service ceased after Waterloo station was bombed in April 1941. This destroyed the platforms used by the necropolis service several years before British Railways came into existence in 1948.

Although the models of the L&SWR hearse vans formerly made by Blacksmith's Models are no longer available, it is still possible to obtain models in kit form of these vehicles in 2mm N scale from Ultima Models. The kits are of the body only and are designed to fit on a Peco chassis. At the time of writing (January 2020) the kits (catalogue reference LSW04) cost £5 and are available from their website: www.ultima-models.co.uk/catalogue/LSWR.html.

There are some scale drawings of the LNC's hearse van in John Clarke's book for anyone brave (or skilled) enough to scratch-build their own model. These were originally drawn by Gordon Weddell for the South Western Circle, the line society for the L&SWR, and are available in 7mm 0 scale under reference SWC/P/50, from the South Western Circle (www.lswr.org/services/drawings/about-drawings.html).

For the even more adventurous modellers – or those dedicated to infinite degrees of accuracy – the original large-scale drawings for these vans still exist and are in the archives of the NRM at York. The drawings are in a collection known as 'Stratford Bench Hole 24', with Drawing 15565 covering the LSWR/LNC's hearse vans. Remarkably, the drawings for the Midland Railway 1888-built corpse vans are also in this collection, as rawing 15567. Both drawings are listed on page 100 of a 215 page document available from the NRM website. It is possible that copies of these drawings are available through HMRS (Historical Model Railway Society).[5]

In August 2015 the author acquired a G-scale model of the Ffestiniog hearse van, hand built as a limited production run (of only forty, it is believed) by a modeller from Cheshire. He was exhibiting a G-scale layout based loosely on the Ffestiniog Railway at the Tramway Village, Crich, and had only a couple of models left of the hearse van, in either 45mm or 32mm gauge, the latter being capable of running on 0-gauge track. For the modest sum of £40 the author could not resist adding this large and unusual model to his collection, though sadly the opportunity for others to do so no longer exists.

Modellers in 00-9 scale are still able to buy kits of the Ffestiniog hearse van, made by GEM as white metal kits. GEM is now part of Lytchett Manor Models from Dorset and the kits (part number 9204, £5.25) are obtainable from them online via their website:[6] www.lytchettmanor.co.uk/lytchett-manor/00-9-rolling-stock.

Perhaps the most famous hearse van of all is Van S2464S as used in the Churchill funeral train and now preserved. A model of the COR PMV from which this van was adapted was in the Hornby catalogue for many years, and indeed was inherited from the earlier Triang range. In 2011 Hornby released a version of the van (R4451) in Pullman livery and with new wheels and bogies, though they made no other improvements to create an accurate model of the Churchill hearse van itself. For example, the centre doors of the van as used in the funeral train had windows fitted, which are not replicated on the model. However, replacement doors can be obtained and fitted, though some painting of the replacements is required.

Inexplicably, having gone to the trouble of applying the correct umber and cream livery to the model, Hornby failed to complete its decoration, adding no numbering or lettering at all. However, in the January 2005 issue of *Model Railway* magazine (to tie in with the fortieth anniversary of the funeral train) there was an article setting out how to convert and repaint the earlier version of the model to create a more accurate representation of the hearse van as used in the funeral train. Considering that this was before the hearse van had been repatriated from the USA, this article was well ahead of its time.

Additionally, incorrect bogies were fitted to the Hornby model, though these can be changed for the correct Bulleid ones. Although this model is no longer in production, occasionally it can be found in the second-hand sections of model railway dealers at shows. The Churchill hearse van had been released as a stand-alone item but was later included in the limited edition (of 1500) special train pack Hornby released in December 2015 under R3300 with a Suggested Retail Price of £239.99.

This includes a model of the Battle of Britain 4-6-2 locomotive 34051 *Winston Churchill*, together with representations (not 100 per cent accurate models) of two of the Pullman Cars from his funeral train, *Perseus* and *Lydia*, as well as the hearse van. Having missed being released in time for the fiftieth anniversary commemorations of his funeral, the train pack perhaps did not capture the market as well as it could have, and occasionally retailers at model railway shows or swap meets do have a Churchill Funeral Train pack for sale. Indeed the author saw one for sale at such an event in December 2019 for £295. No doubt they can be found sometimes on eBay though the usual caveats apply about buying items through that source.

As can be seen from the above, there are quite a number of hearse-van models now or previously available in a variety of scales. These are not often seen on layouts at model railway shows but, depending on the period and location being modelled, it would be quite appropriate to include a hearse van in a train. It would certainly provide a talking point between the layout operator and the visitors.

12

QUIRKS AND CURIOSITIES

As might be expected with a subject that generates a certain degree of 'morbid curiosity', there are a number of stories about corpses and death that have been published in books about unusual incidents on railways. Some are, frankly, far-fetched and not worth repeating but here is one that is plausible, though it cannot be verified. It is followed by some whose veracity has been researched and proved accurate, though sometimes the details need correcting.

The story is told in *Taken for a Ride: A Distressing Account of the Misfortunes and Misbehaviour of the Early British Railway Traveller*[1] of:

a maidservant who travelled second class in a dark, unilluminated carriage of a train from Doncaster to York. In the course of her journey this sensitive young woman tumbled to the disconcerting realisation that the long wooden box under her seat was, in fact, a coffin. Moreover, it was occupied. Later, standing in a state of rigid shock on the platform at York, she watched four porters enter the carriage and emerge bearing the coffin on their shoulders. No explanations or apologies were offered to the girl.

Whilst this story may well be true, no date was given for this episode nor was any source cited for the story's origin, so it must be regarded with a degree of scepticism.

One strange story that turned out to be true concerns a railway accident in Yorkshire in 1912. This mishap resulted in a corpse being spilled from its coffin that was being carried in its own van. The tale was reported at The Halifax Ghost Story Festival @Dean Clough, in 2014 or possibly earlier, in the following way:

> But some ordinary passenger trains have been known to carry coffins in their brake vans. On 21 June 1912, a passenger train running between Manchester and Leeds derailed near Hebden Bridge. The coffin of Mr Charles Horsfield shot out of the brake van, and his body was deposited onto the track. The Halifax Courier reported: "The coffin was found all splintered and the corpse, though unmarked, was pinned under the debris and partly exposed". This was too good a story for the locals to miss, and it was soon rumoured that Horsfield had originally drowned with the sinking of the Titanic and his body had been fished out of the icy ocean, only to end up on a railway track in Hebden Bridge. Accident prone to say the least. (The Titanic had sunk just 10 weeks earlier, and was still fresh in people's minds.)

The Board of Trade (BoT) report into this accident[2] records that a coffin was indeed being carried in a separate six-wheeled third van, No. 1967,[3] forming part of this train. The van had been attached at Manchester, together with a bogie composite van, No. 625, originating from Southport, both being destined for Harrogate. The BoT report records the destruction of the van carrying the coffin in the accident, the evidence of the fireman as given to the investigator being that the 'corpse van [was] broken to pieces'. The BoT report does not mention that the coffin was also damaged, nor does it mention the unfortunate Mr Horsfield by name. This 64-year-old had died in Sheffield and was presumably being taken 'home' for burial. Hopefully he got there in the end, but sadly history does not record his ultimate fate or place of burial.

A similar event occurred in another accident, this time on 15 July 1946, when the 7.05 p.m. Aberdeen Express from King's Cross in London derailed near Hatfield. As noted in the Ministry of Transport (MoT) report into this accident dated 8 November 1946,[4] the train was being hauled by a V2 Class 2-6-2 locomotive, No. 3645, designed by Sir Nigel Gresley.

The train was travelling at about 60mph around a gentle right-hand curve when the locomotive derailed and most of the following fourteen bogie coaches were derailed, the first four overturning. Remarkably no one was killed in this accident, though eleven of the 400 or so passengers were injured seriously enough to be detained in hospital. However, rescue workers attending the scene found a corpse which, on inspection, appeared to have been dead before the accident.

The truth was that this was a corpse being transported north, presumably back to Scotland for burial, a practice that was still relatively common even after cremation had started to become more widespread after the Second World War. The accident had caused the coffin to be thrown from the wreckage, with the corpse being ejected from the coffin itself. Unlike the Hebden Bridge case, history[5] does not record the name of the deceased and the ultimate fate of this unfortunate traveller is not known. One can only hope that he completed his final journey without further problems and now safely rests in peace in the place chosen for him by his loved ones.

There was, however, a fairly regular transport by train of corpses to the University of Aberdeen's Medical School, one of the leading anatomy schools in the UK, from places in England.[6] This was because the supply of corpses for the school was not sufficient within Scotland and corpses had to be brought in from elsewhere. Whether the corpse in this particular accident was one of those destined for the Medical School will probably never be known.

Another amusing story is told in the book *Don't Tell the Management* by author Terry Small, nicknamed 'Tiny', who worked on the railways from 1978 to 1988. He was working as guard out of Eastleigh when the following incident occurred, as recalled on p.47 of his book (grammar and punctuation as in the original):

> Parcels had almost become a thing of the past but we still carried some rather unusual items. One day I found six empty coffins in the brake van bound for an undertaker in Woking. At Southampton two very large baskets were loaded on board "You'll never guess what's in these, 'Tiny'"

said one of the porters, "one of the lids doesn't close properly and we saw what's inside". Taking a look I saw mannequin body parts, en route to a London department store.

This was too good an opportunity to miss. As we came to a halt in the platform at Woking, things got even better, there on the platform was a large barrow with one male and one female porter to unload the coffins. I handed out four and as the lady porter was about to lift the fifth from the van, she let out a terrible scream, for there hanging out of the side of the coffin was an arm, bent at the elbow. She reeled back and was helped to a platform seat to recover herself, "Did you see that, one of them coffins mate, it's got a body in". "Rubbish, you're imagining things" her mate told her, "Tiny and I have just put it on the barrow, they're all empty, see?" She looked at the barrow cautiously coming closer and walking both sides, but of course by this time the arm was safely back in its basket and she was assured that her imagination had run away with her. She was very wary about unloading vans for some time after this, and I wonder if she ever found out what really happened.

The author was alerted to this wonderful, if macabre, story by Terry Small himself, who mentioned it, and his book, at a model-railway exhibition where the author was exhibiting his model railway 'Journey's End', based on a fictional cemetery. The layout was inspired by Brookwood Cemetery near Woking, so the reference to Woking in the story is most appropriate. One of the aspects of this story that is unusual is how late in the life of British Rail it occurred. The transport of deceased people in coffins by train on the UK main line stopped in March 1988, and the carrying of empty coffins by train (especially six at one time) after 1978, when Terry Small started working on the railway, would probably have been a rare event.

Another quirky story of a real corpse being transported in a crate is told by Simon Bradley.[7] A young actor called William Ryder had died of pneumonia whilst on tour in Middlesbrough in 1899. Bradley reports that 'his friends therefore returned the body to his bereaved family in London by encasing the coffin within a simple crate'. This was scrawled with the words 'theatrical properties' and 'this side up'. Carried at the standard goods rate, the cost was 16 shillings 2 pence, but as an acknowledged cadaver, even without the extra weight of the packing case, it would have been

£11. Bradley tells us that 'The ruse was discovered but the Great Northern Railway generously waived the difference.' This story is credited by Bradley to the Liverpool Daily Post on 6 May 1899, but the author has been unable to find any trace of this William Ryder's death in the records maintained by the General Record Office.

A highly unusual story concerns a railway line where the first and almost the last train both carried coffins. This occurred in County Mayo, on the north-west coast of Ireland, now in the Republic of Ireland but at the time of the first event it was under British rule. The line concerned was between Newport and Achill, which was part of the Midland Great Western Railway Company's line that started from Westport. In 1894 it was extended from Newport to Mallaranny[8] and then on to Achill, but before it opened formally to fare-paying passengers it was used to take home the bodies of thirty-two young people who had been drowned in what became known as the Clew Bay Drowning. This occurred when a vessel carrying them to meet a steamer in Newport harbour, that would take them across to Scotland to work in seasonal potato picking, capsized causing their deaths. A monument recoding their names and commemorating their deaths can be seen in the old cemetery in Kildavenet (also spelled Kildownet).

The transportation of these coffins was seen as fulfilling the first part of an ancient prophecy by a local prophet Brian Rua O' Cearbhaim (1648–?). He had prophesised that 'carts on iron wheels with smoke and fire will come to Achill and the first and last carriages will carry dead bodies'. The line was never particularly profitable and just before it closed in 1937 it was used again to carry the coffins of ten potato pickers from Achill, who had been killed in a fire in a bothy at Kirkintilloch in East Dunbartonshire, Scotland. Once again, the railway was used to provide functional transport to take the dead home. The second part of the prophecy was not fulfilled exactly, as this train was not quite the last on the line, which closed only two weeks later.[9] Whether or not any credence can be placed in the prophecy, it is certainly unique that this railway was used for its first and almost last trains to carry coffins. The large number of coffins (thirty-two) transported by the first train, arising from a single accident, was not exceeded within the British Isles in peacetime until 1930, when the forty-eight victims of the R101 airship disaster were transported in a single train[10] from London to Bedfordshire (see Chapter 5).

Although most of the coffins transported by train were carried either in ordinary railway vehicles or specially constructed hearse/corpse vans, research for this book has uncovered one very unusual machine for transporting a coffin by rail. This is a four-wheel velocipede, a human-powered vehicle, which is a variation of a type of device used to inspect or maintain the track before powered machines, such as 'Wickham Trollies', were developed. This velocipede has been named 'Morticia' and is normally kept on the North Yorkshire Moors Railway by its part-owner, Phil Naylor, to whom the author is grateful for permission to use the following story. (See photo in colour section.)

As might be expected with such an unusual machine, it has a made-up backstory featuring the fictional 'Ravenscar Necropolis Railway', which is relevant to the subject matter of this book:

The story has its roots in the North Yorkshire village of Ravenscar. With the opening of the Scarborough to Whitby railway line in 1884, ideas to develop the coast came to the fore and the Peak Estate Company, taking its name from nearby Peak Hall and the adjoining estate was set up. The company drew up plans for a 'new town' to include shops, tea rooms, guesthouses and hanging gardens. Roads, drains and a mains water supply were laid down. The land was divided into 1500 plots for building and offered for sale.

It was decided to rename the town Ravenscar, possibly to avoid confusion with the Peak District in Derbyshire, or just simply to sound more attractive. Sadly, the dream did not come to fruition, investors did not buy plots of land and the town was not built. Access by train proved to be difficult, with trains often struggling to overcome the line's steep gradients. With Ravenscar's exposed cliff top location often at the mercy of the wind and rain, a rocky shoreline hundreds of feet below with difficult access, and no proper sandy beach, the venture failed. [So far, this much of the story is true.]

A little-known offshoot was the Ravenscar Necropolis Railway (R.N.R.). Modelled on the better-known Brookwood Necropolis Railway (1854-1941) run by the London Necropolis Company (LNC), the aim was to establish a clifftop cemetery to be furnished with corpses by the railway line. The LNC was set up to solve the problems of full cemeteries in the capital, carrying 200,000 bodies to its cemetery at Brookwood during the 87 years that the railway ran. [This sentence is also true, see Chapter 3, though the number of bodies carried by train may have been overstated.]

The raison d'être for the Ravenscar venture was to provide the same service for Northern towns and cities, but it was fatally flawed. A ¾ mile long siding was laid from just south of the station to a five acre site twenty yards from the cliff edge, where a Mortuary Chapel built over the line was planned for the funeral service to be conducted. Bodies and mourners were to be taken from the station to here by horse powered hearse and funeral carriages adapted to run on the rails.

A particularly lucrative source of income for the R.N.R. was expected to be the transport of pauper corpses relieving parishes of the responsibility of burial and with economies of scale giving a healthy profit. For the movement of these bodies from the station a more economic method was proposed.

A velocipede of the type usually employed in the maintenance of railway lines was purchased from the USA and modified to take a coffin, the same vehicle doubling as a means of transporting grave diggers and other workmen along the track. When this was required the coffin was replaced by a crude wooden box for tools and other goods.

Great things were expected from this enterprise, but along with Ravenscar town, success eluded it. A hint of things to come was when a trial grave was dug, the men hitting sandstone after two feet of digging, resulting in three days being taken to reach the required six feet. The work was undertaken in high winds and sleet leading to one of the grave diggers getting pneumonia and barely living, it being joked by his workmates that at least the grave wouldn't have been wasted should he have died. With hindsight a trial dig should have been carried out before the siding was built. No pauper burials ever materialized, the local authorities of the time finding it cheaper to do the job in-house digging deeper and stacking the coffins.

So here the scheme died, the siding remained, falling into disrepair until the advent of the Great War. It was then used to supply materials for six 12-inch guns being constructed on the excellent rock foundation. The guns came into operation on the 22nd of December 1914, six days after the passage of the German Imperial Fleet following its bombardment of Scarborough. [This bombardment did actually occur; Hartlepool and Whitby were also shelled by the German fleet.]

The velocipede was sold to the North Eastern Railway finding use for the next sixty years on track repair duties. It disappeared from view until being discovered in a disused engine shed in the North West of England. Sadly beyond repair, the remains were used as a pattern by Mr Graham Hughes of Stafford to construct the present day machine. Graham was not aware of the machine's unusual history, his intention being that it would be used as a track maintenance vehicle on the preserved Churnet Valley Railway. Strangely though, comment was often made to Graham that it would make a good coffin carrier.

In 2005 Graham offered the machine for sale, it being bought by six members of the North Yorkshire Moors Railway's locomotive department at Grosmont and returned home to its roots. Following the purchase, research was undertaken into its history and the above story came to light. A coffin was made to complete the machine and it was given what its owners think is an appropriate name.

Morticia sees regular use being taken to rallies at preserved steam railways and starring in locally made feature films. The owners' greatest pleasure though is taking her to Whitby during Goth weekends, where coffin rides are given in aid of the town's lifeboat.

Though the Ravenscar Necropolis Railway is obviously the figment of a vivid imagination, 'Morticia' clearly is not, though its practical use for transporting coffins is limited to only one at a time. However, coffin transport is not its real purpose, that being to bring a bit of amusement to what might otherwise be a sombre subject. Its inclusion here is done with the same purpose.

A world away from the fictional Ravenscar Necropolis Railway, and in a very different geographical part of the country, there are two incidents that occurred on the Great Western Railway (GWR) which are worthy of mentioning in this chapter. The first happened in 1924 and was reported in the *Paddington, Kensington and Bayswater Chronicle* on 27 December 1924.[11] Their report, reproduced here in full, was as follows:

G.W.R. EXPRESS HELD BACK
PLIGHT OF MOURNING PARTY

There was consternation at Paddington Station on Sunday night when the 9.15 p.m. express to Aberystwyth was about to depart.

A party of mourners had arrived with wreaths, for whom accommodation had been provided, but the coffin containing the corpse had not arrived. The express was held up for ten minutes in the hope that the undertaker would arrive.

It then transpired that one of the undertaker's assistants who lived about a mile away had gone home, taking with him the keys to the entrance to the yard leading to the mortuary.

An attempt to break down the gate to get the coffin out had failed, and eventually the train departed with the mourners. The coffin followed on Monday.

To report that the delay caused 'consternation' was no doubt a huge understatement, as the mourners were almost certainly very upset at not being able to accompany their deceased loved one and the staff of the GWR would have been extremely displeased at the delay to their express train. (The GWR always prided itself on running its express trains on time.) Much form-filling and reporting of the event to senior railway officials would have followed and no doubt the undertaker's assistant received a few choice words on his return to work on Monday!

The second incident also happened at Paddington Station, a few years later in 1935. The event was witnessed by C. Hamilton Ellis and his report of it was published in *Trains Illustrated* in 1953.[12] He and his wife were trying, late in the evening, to get to Barnstaple to see the Lynton & Barnstaple Railway in the last week of its operation.[13] Having failed to get a direct train from Waterloo, they went to Paddington where the lady ticket clerk suggested they caught an excursion train to Plymouth leaving at midnight and then change at Taunton to catch another train to Barnstaple.[14] The important part of the report reads as follows:

So, late at night, we were at Paddington again and it was a lively place. Drinking coffee, we met a spruce traveller in shirts, disconsolate because he had missed the 9.50 to the West. We told him that if he came on the excursion he would gain on the train he had missed. He gave me a black cheroot with a straw mouthpiece and rushed off on some late night mission in high spirits. I smoked his gift, we finished up the coffee, spent a happy time looking at the engines and joined our train. Competently headed by a 'Castle' it was a uniform Great Western express of the period save, as usual, for the odd vehicle. This was an old gaslit composite clerestory, all reserved for a party going to Taunton. The luggage compartment was sealed; I squinted inside then held my peace. We found two corners elsewhere and watched the other passengers. The large party arrived, with hampers. They walked and talked gravely and gravely black were their clothes.

My wife said: "Why, it's a funeral!"

There was nothing else funereal about the train. It got away smartly and we were comfortable with two men in the other corners.... [The final part of the article is not relevant to the funeral aspects of the story.]

What these two stories confirm is that the functional transportation of coffins by train was an everyday occurrence on the railways. It may not often have been photographed or even reported, unless the deceased was someone noteworthy, but these two cases are good examples of the railways doing what they were good at: transporting people and freight without fuss, to wherever the passengers wanted to go or wherever the freight needed to be.

Perhaps one little-known aspect of modern funerals is the wide choice of coffins that are available. This is of direct relevance to the subject matter of this book in that it is possible to obtain coffins with transport-themed images on them. Chapter 10 has already shown a coffin decorated with an image of a tram, and the company that made it, Colourful Coffins, based near Oxford, list a range of coffins decorated with various types of trains on their website, www.colourfulcoffins.co.uk. These include images of various steam locomotives, including 4472/60103 *Flying Scotsman*, and even a coffin decorated with a Pendolino train in the now historic Virgin Trains livery for railway enthusiasts with a liking for modern trains. As a supporter of the former Great Western Railway (GWR), the author's attention was caught by a coffin showing a preserved GWR 'King' class steam locomotive, 6024

Special coffin made by Crazy Coffins for Brian Holden, who is sitting on it during an exhibition at London South Bank Centre, January 2012. (Photograph © Nicolas Wheatley)

King Edward I, pulling a rake of chocolate and cream coloured coaches on the line at Cockwood Harbour, between Exeter and Teignmouth, on the famous stretch of railway that runs next to the sea between those south Devon stations (see photo in colour section).[15]

Even more special than these coffins, however, was one specially made for railway enthusiast Brian Holden from Manchester by a firm called Crazy Coffins,[16] based in Bulwell near Nottingham. The firm, a subsidiary of the well-known funeral firm Vic Fearn and Company Ltd, was commissioned by Brian Holden in 2007 to make a special coffin in the shape of a railway carriage. This was decorated as one of the carriages in the 'Northern Belle' luxury train, in which Brian and his late wife Jean travelled regularly. The carriages carry the names of British castles or stately homes and *Alnwick* was the favourite of Brian and Jean, being the carriage in which they often journeyed. After her death Brian decided to remember their trips by having this special coffin ready for his use in due course and it was displayed at London's South Bank in January 2012 during an exhibition about death and funerals.[17]

During that exhibition this coffin attracted much attention, both from the visitors and from several media organisations. The author was privileged to speak with Brian Holden to glean some more information about this unique coffin. Apparently, to make sure the correct paint colours were used, Crazy Coffins contacted the operators of the Northern Belle train and were rewarded by being provided with some of the actual paints used on the real train, together with some of the fabric used on the seats. It is not possible to get more authentic than that! The design and decoration of the carriage, including its lining-out, is therefore a very accurate representation of the real thing, including the material used in the interior lining, though obviously on much smaller scale.

Sadly, Brian Holden died aged 88 on 7 September 2017 and his coffin was used at his funeral in Manchester. A report of it appeared in the *Manchester Evening News*,[18] complete with several photographs, including one showing the coffin within which Brian made his final journey in the hearse. The author understands from his conversation with him in 2012 that Brian wanted to be cremated inside the special coffin, and it is believed this wish was carried out. Whilst the destruction of such an interesting and unusual coffin was an unfortunate loss to funeral heritage, as Brian had paid for it himself[19] he was perfectly entitled to decide its fate. Although Brian Holden's funeral did not involve the transport of his body by a train, the fact that his coffin was in the design of a luxury railway carriage, unique as it was, more than justifies the inclusion of the story in this book.

A very different funeral took place in 1936 that involved real luxury railway carriages and the transportation of a coffin draped with a Nazi swastika flag. In 1936 two Pullman cars were used in a train which transported a coffin, as well as some mourners, in circumstances which now seem quite extraordinary. Occurring during an episode of British history that has been largely forgotten, possibly conveniently, the deceased was Dr Leopold von Hoesch, who had been the German Ambassador to Britain since 1932. He died suddenly in London from a heart attack aged 55, on 10 April 1936, during the short reign of King Edward VIII, who was suspected of having Nazi sympathies.

However, the Ambassador was not a Nazi and indeed was highly respected by senior figures in the British establishment. This led to the Ambassador being given a full ceremonial military funeral, with swastika flags being flown as the cortege processed down The Mall in London. The coffin was also draped in the Nazi flag, a diplomatic courtesy as it was the national flag of Germany at the time. Some in the funeral procession gave a Nazi salute as it set off, and a nineteen-gun salute was fired in Hyde Park, this number being dictated by protocol as appropriate for five-star generals, prime ministers and, crucially, ambassadors. The Foreign Secretary, Anthony Eden (who later became Prime Minister), and the Home Secretary, Sir John Simon, were amongst the people walking behind the coffin as the procession made its way to Victoria Station.

From Victoria a special train left for Dover, whilst the German National Anthem was played by a military band. The train included Pullman cars *Marjorie*, a kitchen car with its celebrated interior scheme, and *Leona (II)*, together with three four-wheeled vans for the wreaths and a bogie van carrying the coffin. At Dover the guns at the castle fired another salute whilst the coffin was loaded onto a British destroyer, HMS *Scout*, which then transported the late Ambassador back to Germany. It has been easier to find reports of these extraordinary events in the American press – *The New York Times* – than in the archives of British papers (though some rare footage can be found on YouTube). This leads to the suspicion that this occasion when Nazi flags were ceremonially displayed in London is an event that some people would prefer to forget. The use of Pullman cars in a funeral train which transported a coffin draped with the Nazi swastika flag was certainly one of the more unusual workings of these vehicles. It was, however, perhaps understandable in the political circumstances of the time, when a policy of appeasement was being followed, before the Second World War became inevitable. In a curious twist of history, Pullman car *Leona (II)*, as used in the late Ambassador's train, was later converted to *Car No. 208*, and in 1965 it was used in the Churchill funeral train.[20]

Perhaps one final curiosity should be allowed to complete this chapter, a poem by a writer who sadly committed suicide in 1914 at the age of only 33. His name was Alphonse Courlander and the poem[21] is as follows:

The Phantom Train

When the night is dark and stormy,
And the clouds are black o'er head,
When the screech-birds cry in chorus,
As if mourning for the dead,
When the wild winds are roaring,
And the air is thick with rain,
Then on such a night, with a shriek of affright,
Is seen the Phantom Train.

With a roar and a hiss the engine
Rushes on its phantom road,
With its ghostly phantom driver
And its grisly phantom load:
And the villagers in their terror
Cross themselves again and again-
But no one knows how the story goes
Of the fearsome Phantom Train.

There are whispers of a collision-
Of a driver who blasphemed the Lord,
And was doomed therefore in this manner
To suffer ever afterward.
But not one knows the story,
Tho' the gossips guess in vain-
Yet on stormy nights, with a shriek of fright,
Runs the terrible Phantom Train.

Now, who can solve the mystery
Of this Phantom Train of Fear,
And who can say where it comes from
And why does it run each year,
With its headlights flashing brightly,
And who can ever explain
The skeleton crew, and the driver too,
Of the fearsome Phantom Train?

13

ENDING AND CONTINUATION

Part 1: Ending on the Main Line

Previous chapters have sought to differentiate between the functional transportation of coffins by train and the ceremonial aspects that often accompany such transport. As noted above, much ceremony often attaches to the funeral transport (by whatever means) of high-status individuals or those who have died prematurely, particularly in military service. The use of trains to convey coffins was a development of funeral transport based on a new technology, when previously the distance a coffin could be transported was largely based on the technology of horse-drawn hearses or carts and the stamina of the horses to travel the distance required. There were some exceptions, as noted in Chapter 2, including the transportation of Queen Eleanor of Castille's remains to London in 1290 and the repatriation of Admiral Lord Nelson's body to England in a barrel of brandy in 1805. However, these exceptions were of very high-status individuals where the cost of such repatriations was not an obstacle. For ordinary, albeit relatively well off financially, families the opportunity to take or send their loved ones' remains 'home' by train for burial generated much traffic for the railways for nearly 150 years.

For the last seventy or so years, however, the level of this traffic had been declining, due largely to two factors outside the railways' control. Changes to the railways themselves also played a part and were ultimately the reasons given for the termination of functional coffin transport on the main line. Briefly, the two external factors were the development of motor hearses and the acceptance and spread of cremation as a method of disposal. The first motor hearses were introduced in the decade after 1900, although the first vehicle in 1900 was used for the distant delivery of coffins rather than for funerals. By 1904 a motor hearse had been used to convey a coffin over a long distance, some 74 miles from London to Eastbourne, but by January 1910 a trade publication for funeral directors, *The Undertaker's Journal*, commented that: 'The motor is entering so much of our daily life that it was inevitable that it should be eventually called in to serve the undertaker in his dealings with the dead.'[1]

This did indeed prove to be the case and had a direct impact on the use of trains to transport coffins. For example, the west London firm of funeral directors W.S. Bond in 1915 acquired a 25hp motor hearse, with pneumatic tyres, electric lighting, side curtains and full ventilation. It could also accommodate five passengers along with a large coffin and was known as the 'Railway Train Competitor'.[2] W.S. Bond also possessed a Napier hearse which resembled a customised delivery van, but both vehicles were mostly used to transport coffins over a distance where horses or the rail system were impractical.[3] This would particularly be the case for long-distance transportation of coffins, but trains were still used for even relatively short distances for many decades, as many examples in this book have demonstrated. The service to Brookwood Cemetery near Woking covered only 25 miles from Waterloo, but the trains still operated to there, albeit with decreasing frequency, until 1941.

The other factor that undermined the transportation of coffins by train was a change in funeral practice with the growth of cremation. The history of cremation in the UK is outside the scope of this book, and is covered in many other sources, one of them being by Professor Hilary Grainger OBE in her book *Death Redesigned: British Crematoria, History, Architecture and Landscape*, published in 2005.[4] In his Foreword to this book Reverend Dr Peter Jupp refers to the development of new forms of cemetery (covered in Chapter 2 of this book) and notes that:

the new public cemeteries could not solve the disposal needs of an increasingly urbanising society. Cremation offered a second solution but this radical concept only became of interest to the general public when attitudes to death, mourning and memorialisation had been drastically challenged by the First World War. Indeed cremation only became more available to the general public as local authorities increasingly turned to crematoria building projects between 1918 and 1939.

One unintended consequence of this was that initially there was an increase in the number of coffins being transported by train. This was to take coffins to the very few crematoria that were at first built in the UK. The first rudimentary 'crematory' in the UK was built at Woking and opened in 1879. It was not part of Brookwood Cemetery, though it was built on land sold for £200 by the London Necropolis Company (LNC) which operated the cemetery and its railway service. The facility was provided by the privately constituted Cremation Society but did not carry out its first cremation until 1885, a year after the practice had been declared legal in Britain.[5]

From its first cremation the numbers of cremations at Woking grew very slowly, and initially coffins were transported to the crematorium by horse-drawn hearse. From central London this distance of 25 miles would have been fairly exhausting for the horses. Quite soon the coffins were placed on scheduled trains and taken to Woking station, less than 2 miles from the crematorium. However, by 1890 the Cremation Society had developed links with the LNC and made arrangements so that coffins which were to be cremated, together with any accompanying mourners, could be transported on the regular necropolis service trains to Brookwood. From there the coffins were taken to the nearby crematorium and the mourners sometimes stayed at the cemetery, no doubt enjoying the facilities of its refreshment rooms, until the urn containing the ashes was handed back to them.[6]

One example of a person whose remains were transported by train for cremation at Woking was Thomas John Barnardo (1845–1905). He was a Dublin-born philanthropist who is most famous for having set up a 'ragged school'[7] and later homes for poor and orphaned children in the East End of London. Though he never completed his medical training, he called himself 'Dr' and the orphanages became known as Dr Barnardo's Homes.

Coffin of Dr Thomas Barnardo in procession from Barkingside station, September 1905. (Author's Collection)

The organisation he founded still operates, now simply called 'Barnardo's', with its headquarters in Barkingside, East London. On his death in September 1905, his body lay in state at the Edinburgh Castle Mission Hall and then a procession took place from Limehouse through the East End to Liverpool Street station. From there his coffin was taken by train along the route then operated by the Great Eastern Railway to Barkingside. From that station six bearers carried the coffin the short distance to the Children's Church in the grounds of the Girls' Village Home. However, after the service his body was taken by train for cremation at Woking[8] before his ashes were buried in front of Cairn's House, the headquarters of the organisation. The railway line is now operated as part of Transport for London's Central Line, but some reports that this was an example of coffin transport on the London Underground are incorrect. The line was not part of that network in 1905,[9] indeed it only became used as part of the Central Line in 1948.

Another example of a person whose body was transported by train for cremation occurred in 1911. On 21 September of that year the coffin of His Highness the Nineteenth Maharajah of Cooch Behar, (Sir Nripendra Narayan), who had died on 18 September in Bexhill, Kent, was

Coffin of Nineteenth Maharajah of Cooch Behar being loaded into train at Bexhill station, Kent, September 1911. His coffin was taken to London for cremation at Golders Green crematorium. (Image courtesy of Brian Parsons)

transported by train to Victoria. The coffin was then taken to Golders Green Crematorium in north London, which had opened in 1904 and was the nearest facility (though Woking crematorium was open by that date). After the cremation had taken place his ashes were taken back to India for interment and a plaque was erected in the West Chapel at Golders Green.[10] In passing, it can be noted that his son, Raj Rajendra Narayan (the twentieth Maharajah), died in 1913 in Erpingham, Norfolk, and his coffin was also possibly taken by train to London for cremation.

It was only after the passing of the Cremation Act in 1902, which gave powers to local authorities to provide crematoria, that many more were built in other parts of the country, although some were also provided by private companies. One such privately provided facility was opened in 1928 within Arnos Vale Cemetery in Bristol, becoming the first crematorium in the south-west of England.[11] This resulted in a number of coffins for cremation being sent by train from further parts of the West Country to Temple Meads station in Bristol, only a mile or so from the crematorium. The scale of this traffic is still being researched.

The choice of cremation over burial as a method of disposal did, however, take several decades to gain ascendancy. Partly this was because of religious opposition, including from the Church of England which did not formally approve cremation until 1944. The Roman Catholic Church had declared cremation illegal in 1886 and this ban remained in place until 1964. Indeed it was not until 1967 that cremation reached a level of 50 per cent of disposals, having been only 9.1 per cent in 1945.[12] During this time better roads were being built across the UK, particularly with the development of the motorway network, starting in the 1960s and continuing through the 1970s and early 1980s. Improvements to the road network enabled funeral directors to transport coffins more easily themselves, using vans that were either unmarked or discreetly marked as 'private ambulances'.

The use of roads also enabled more freight to be transported by lorries, often at more competitive prices than the railways were able to charge in view of the standing costs incurred to maintain all their infrastructure. This modal shift was particularly pronounced in relation to small consignments of freight, i.e. less than one wagon load. Even by 1949, British Railways was concentrating the collection and despatch of such types of freight into larger centres, as evidenced by a letter in the author's collection.

This letter is dated 4 July 1949 and was sent by British Railways (Southern Region) Southern Division Superintendent's Office in Southampton. It set out details of a new system being introduced throughout the country for dealing with small consignments of freight. Bournemouth Central Goods Depot was to become the focal point for dealing with traffic in less than whole wagon loads within a wide but defined area surrounding Bournemouth. The aim was to speed up the collection and delivery of small consignments of freight and no doubt similar arrangements were being put in place across the rail network. One effect was to reduce the number of stations from which goods could be despatched, or from which they could be collected. Although the shipment of coffins was undoubtedly a special type of freight, they would certainly have been less than one wagon load, though often they would have been placed separately in a van on their own. However, the overall effect of the changes announced in this letter from 1949 would have been to reduce the opportunities to send or receive coffins at many smaller stations.

At the same time the railway network was in a period of decline, which started before the Second World War. It was accelerated by the many closures that followed the publication in 1963 of Dr Beeching's report *The Reshaping of British Railways*.[13] In truth, more miles of track were closed before, and a few after, the Beeching Repot than were closed as a result of its recommendations. However, one major consequence was the closure of many smaller stations and goods-handling facilities, even on lines that stayed open. This had an adverse effect on the ability to send freight – including coffins – from almost anywhere to almost anywhere else. For example, the following photograph[14] shows a train arriving at Cinderford station in the Forest of Dean, Gloucestershire, sometime around 1910 (it is believed). There is a horse-drawn hearse waiting outside the station building, so the train is probably carrying a coffin 'home' for someone's burial. Unfortunately, research has not yet identified the exact date of the event or the name of the deceased. The station itself was opened in 1900, closed to passengers in 1958 and to freight in 1967, reflecting a typical history of many small country stations.

A better view of a horse-drawn hearse, with a separate carriage for the mourners, waiting for a train, can be seen in the view from Euston station, from about 1905.

The reduction in the amount and types of freight carried by the railways has been covered in many other books and articles and the exact number of coffins transported by train is not known, as no statistics were collected for this traffic. However, there is some evidence that coffins were still being transported by train well into the 1960s and 1970s. Indeed, research for this book has discovered that the coffin of the US-born writer and poet Sylvia Plath (1932–1963) was transported by train from King's Cross station in London to Hebden Bridge following her death by suicide in 1963. Although estranged from her husband, the writer and Poet Laureate Ted Hughes (1930–1998), he remained her next of kin for the purposes of arranging her funeral. As part of that he arranged for her to be buried in the churchyard of St Thomas the Apostle, Heptonstall, near Hebden Bridge in Yorkshire.

This village is close to where Hughes was born and spent the first few years of his life, in nearby Mytholmroyd. That village's location in the Calder Valley is prone to flooding, so a new cemetery was developed up

Cinderford station, Gloucestershire, around 1905–10. Horse-drawn hearse waiting at station for incoming train. (Image courtesy of Ian Pope)

London Terminus. Waiting arrival of Train.

A hearse and carriage waiting at Euston Station.

Euston station, around 1903. Horse-drawn hearse and carriage for mourners waiting for train. (Image courtesy of Brian Parsons)

the hill as an extension to the existing churchyard in Heptonstall. The cost of Sylvia Plath's final journey by train in February 1963, of about 200 miles, was £30,[15] which equates to approximately 3 shillings per mile, which was the standard rate at the time. It is believed this was also the rate charged for the transportation of Sir Winston Churchill's coffin two years later, though there were many other costs associated with his final journey, such as hiring the Pullman cars at a cost of 15 guineas (a guinea was 21 shillings) each.[16]

The transportation of coffins by train certainly carried on into the 1960s and beyond, and Chapter 12 records an incident involving the transportation of some empty coffins during the late 1970s. In the course of research for this book the author has been told many stories, some of which cannot be verified, but one which comes from a reliable source[17] concerned a railway worker who died on holiday in Spain during the late 1970s or early 1980s. Apparently his union paid for the cost of repatriating his body, which appropriately was undertaken in a railway wagon of the type then used for the international transport of freight.

However, the number of coffins being transported was obviously decreasing and on 3 March 1988 British Railways wrote to the secretaries of five railway staff unions notifying them that: 'The [British Railways] Board had decided to discontinue from the 31 March the conveyance of corpses.' The reason given for this decision was that:

> with the streamlining of our network the special vans in which corpse conveyance must take place have become increasingly difficult to organise in the short notice that funeral directors require. Due to this it is invariably cheaper and more convenient that the transportation be by road. ... as a result of this withdrawal the facility currently available for active/retired staff and dependants, of a 50% reduction on the public corpse conveyance charges will also be discontinued from the same date'.

The writer of the letter, D.J.T. Goodall, Personnel Services Manager, continues by stating that 'steps will be taken to notify staff and any assistance you can give to publicise the discontinuance of this concession would be greatly appreciated.'

Presumably this decision was reported to members of the five unions affected in newsletters sent out to them after the letter was received. As yet it has not been possible to find any copies of such newsletters or to establish when the last coffin of a railway union member was transported by train. An organisation called the 'Branch Line Society' did report the ending of coffin transport by train in the 5 May 1988 edition of their publication, called *Branch Line News*,[18] though it was not until the 4 October 1990 issue of that publication[19] that it was reported that this also applied to the ending of coffin transport by train for BR staff.

The announcement of the ending of coffin transport by train may still have been of some interest to the railway unions and their members, but apparently it was of no consequence to funeral directors, who presumably had by then stopped using trains for coffin transport. Parsons notes that: 'when in March 1988 it was announced that coffins could no longer be taken on the national network it didn't even warrant a mention in the trade journals'.[20] Reference to the stopping of coffin transport by train appears in some books on death and funerals from relatively soon after it occurred, for example on page 120 of Julian Litten's landmark 1991 book *The English Way of Death: The Common Funeral Since 1450*.[21] Research for this book has, however, resulted in the production of a copy of the letter,[22] which is reproduced below, it is believed for the very first time. It could be said that this letter is the 'Holy Grail' of coffin transport by train in the UK, being the only known document that formally announces its termination.

Following this termination of coffin transport on the main line only one exception has been made and that was in August 2001. This was for the final journey of Jimmy Knapp, who was general secretary of the NUR (National Union of Railwaymen) in 1988 and one of the people to whom the letter giving notice of termination was addressed. By the date of his premature death from cancer aged 60, he was leader of the larger RMT (National Union of Rail, Maritime and Transport Workers), and in view of his associations with the railway industry his coffin was taken by train from Euston to Glasgow. Further details and a photo of this event are set out in Chapter 9.

In line with past royal precedent, it might have been expected that the deaths of two senior members of the Royal Family in 2002 would result in their final journeys being by train to Windsor. However, this

British Railways Board

J.M. Dalgleish, Esq.
National Secretary
British Transport Officers' Guild
Room 204/205, East Side Offices
King's Cross Station
London N1 9AX

date 3rd March 1988
o/r 70-16-9
y/r
tel ext 30493

J. Knapp, Esq.
General Secretary
National Union of Railwaymen
Unity House
Euston Road
London NW1 2BL

N.F. Milligan, Esq.
General Secretary
A.S.L.E. & F.
9 Arkwright Road
Hampstead
London NW3 6AB

C.A. Lyons, Esq.
General Secretary
Transport Salaried Staffs' Association
Walkden House
10 Melton Street
London NW1 2EJ

A. Ferry, M.B.E.
Joint Secretary
Trade Union Side
R.Sh.N.C.
Confederation of Shipbuilding
and Engineering Unions
140-142 Walworth Road
London SE17 1JW

Dear Sir,

CONVEYANCE OF CORPSES

I thought I should advise you that the Board has decided to discontinue
from the 31st March the conveyance of corpses. The reason for this is
that with the streamlining of our network the special vans in which
corpse conveyance must take place have become increasingly difficult to
organise in the short notice that funeral directors require. Due to this
it is invariably cheaper and more convenient that the transportation of
the corpse be by road.

As a consequence of this withdrawal, the facility currently available to
active/retired staff and dependants, of a 50% reduction on the public
corpse conveyance charges will also be discontinued from the same date.

Steps will be taken to notify staff of the foregoing and any assistance
you can give to publicise the discontinuance of this concession would be
greatly appreciated.

Yours faithfully,

for D.J.T. GOODALL
PERSONNEL SERVICES MANAGER

Departure Side Offices, Platform 1, Paddington Station, London W2 1FT Telephone 01-928 5151 Telex 299431 BRHQLN G quote HQZA

BR 27/7:

Letter sent in March 1988 to five trade union officials announcing the ending of
corpse transport on British Rail. (Image courtesy of Great Western Trust, Didcot)

did not occur and the coffins of both HM Queen Elizabeth The Queen Mother (1900–2002) and HRH Princess Margaret (1930–2002) were both transported by motor hearse, as noted in Chapter 6. At the time of her premature death on 31 August 1997, Diana, Princess of Wales (b. 1961), was no longer a member of the Royal Family and, following her large ceremonial funeral in London, her coffin was transported by motor hearse rather than by train. The coffin was taken to the Spencer family's ancestral estate, now home of her brother, Charles 9th Earl Spencer, at Althorp in Northamptonshire for burial privately. However, the Royal Train was used in connection with this final journey, transporting many mourners including HRH Prince Charles and Diana's two sons, TRH Princes William and Harry, as well as Earl Spencer, to the nearby station at Long Buckby, from where they travelled to Althorp by car.[23]

The ending of coffin transport by train could be seen in the context of the 'life-cycle theory', which has been applied to railways by the academic Zdenek Tomes,[24] though not specifically in relation to coffin transport. He compares the development of railways generally to the introduction and subsequent rise and decline of products in the marketplace. He opines that railways follow a discernible path of 'introduction, growth, maturity and decline', and it is possible to see the transport of coffins by train in the same sequence of development. It was introduced as a new form of technology to meet a need, grew as the network expanded, reached maturity as more people died away from home and were taken back for burial, but declined when the new technologies of cremation and motor hearses proved more practical and cheaper than rail transport. The flaw in applying this theory generally to railways is that it cannot accommodate the resurgent growth, within the last few years, of passenger numbers and some bulk freight transportation, though not of coffins. The other problem with this theory in relation to the transportation of coffins by train is that it takes no account of the practice of giving a ceremonial final journey on heritage railways to certain favoured volunteers or other people with significant links to those railways. This now forms the second part of this chapter.

Part 2: Continuation on Heritage Railways

It is not known for certain when the first ceremonial final journey took place on a heritage railway but Chapter 9 refers to a case on the Talyllyn Railway in 1989 where the coffin of Hugh Jones was transported in Guard's Van No. 5 on that line. There are no known photos of that event, but from the written reports there was clearly a degree of ceremony involved. There may have been other ceremonial final journeys on other heritage railways before that, but none have come to the author's knowledge as yet.

However, a good starting point for this part of this chapter is the event which is depicted on the front cover of this book. This took place on 15 September 2003 and involved a final journey for Jack Rowell, who had been a member of the Keighley & Worth Valley Railway (KWVR) in Yorkshire since 1961. During his forty-year-long association with the railway, he had spent ten years as Station Master at Oxenhope, and later became chairman of the railway's sales department, managing gift shops at Oxenhope, Haworth and Keighley stations. He also acted as a real-life Father Christmas on the railway's Santa Specials, growing a magnificent beard for that role. He also had several important roles in the local community, including being a churchwarden at St Mary's Church, Oxenhope, where his funeral service was held.

Following his death after a long illness, the KWVR organised for him to have a final journey from Oxenhope, where the photograph was taken, to Oakworth station, from where his coffin was taken to the crematorium within Oakworth Cemetery. The train also carried his family and friends and after a further service at the crematorium they travelled back by train to Oxenhope for a wake. A report on the event, together with a large photograph of the coffin being loaded onto the train, appeared on the front page of the *Yorkshire Post* newspaper on 16 September 2003.

One heritage railway that has had no fewer than four ceremonial funeral trains is the South Devon Railway (SDR) that runs from Buckfastleigh to Totnes Riverside. These occurred in 2011, 2013, 2018 and 2019. The first of these was for volunteer Brian Cocks (1940–2011), who had started his working life on British Railways in London. His early days of volunteering on what was then called the Dart Valley Railway saw him driving ex-GWR 0-6-0 tank locomotive 1369 for the first time in 1967, which

South Devon Railway, 2013. Coffin of Chris Woodland being carried to train at Buckfastleigh station. (Photograph © John Brodribb)

his wife June had helped to repaint. He drove one of the first public trains when the railway reopened as a preserved line in April 1969. It had originally closed to passengers in 1958 and then completely in 1962, but the reopening ceremony in May 1969 was carried out by none other than Dr Richard Beeching who joked, incorrectly, that he would not have been able to reopen the railway if he had not closed it in the first place.

Brian Cocks left the DVR in 1975 but after his retirement he became increasingly involved with the newly reconstituted South Devon Railway during the 1990s, working in a variety of roles and being Carriage and Wagon Supervisor at the time of his premature death from leukaemia. He was also a former Chairman of the South Devon Railway Association.[25] Fittingly, his funeral train was hauled by locomotive 1369, driven by his friend Dave Knowling, who was honoured with his own funeral train in 2018, as below. The photograph shows the Reverend David Hardy leading the procession carrying Brian Cocks' coffin towards the train at Buckfastleigh station on 15 July 2011.

Just two years later, on 22 June 2013, the SDR provided another funeral train for Chris Woodland, another respected volunteer who had many roles on the railway. Both he and his wife Sheree worked as crew on the loco-motives, sometimes with him as driver and her as fireman (or should that be 'firewoman'?). The photograph shows his coffin being carried across the platform at Buckfastleigh to be placed on the train for his final journey. The locomotive used for this special train was an ex-GWR 0-6-0 pannier tank based on the SDR which is owned by the Worcester Locomotive Society. In GWR times the locomotive was numbered 5786 but was renumbered L92 when it was sold to London Transport (LT) in 1958. It was repainted by LT into their maroon livery, in which guise it hauled Chris Woodland's funeral train.

The longest-serving driver on the SDR was Dave Knowling (1939–2017), who had spent a career on British Railways as a fireman and later as a driver. Within the SDR family he was a legendary figure and when he died on 23 December 2017 the railway decided that he was more than deserving of a final journey along the line. After an interrup-tion caused by the Christmas and New Year break, a special funeral train was organised for 15 January 2018. This was hauled by ex-GWR 0-6-0 pannier locomotive 6412, which has long associations with the SDR. No fewer than five coaches were provided to accommodate Dave Knowling's family and many other mourners (see photo in colour section). It will be noted that Dave Knowling's coffin is being transported in the guard's compartment of a passenger coach, much like many coffins would have been transported in trains on the main line before 1988. A guard and a representative of the funeral directors are keeping a respectful watch over the coffin during Dave Knowling's final journey.

After the return of the ceremonial final journey to Buckfastleigh, his funeral took place in the ruins of the old church on the hill above that village and he is buried in the adjacent churchyard. Even some torrential rain in the roofless structure did not dampen the warmth and affection that those attending felt towards this much respected figure, who had truly become an integral part of the SDR.

The fourth funeral train on the SDR was run on 18 March 2019 for another respected volunteer, John Bunting. On that date a special train again hauled by ex-GWR 0-6-0 pannier locomotive 6412 carried his coffin as far as Staverton station, from where the funeral directors took it to Torbay Crematorium, as there is no road access at Totnes Riverside.

This first train did not carry a wreath or headboard but a second train the following day did, whilst conveying John Bunting's ashes to a particular location along the line where his ashes were deposited and the wreath placed above that spot. The photograph in the colour section shows the first train at the photogenic location of Hood Bridge, where the A384 road crosses the railway and the River Dart.

Another preserved or heritage railway that has run more than one funeral train is the Bluebell Railway in Sussex, which now runs from Sheffield Park to East Grinstead, some 14 miles (23km) to the north. In October 2012 the railway's long-serving President, Bernard Holden MBE, died at the age of 104 and his coffin was carried for a final journey along the line, which at that time only reached as far as Kingscote, south of East Grinstead. He had been born in Barcombe station, to which the coffin of Sir William Grantham was returned in 1911, as mentioned in Chapter 8. Bernard Holden's father was Station Master at Barcombe at the time and Bernard went on to have a long career with the Southern Railway and then British Railways from 1948.

He was one of the founder members of the Bluebell Railway Preservation Society, and was its President for the last twenty years of his life. It was therefore most appropriate that he should have a final journey along the line, with his coffin draped with the flag of the Royal Engineers, his old regiment, topped with his bowler hat and various medals, including the Burma Star and his MBE. The coffin was carried in ex-LSWR brake carriage No. 63, one of the first carriages on the Bluebell Railway, with the train being topped and tailed by two steam locomotives.[26]

In 2016 a tragic event resulted in another funeral train being run on the Bluebell Railway, for one of the railway's young but important volunteers, Simon Brown. He was accidentally killed aged 24, leaning out of a window on the Gatwick Express train in August 2016, but he had already been a volunteer on the Bluebell Railway since he was only 9 years old, when he was one of Santa's elves. He had served in many volunteer roles on that railway and was working full time on the main-line railway, having moved from being a fitter with Southern Railway to an engineer's role with Hitachi shortly before his premature death. It was only fitting that the Bluebell Railway ran a special train in his honour, described as a 'Celebration of Life' rather than a funeral train, much like funerals themselves have changed their emphasis and even their names. However, it is understood that Simon Brown's coffin was carried on this train, for one final journey.

Between these two occasions the Bluebell Railway ran another special train for one of their former long-serving volunteers, Jack Owen. He had been in charge of the locomotive department for many years before moving to Shropshire, where he died. To overcome the practicalities, and possibly the cost, of conveying his coffin to Sussex, he was cremated and his ashes were transported on a special train on 29 March 2014. This train, hauled by the famous Bluebell locomotive 55 *Stepney* and another locomotive, carried Jack Owen's ashes together with his widow, family, friends and other mourners, of whom the author was privileged to be one. Although it was not a funeral train carrying a coffin, it was a special train carrying the ashes of a person for the ceremonial purposes of honouring that individual and, on that basis, qualifies for a mention in this book.

Another heritage railway that has had two funeral trains carrying coffins for their former volunteers, is the Swanage Railway in Dorset. In 2016 the coffin of Mike Stollery was provided with a final journey and in 2017 the coffin of Frank Mead received a similar honour. Mike Stollery was one of the founder members of the Swanage Railway and was its Chairman at one time. He was associated with the railway for forty-five years but following a long illness he died aged 71, in January 2016. The following month he was given a final journey from Swanage to Norden, from where his coffin was taken by motor hearse to Poole Crematorium. His funeral train comprised two Bulleid coaches, including No. 4365, the railway's first coach and one which Mike Stollery had helped to restore. It was therefore fitting that his coffin was carried in the luggage compartment of this coach for his final journey. The coaches were hauled by the railway's own M7 tank locomotive, No. 30053, details of which appear below.[27]

Frank Mead died suddenly aged 71, but he was still employed as a locomotive fitter at the Swanage Railway and was their longest-serving staff member. He was honoured with a final journey[28] from Swanage to Norden, hauled by locomotive No. 30053. This M7 0-4-4 tank locomotive was designed by Dugald Drummond, who had his own funeral train in 1912 to take him for burial in Brookwood Cemetery. It was M7 tank locomotives that provided the regular motive power for the Brookwood necropolis services after their introduction in 1897. It was therefore most appropriate that Frank Mead's funeral train was hauled by this locomotive, though it is not known whether this particular member of the M7 class ever hauled the necropolis trains.

Two other heritage railways are known to have transported coffins as part of a person's final journey, and there may be others that have kept the event private.[29] One event that was reported in the local newspaper at the time was on the Dean Forest Railway in Gloucestershire in 2012. One of their volunteers, Richard Eagle, was a keen enthusiast of the railway's diesel multiple unit (DMU) and also of teddy bears. At the age of 60, after a fatal fall from Symonds Yat Rock, his final journey was in the railway's DMU, as shown in a photograph in the colour section.

This picture, taken in February 2012, shows Richard Eagle's coffin on the platform at Norchard station's low-level platform, being wheeled away from the train. It is possible to see two of his favourite teddy bears on top of the coffin, with the one on the left wearing a jumper reading' Don't just do it, DMU it', whilst the one on the right has a jumper reading 'To Richard, Happy 50th birthday'. He was also keen on the wartime event on the railway, explaining why some of the mourners are dressed in military uniforms, which might otherwise seem inappropriate outside the context of a military funeral.

Later in 2012 another funeral train was run on a heritage railway, this time the Gloucestershire Warwickshire Steam Railway. This was for Mary Molesworth, wife of Roger Molesworth, one of the key personalities behind the restoration of the Cotswold Steam Preservation Group's ex-GWR Churchward 2-8-0 heavy freight locomotive 2807. Sadly Mary died unexpectedly, after a short illness, before she could fulfil her ambition of travelling up the extended line to Laverton, then the northern-most limit of the railway.[30] However, as part of her funeral celebrations on 13 December 2012 she was treated to a trip on the line with the intention of reaching that location, appropriately on a train hauled by locomotive 2807. Unfortunately, due to a number of problems mostly caused by some extremely cold weather, the train was unable to complete its trip to Laverton. Nonetheless, Mary was given a very fitting return final journey to Cheltenham on the line she loved so much. To commemorate her close association with the restoration of locomotive 2807, an image of it

GWSR – Gloucestershire Warwickshire Steam Railway, 2012. Headstone of Mary Molesworth in Winchcombe Cemetery. (Photograph © Nicolas Wheatley)

has been incorporated into Mary's headstone, where she rests at peace in Winchcombe cemetery.

It was noted in Chapter 9 that the Ffestiniog Railway has a hearse van that was used for functional purposes to transport bodies from remote locations close to the railway line, taking the deceased to a place where they could have a funeral service and be buried. This van has not been used to transport coffins since at least 1946,[31] though as noted it has been used on a very few occasions to convey a person's ashes in a ceremonial funeral train. In 2016, however, a coffin was transported on a train on the Ffestiniog Railway (FR), this being a special funeral train run on 30 June for long-serving volunteer Bob Washington (1940–2016) who had died on 19 June.

As reported on p.97 of the August 2016 issue of *The Railway Magazine*, Bob Washington built and, until shortly before his death, operated the 7¼-inch gauge Porthmadog Woodland Railway at Gelert's Farm on the Welsh Highland Heritage Railway (WHHR). The special funeral train was hauled by the WHHR's Hunslet 2-6-2T *Russell*, tailed by Hunslet 0-4-0ST *Britomart*. The train itself comprised FR brake van No. 7, open bogie wagon No. 63, within which the coffin was conveyed, and FR brake coach No. 10, which carried the mourners. The report continues:

> It left the WHHR's Tremadog Road station just after 9.45. At Pen-y-Mount Russell was uncoupled and Britomart took the train on over WHHR metals, across Britannia Bridge and up the FR to Penrhyndeudraeth. There the coffin was taken to Capel Fron, opposite the station, for the 11.00 service, and subsequently by road to Bangor crematorium.

A photograph of the event accompanying the report shows that the bogie wagon which carried the coffin was draped in black and many railway workers stood, heads bowed, by the lineside as the train passed by. This funeral train was both functional, in terms of carrying Bob Washington's coffin to the chapel for the funeral service, but also ceremonial in the way it was carried out. It is believed to be the first time a coffin had been taken on a final journey on the FR since the railway was restored to operation, starting in 1954.

The Ffestiniog Railway is not actually a heritage railway, as it has been operating under the legislation that first authorised it back in 1832. Following construction of the line the railway started operations in 1836, though this was by horse-drawn wagons going uphill and gravity operating downhill. Steam locomotives were introduced in 1863, and when operations ceased in 1946 the line was never formally closed, nor was the Act of Parliament that authorised it ever amended. Its reopening, in stages from 1954, therefore does not make it a heritage railway, though many people think of it as being one. What it undoubtedly is, however, is a narrow-gauge railway, having a track gauge of only 1ft 11½in (597mm), less than the standard gauge of 4ft 8½in (1,435mm) of the UK main line and most heritage railways. The relevance for this book is that the Ffestiniog Railway is not the only railway of less than standard gauge size that has operated a funeral train.

Research for this book has found at least four funeral trains carrying coffins, on railways of less than standard gauge, and also another funeral train on a standard-gauge private railway. The first of these trains took place in 2006, on the privately constructed and operated Lavendon Narrow Gauge

Railway. This miniature railway, in the village of Lavendon, north of Olney in Buckinghamshire, was created by a transport enthusiast called Brian Collins, and is now operated by his son Tony and Tony's wife Pam. The 10¼in (260mm) gauge railway took sixteen years to build, starting in Tony and Pam's garden and passing behind some neighbours' houses before finishing in Brian's garden. Sadly, shortly after it was completed Brian died aged 74 after battling cancer for many years. His granddaughter Harriet recalled a conversation where Brian had told her he would like to be buried in the sunniest spot in his own garden, which is entirely lawful in the UK, within certain parameters.

A large funeral gathering took place in the garden, attended by over 200 people, and they were delighted to see Brian's coffin being transported along the line he and his family had built, hauled by a diesel-outline petrol-driven locomotive that he had also built specially for the private railway.[32]

The photograph in the colour section shows the funeral train travelling along part of the line, which has since been considerably extended, being followed by Brian's son Tony and other mourners. At the end of his final journey Brian Collins was buried in his garden, in accordance with the wish he had expressed to his granddaughter. In this case the final journey was a purely ceremonial one but is a rare case of a funeral train not only hauled by a diesel-outline locomotive but also one on a person's own private railway. Although essentially private, the railway is normally open to the public once a month during the summer,[33] details of which can be found on the website for Lavendon village.[34]

Another miniature railway on which a funeral train was run is the Audley End Miniature Railway, near Saffron Walden in Essex. This operates around the grounds of Audley End House, once the home of Lord Braybrooke and his family but now owned by English Heritage. Robin Neville, 10th Lord Braybrooke (1932–2017) had started the 10¼in (260mm) gauge Audley End Miniature Railway (AER) in 1964 which was (and still is) open to the public, and operates quite separately from the stately house. The Saffron Walden & District Society of Model Engineers (SWDSME) also has their miniature 7¼in-gauge railway line adjacent to the AER. When he died in 2017, part of Lord Braybrooke's funeral commemorations on 21 June included putting his coffin on a wagon and taking it for a ceremonial final journey along at least some of the 1½ mile (2.4km) long AER. Several members of the SWDSME brought their steam locomotives to the AER and gave a blow on their whistles as the funeral train steamed past. The photo in the colour section shows Lord Braybrooke's coffin in a short train being hauled by locomotive 3548 driven by Terry Hartga, the longest-serving driver on the AER, with forty-seven years of service. Also of note in the photograph are the mourners, railway workers and family[35] alike, standing respectfully as the train passes by, as has been seen in many photographs of funeral trains in this book.

Within the British Isles, funeral trains are not just limited to the UK mainland. As was noted in Chapter 12, there were two instances of trains transporting coffins, both in tragic circumstances, in County Mayo. On the first occasion, in 1894, the area was under British rule, though by the time of the second train, in 1937, the area was part of the Republic of Ireland. Although the Isle of Man has been self-governing for centuries, it could still be regarded as part of the British Isles, so a funeral train that was run there in 2009 is within the scope of this book. The train was run to provide a ceremonial final journey for Tony Beard, who was the chairman of the Isle of Man Steam Railway Supporters' Association.[36] The railway on the Isle of Man was built in 1873 to a gauge of 3ft (960mm) and has been operated mostly by steam locomotives ever since, with a brief interruption in the mid 1960s. In past decades it carried a very large number of visitors to the island when it was a major holiday destination. Even today it still carries a considerable number of tourists, as well as significant numbers of railway enthusiasts, visiting from the mainland.

The train comprised three coaches, F10, F26 and luggage van F49, within which the coffin was carried.[37] Motive power was provided by one of the Isle of Man Railway's (IoMR) regular steam locomotives, No. 13 *Kissack*, built in 1910 by Beyer Peacock in Manchester and named after IoMR company director Edward Thomas Kissack. At the time of the funeral train this locomotive was painted Indian Red, but it now carries the lined green historical livery in which she first appeared. The funeral train ran on Monday, 16 March 2009, between Douglas and Santon, carrying not only Tony Beard's coffin but many of his family and friends, and was run purely for ceremonial purposes as his funeral was the following day. The locomotive crew were James Maddrell, driver, and fireman Jack Dibnah, son of the famous Fred (see photo in colour section). There are believed to have been other occasions when coffins were carried on trains in the Isle of Man, either for functional or ceremonial purposes, but details of these events are still being researched.

A unique funeral train ran in March 2018 on a private standard-gauge railway in England. This train carried the coffin of Sir William McAlpine Bt FRSE FCILT and ran on his estate at Fawley Hill near Henley, in Berkshire. Sir William (1932–2018) was a successful businessman, deriving his wealth from the family firm of Sir Robert McAlpine & Sons, but he was also a well-known supporter of a great many railway projects and activities. The full range of his many contributions to the world of railways, including the many organisations of which he was patron, chairman or other supporter is beyond the scope of this book. However, they have been well documented in his obituaries or biographies of his life. Nevertheless, it is important to note his involvement with the preservation of two particular two locomotives. The first of these was buying and saving ex-GWR Castle-class 4-6-0 locomotive 4079 *Pendennis Castle,* the restoration of which is soon to be completed at the Great Western Society's base at Didcot. Perhaps most famously, Sir William's name will be forever associated with ex-LNER A3 Pacific locomotive 4472/60103 *Flying Scotsman*, now in the National Collection. Sir William stepped in to rescue and repatriate *Flying Scotsman* in 1973 after it was left stranded in the USA following the bankruptcy of Alan Pegler who had taken the locomotive on two tours of that country starting in 1969.

Sir William was also a founder member in 1985 of the Railway Heritage Trust (RHT), which has provided funding to preserve and restore many items of railway-related infrastructure, including buildings and their interiors as well as many other historic artefacts. Sir William was chairman of the RHT until his death, but sadly he did not live to see the restoration in 2019 of Captain Fryatt's grave in Dovercourt, which was partly financed with some money from a special fund from the RHT.

After his death on 4 March 2018, his funeral service took place on 24 March at the parish church of St Mary the Virgin in Fawley, close to his estate on which he had built a short private railway line. After the funeral service itself a large number of people assembled at Fawley Hill, to which his coffin was taken. The coffin was placed on an open wagon, which was driven down the railway's 1-in-13.4 gradient to the valley below. The locomotive for this unique funeral train was 1913-built Hudswell Clarke

0-6-0ST No. 31, which Sir William had bought for £100 in 1965 from his family firm, which had owned it since new. Following his final journey Sir William was buried in a wooded place on his estate, where he rests surrounded by the unique railway setting that he created. Though it is not generally open to the public, there are occasionally special open days when the public can visit Fawley Hill and its railway.[38] The site was also the location for the filming of a TV programme, *The Great Model Railway Challenge*, which was broadcast in 2018 and 2019.

Though they were very different people, with very different private railways, it is worth noting that both Brian Collins, on his Lavendon Narrow Gauge Railway, and Sir William McAlpine, at Fawley Hill, shared the rare experience of having a final journey on their own private lines. Each journey was unique in that the gauge of their separate railways was different. Lord Braybrooke's final journey was on a railway that he had created, though it was open to the public, so it was unique in its own way. All three final journeys demonstrate that railways are still being used to transport coffins for ceremonial purposes, even if their original role, as in Victorian times, of getting someone 'home' for burial is no longer required. Just to show that some railways continue to provide ceremonial final journeys to honour people with close links with them, the last case to be mentioned here took place only a few weeks before writing for this book was completed.

This was a final journey for Richard Batten (1943–2019), a long-serving driver on the Romney Hythe & Dymchurch Railway (RH&DR) in Kent. This wonderful railway runs on a track gauge of only 15in (381mm) and was conceived by racing-car drivers Captain John Howey and Count Zborowski, though the latter was killed in a racing accident in 1924 before the line was built. The first part of the line opened in 1927 and was later extended. It now runs for nearly 14 miles (23km) along the coast, from Hythe in the east to Dungeness in the west. For many decades it could boast that it was the world's smallest public railway, but it lost this title in 1982 when a 10¼in (260mm) gauge railway was built in Norfolk,[39] providing a public, though seasonal, service between Wells and Walsingham,[40] a distance of some four miles (6km).

Richard Batten had been associated with the RH&DR for many years, including being a locomotive driver, and after his death on 18 December

2019 his funeral was deferred until a final journey could be arranged. This took place on 17 January 2020, on what would have been his 77th birthday. A train of four coaches, hauled by 1927-built 4-6-2 locomotive No. 8 *Hurricane*, took Richard Batten's coffin, with accompanying family and other mourners, on a final journey along the line, driven by his son, Simon. This train, shown near Dungeness (see colour section), is identifiable as a special by the lack of indicator discs, as usually displayed by RH&DR service trains. There will undoubtedly be more final journeys provided by other heritage (or non-national-network) railways in due course, but Richard Batten's funeral train is the last one known at the time of completing this book.

It is perhaps little known, but it is not necessary to be a volunteer, staff member or supporter of a heritage railway to have a railway funeral. Research for this book has identified that the West Somerset Railway (WSR) actually has a section of its website entitled 'Policy on Funeral Trains',[41] where information is given about hiring a train on that railway as part of a funeral. There is no requirement for the deceased to have had any particular links to the WSR. There is also information given about disposing of a person's ashes into the firebox of a steam locomotive, either on a privately hired train or on a timetabled train. However, there is no specific mention of carrying coffins, though in theory this could be done on a privately hired train, after any necessary discussions had been concluded. No doubt many other heritage railways would be willing to arrange for the disposal of a person's ashes through the firebox of one of their locomotives, though the WSR appears (as far as found so far) to be the only railway that publishes its policy on its website.

If the particular desire is to have a coffin transported on a train, it is possible to do this at the Midland Railway- Butterley (MR-B), near Ripley, Derbyshire.[42] The MR-B has a commercial association with a firm of funeral directors, Peace Funerals, based in Sheffield, to provide a railway funeral at Butterley. Several options[43] are possible, including a funeral service in the small tabernacle, St Saviour's Church. This building was relocated to Butterley from its former location at nearby Westhouses, where it had been built in 1898 with support from the Midland Railway company. It is possible for a coffin to be carried either on the standard-gauge railway at the site or on the narrow-gauge Golden Valley Light Railway line that runs eastwards to a natural burial ground. Here the deceased could be laid to rest in a site adjacent to the standard-gauge line, perhaps a fitting burial place for a train enthusiast.

What the final journeys in the second part of this chapter demonstrate is that funeral trains are not just of historical interest. Although the functional role of main-line railways to transport a person's coffin home for burial has ended, the ceremonial aspects of funeral transport continue to provide opportunities for non-main-line railways to play their role in providing final journeys for some people. As has been seen, the range of railways on which this has occurred is considerable, from standard-gauge heritage lines, narrow-gauge lines, miniature railways and private lines of more than one gauge. Ceremonial rail-based funeral transport has also occurred on heritage tramways, as noted in Chapter 10. Now that the story of funeral trains has largely been told, and their existence highlighted, maybe more such ceremonial railway transportation will be desired and provided.

14

CONCLUSIONS

Railways in the UK were developed from 1825 to transport freight, particularly coal in the north-east of England. The Liverpool & Manchester Railway's opening in 1830 was intended to provide a railway connection between those two places to carry freight, though it was overshadowed by the accidental death of William Huskisson MP. That railway soon became very popular with passengers, as did many other lines that were rapidly developed across the country. This was despite the initially high risk of accidents, often fatal, though this did not ultimately prevent railways becoming an everyday part of many people's lives. Railways also became, from an early date, an important part of the deaths of hundreds, indeed thousands, of people. This arose either from fatal train crashes or from the ability of relatives to bring or send their loved one's remains 'home' for burial.

Transporting the bodies of dead people by train could be said to fall somewhere between carrying passengers and transporting freight, though in truth it is closer to the latter. This book has shown that this was largely done for functional purposes but also with a degree of ceremony, as part of the respect shown for the dead during the funeral rituals. As might be expected, the degree of ceremony increases with the status of the deceased, either during their lifetime, such as Sir Winston Churchill, or because of the manner of their untimely deaths, such as the victims of various accidents or military conflicts.

Like the transport of many types of freight, some specialist vehicles were developed to transport the dead, namely the hearse/corpse vans built by several railway companies, as evidenced in Chapter 9. However, the transport of coffins was more often undertaken in ordinary railway vehicles, either in the guard's compartments of coaches within passenger trains or in separate vans attached to those trains. Sometimes in these cases a party of mourners would accompany the deceased in a separate carriage attached to the same train. There was also some specialised equipment used at stations to handle the coffins, keeping them out of sight, as far as possible, from ordinary travellers. This may have contributed to the general lack of knowledge about the use of trains to transport the dead. It is certainly an aspect of railway operation that is not even mentioned by most books on the history of railways. Except for the works on Queen Victoria's funeral train and the services to the cemeteries at Brookwood and Southgate, the subject is only briefly covered in a very few published books. Hopefully this book has shone a light into this previously little-known area of railway operation.

The early chapters of this book covered the ways in which trains were used in funeral transport from the very early days of railways and how they were intended to assist, though not always successfully, with the development of new forms of cemeteries beyond the outskirts of major towns. The development of cremation as a new method of disposal of the dead gave a small boost to the transportation of coffins to the initial few crematoria that were built. However, once cremation became a more accepted practice and more crematoria were constructed, the need for trains to transport coffins to a place of burial diminished. This was hastened by two other significant changes of technology.

Firstly, the development of motor hearses from 1900 onwards gave undertakers much greater flexibly in their traditional role of providing funeral transport; this reduced the need to send coffins by train. Secondly, the changing nature of the railways themselves, with reduced facilities to handle coffins, made handling such traffic more difficult to accommodate. It will be recalled that the BR letter of March 1988, notifying several trade-union officials of the termination of the service, specifically mentioned that 'the special vans within which corpse conveyance must take place have become increasingly difficult to organise in the short notice that funeral directors require'.

Trains had also changed, with multiple-unit trains having limited space for carrying goods, parcels, luggage or even, these days, bicycles. It would certainly be difficult to find space for a coffin on most modern trains, though a BBC news story in October 2015 reports that Virgin Trains did receive a query via Twitter from a grieving relative asking 'how to get a coffin on a Pendolino'.[1] It would be interesting to know the reply, which unfortunately is not recorded in the story. Curiously, a coffin was recently listed as one of the items of lost property once held by Transport for London,[2] though whether it was left on a train is unclear, nor is there any explanation of how it may have been taken onto a train.

This book has sought to show how railways were not only part of the development of cemeteries and funeral practices in the nineteenth century but also influenced them. However, funeral transport by train was eventually rendered obsolete in the late twentieth century, at least as far as the functional transport of coffins is concerned. Nevertheless, trains continue to have a role in providing ceremonial transport, at least on heritage railways, with the last recorded occasion taking place only a few weeks before this book was completed.[3] References to trains have also become embedded in the funeral services for some railway enthusiasts or railway workers, as the following poems demonstrate. There are undoubtedly many other examples that exist.

'Will The Lights Be White?'
by Andy Seatherton (1963-present)[4]
In memory of his father, Arch.

Oft, when I feel my engine swerve,
As o'er strange rails we fare,
I strain my eyes around the curve
For what awaits us there.
When swift and free she carries me
Through yards unknown at night,
I look along the line to see
That all the lamps are white.

A green card marks the crippled car,
The yellow light signals slow;
The red light is a danger light,
The green light, "Let her go."
Again the open fields we roam,
And, when the night is fair, I look up in the starry dome
And wonder what's up there.
For who can speak for those who dwell
Behind the curving sky?
No man has ever lived to tell
Just what it means to die.
Swift toward life's terminal I trend,
The run seems short tonight;
God only knows what's at the end –
But I know the lamps are white.[5]

Last Train Home
by Jessica Green[6]

You are standing on the platform; of the station they call life,
It is time for you to move on, from any suffering, any strife.

You hear the whistle sounding, like music to your ears,
It's the sound that's always brought you joy, for many many years.

And as the train approaches, and the steam begins to fade,
You see it's the engine, of which your dreams were made.

And as the train slows down and stops, and the door it opens wide,
You see that all your closest friends, and family are inside.

With beaming faces filled with joy, arms ready to embrace,
Ready to welcome you on this train, to a very special place.

You are sad to leave your loved ones, but you know you'll meet again.

This book on funeral trains has endeavoured to tell the story of how railways in the UK have been used to transport the physical remains of deceased people to places of burial. These have been either a place of significance to the deceased, their family or, in the cases of many high-profile individuals, to the nation. This was often undertaken with a considerable degree of ceremony to honour and show respect to the dead. It is that aspect of funerals that ensures that coffins are still carried on trains right up to the present day. The desire to provide a ceremonial final journey to commemorate important volunteers and others with significant links to heritage railways has resulted in many occasions when that has been done. Many of these have not been reported in the railway press, though there are some exceptions. The author is grateful to the families of a number of people whose coffins have been given a final journey by train for allowing their stories to be told and, importantly, illustrated by some of the photographs included in this book. The author invites readers to view these stories as a way of maintaining the memories and showing ongoing respect to the people involved, both the deceased and their families.

Death is an inevitable event for everyone, but few people look forward to it with any degree of joyful anticipation. This might be considered surprising in some ways for those with religious beliefs, as the promise of a better life in heaven is a key tenet of many faiths. On a less religious basis, the opportunity to be reunited with friends and loved ones who have already died is one way of looking at death that is appealing to many people. Indeed, it forms an important part of the second poem set out above and also features in the poem set out below.

As was seen in Chapter 2 with the 'tombstone' in Ely Cathedral that refers to 'The Spiritual Railway', the link between trains and getting to the hereafter has a history going back to the very early days of railways.[7] The poems reproduced earlier in this chapter are modern-day examples of metaphors in which trains are used to assist a soul's progress to the next world. They were written with funerals specifically in mind and used in circumstances where a death had already occurred. However, to complete this story about final journeys, the final word goes to a poem written from the point of view of a living person and it asks a question that probably no one wants to answer. Read on to see what it is and contemplate your own response.

If My Train Will Come

by Katrina Porteous (1960–present)[8]

If my train will come,
Quietly in the night,
With no other sound than the slow
Creak of wheel upon wheel;
If, huge as a house but brighter,
Crouched at the edge of the fields
Like a steaming beast, it is waiting
Down the deserted road;
Though the colliery gate and the church
Where my mother and father were wed
Are all grown over at last
And the people I knew dead now,
If a stranger alights
And, holding my breath, I see
That he has your eyes, your hair,
But does not remember me;
And if there follows a girl
With my face from years ago
And for miles by the sides of the tracks
The Durham grasses blow–
O, if my train will come
With its cargo of souls that have passed
Over this world to find me,
Will I go? Will I want to?

EPILOGUE

With a topic as wide-ranging as this it is inevitable that much more material will come to light in due course and hopefully more research will be undertaken into the various aspects of this topic. What this book seeks to do is to present the findings of several years of research carried out in an eclectic range of sources, though information gleaned from historical newspaper reports of funerals involving train transport of coffins is under-represented. There is also no doubt much more information to be found in many other sources, including family history records. The author recalls being asked by one family researcher whether there was a list anywhere of everyone whose coffin was transported by train. The researcher was hoping such list would record her ancestor's final journey – if only it was that simple! This book can go only a very small way towards creating such a list.

However, one valuable source of information is at risk of being lost in the coming years. It is to be hoped that a project could be set up to record the oral testimony of former railway workers – and perhaps funeral directors – who had practical experience or personal knowledge of the transport of coffins by train before British Rail stopped the practice in 1988. Age is beginning to catch up with these people and the story of the transport of coffins by train would be enriched if their stories could be recorded before it becomes too late.

There will also be further cases of ceremonial transport on heritage railways to be added to the story in due course. Indeed, the author has requested – and provided for in his will – that, when the time comes, his coffin be given a ceremonial final journey on the line where he volunteers, the Gloucestershire Warwickshire Steam Railway. Perhaps the biggest unanswered question is whether there will be a funeral train for Her Majesty The Queen when her time comes.

Although there has not been a funeral train for a member of the Royal Family since 1979, since when much has changed on Britain's rail network, the author believes that a funeral train for Her Majesty should not be ruled out. In functional terms a motor hearse to Windsor, for burial at Frogmore or in St George's Chapel, would be an easy option. However, the ceremonial aspects of a royal funeral train for the longest-serving monarch in British history mean that such a train would have considerable advantages over Her Majesty's final journey in a motor hearse. The future will reveal all in due course and maybe another chapter will need to be added to a revised edition of this book. Let us hope that such a chapter is not needed for many years to come, and as far as Her Majesty is concerned – 'long may she reign over us!'

GAZETTEER

Keys:

★ Denotes train transport almost certainly used, though details still to be verified.

★★ Denotes train transport likely to have been used, though details to be verified.

★★★ Denotes train transport possibly used, details still to be verified.

No star = train transport used, details verified.

JHK = funeral carried out by firm of J.H. Kenyon

Garstin = funeral carried out by firm of Garstin

Leverton = funeral carried out by firm of Leverton

Categories of people whose coffins were transported by train

Transport related

RAIL

1856   *John Rastrick (1780–1856) Loco engineer (died in Chertsey, buried in Extra-Mural Cemetery Brighton)

1860   *Joseph Locke (1805–1860) Early railway engineer (died in Moffat, Dumfriesshire, Scotland, buried in Kensal Green cemetery)

1861   ***William Baly (1814–1861) Well-known physician (including to Queen Victoria) (died in Wimbledon train crash, buried in Kensal Green cemetery)

1865   John Spencer (1838–1865) fireman on L&SWR (killed in accident on locomotive at Winchester, buried in Brookwood cemetery, Plot 47)

1871   George Hudson (1800–1871) 'The Railway King' (died in London, by Midland Railway train from St Pancras then via North Eastern Railway to York, for burial at Scrayingham)

1874   Shipton on Cherwell accident, GWR's worst, with thirty-four dead (some victims taken by train back to Oxford, believed some taken 'home' by train)

1875   *Charles Vignoles (1793–1875) Early railway engineer who introduced flat-bottomed rail to UK (died in Southampton, buried in Brompton Cemetery)

1889   *William Stroudley (1833-1889) loco designer (died in Paris, buried in Extra-Mural Cemetery Brighton)

1889   3rd Duke of Buckingham & Chandos (1823–1889) Chairman of LNWR (died in London, buried on family estate in Wotton, Buckinghamshire) (NB his father, 2nd Duke (1797–1861), died at the Great Western Hotel, Paddington. Not clear where father is buried, but possibly at Stowe or at Wotton, in which case train almost certainly used to transport coffin there, possibly to Buckingham)

1892   *Sir James Allport (1811–1892) Railway Manager, Midland Railway, first railway manager to be knighted, 1884 (died at Midland Grand Hotel, St Pancras, buried in Belper cemetery, Derbyshire)

1893   Edgar William Verrinder (1837–1893) Chief Traffic Superintendent of LSWR, special funeral train stopped at Clapham Junction to collect coffin on way to Brookwood Cemetery, 3,000 people attended his funeral, two extra trains needed for mourners (see further details in *South Western Gazette* 1893, August, pages 3 & 9) (funeral arrangements personally overseen by F.E. Smith of London Necropolis Company)

1897   Welshampton railway accident – twelve victims taken back home to Oldham by train

1898   *Sir John Fowler (1817–1898) Engineer, Forth Bridge (died in Bournemouth, buried in Brompton cemetery)

1906   Salisbury train crash victims (some bodies taken by train to Plymouth for repatriation to USA, others taken to Liverpool and taken on Cunard liner to New York)

1906   Edwin Booth (1881–1906) Fireman on loco that crashed at Ulleskelf near York (buried in Hull Western Cemetery, headstone is Grade 2 listed)

1907   *Sir Benjamin Baker (1840–1907) Engineer, Forth Bridge (died in Pangbourne, Berkshire, buried in St Nicholas churchyard, Idbury, Oxfordshire)

1912   Dugald Drummond (1840–1912) loco designer (died at home in Surbiton, buried in Brookwood cemetery- more details in John Clarke book)

1915   Quintinshill crash (Military victims returned to Edinburgh for burial, also some ordinary passengers returned to Newcastle on Tyne for burial)

1918   *Stephen Dewar Holden (1870–1918) Son of James Holden, Locomotive Superintendent of Great Eastern Railway 1908–12 (died in Rochester, Kent, buried in Wanstead Quaker Burial Ground, Essex) (*Steam Magazine* [SM] 440)

1919   Frank Potter (18??–1919) General Manager of GWR (died at Tregenna Castle Hotel, St Ives, taken by train to Paddington for burial in Harlington) [info from *The Great Western Railway in the First World War*, Sandra Gittins, 2010]

1925   **James Holden (1837–1925) Father of Stephen Dewar Holden, Locomotive Superintendent of Great Eastern Railway 1885–1907

(died in Bath, buried in Wanstead Quaker Burial Ground, Essex)
(SM 440)

1930　Towcester, Tom Holton's sister (child daughter of station-master)
(Quinn book, unverified)

1931　Sarah Eleanor Smith (1861–1931) widow of Edward John Smith,
Captain of *Titanic* (died in London of injuries sustained in collision
with taxi, special funeral train to Brookwood, buried in Plot 32)
(p.159 of JMC'S London Necropolis, 2nd edition)

1934　**Sir Vincent Raven (1859–1934) Chief Mechanical Engineer,
North Eastern Railway, 1910–22 (died in Felixstowe, buried in
Brookwood Cemetery)

1937　**Sir John Aspinall (1851–1937) Chief Mechanical Engineer of
Lancashire & Yorkshire Railway 1886–99, then became General
Manager (died in Woking, buried in St Edward's Cemetery, Sutton
Coldfield) (SM440)

1941　*Sir Nigel Gresley (1876–1941) (died at daughter's home in
Hertfordshire, buried in cemetery of St Peter's Church, Netherseal,
Derbyshire; train transport of coffin awaiting confirmation)

TRAMS (used in funerals or for coffin transport)

1901　Martin Cadman (born 1862, died aged 38) (Dudley, Stourbridge
and District Electric Traction & Kinver Light Railway)

1902　LUT 'social saloon' (could be hired by mourners)

1902–10 Great Orme Tramway (functional transport to St Tudno's church)

1907　Pye Nest crash, Halifax

1912　Alexander Hollas (1865–1911) (Blackpool Tramways)

1915　Rev Ernest Hexall (18??–1915) (Kinver Light Railway)

1916　Streatham (funeral of tram crew killed in air raid)

1917　Dover (Britain's worst tram accident – eleven killed, sixty seriously
injured, some victims returned home by train)

1985　Richard Fairbairn (1895–1985) (Crich Tramway Village)

2008　Winstan Bond, OBE (1936–2008) (Crich Tramway Village)

2019　Robert Hall (1938–2019) (Crich Tramway Village)

ROAD

1906   ★Orpington etc. Fire Brigade (major bus accident at Handcross, Sussex)

1927   ★★J.G. Parry Thomas (1884–1927) Welsh land-speed record holder (killed attempting to regain land-speed record on Pendine Sands, Wales, buried in Byfleet, Surrey)

1933   ★★Sir Henry 'Tim' Birkin (1896–1933) one of the 'Bentley Blower Boys' (died in London, buried in Blakeney, Norfolk)

1933   Sir Henry Royce (1863–1933) (died in Wittering, Sussex, body collected Sunday 23 April in Rolls Royce hearse, cremated at Golders Green, 25 April, ashes reburied near Peterborough after initial burial in Derby) (Leverton) (see also Charles Rolls, 1910)

1952   ★★Captain John Rhodes Cobb, land-speed record holder (died attempting water-speed record, Loch Ness, Scotland; buried in Esher, his place of birth)

AVIATION/MILITARY

1890   ★Ernest Richard Hamilton (1869–1890) soldier, son of Thomas de Courcy Hamilton VC (died aged 21 in Kensington, London; buried in Bouncers Lane cemetery, Cheltenham, family's home. NB parents buried in same grave, father died 1908 and mother died 1913)

1901   ★Colonel Sir Henry Wilmot VC KCB (1831–1901) Soldier and MP (died in Bournemouth, buried in St Mary's churchyard, Chaddesden, Derby- town of birth)

1907   ★Henry Lysons VC soldier (died aged 49 in London, Marylebone, buried in Rodmarton, Gloucestershire)

1910   Charles Rolls (1877–1910) Aviator and motor-car pioneer (killed in air crash in Bournemouth, by train to Monmouth Troy for burial near family home – the station is now rebuilt at Winchcombe, Gloucestershire) [see also 1933 entry for Sir Henry Royce]

1912   Edward Hotchkiss (1883–1912) pioneer aviator (killed in accident near Oxford, coffin by train to Craven Arms, buried in Stokesay churchyard, Shropshire, also stained glass window in Stokesay church and memorial plaque on Old Toll Bridge, Godstow Road, Wolvercote, Oxford, near scene of accident)

1914　*Sir James Moncrieff Grierson, Commanding Officer II Army Corps, General Staff (died aged 55 on train near Amiens, returned to UK and buried in Glasgow Necropolis) (see CWGC entry)

1914　Norman Champion de Crespigny (18??–1914) Soldier (killed 1 September at Nery, France, repatriated after initial burial, taken by train to Maldon, Essex, buried 13 November 1914 in family mausoleum, since demolished)

1915　W.G.C. Gladstone (1885–April 1915) grandson of PM (died in France, buried at Hawarden, North Wales, near family home; repatriation was specially authorised by King George V)

1915　(May) Quintinshill crash (Military victims returned to Edinburgh for burial; two civilian victims returned to Newcastle upon Tyne for burial)

1915　*Reginald ('Rex') Warneford VC (1891–June 1915) won VC for shooting down a Zeppelin airship (died in France, buried in Brompton Cemetery)

1915　*(John) Aidan Liddell VC (1888–August 1915) (died on active service in Belgium, buried in Holy Ghost Cemetery, Basingstoke)

1916　*Jack Cornwell VC (1900–1916) Boy Sailor, injured in Battle of Jutland (died in hospital in Grimsby, buried in Manor Park cemetery, London)

1917　**R. Harold Barnwell (1878–1917) (killed in air crash at Joyce Green airfield near Dartford, buried in Byfleet, Surrey) (same cemetery for JG Parry Jones and Constable Walter Choat)

1917　*Bere Ferrers tragedy. Ten victims of accident at Bere Ferrers station (New Zealand soldiers killed by train, buried at Efford Cemetery, Plymouth, with CWGC headstones)

1918　**Harold Messenger aged 29, Royal Engineers (death on 18 November 1918 registered in Bristol, buried in Minster Lovell churchyard, Oxfordshire)

1918　*William Douglas Henderson (1893–1918) Flight Cadet, thrown out of cockpit of plane whilst flying from Montrose airfield, Scotland, 28 November 1918 (Body recovered and buried in Gloucester Cemetery 'a few days later') (CGWFA Newsletter No.152, June 2019)

1919   Sir Jack Alcock (1892–1919) pioneer transatlantic aviator with Sir
        Arthur Brown (killed in France, by train to Waterloo, buried in
        Manchester)

1921   R38 airship disaster (sixteen American victims taken by train to
        Devonport, Plymouth for repatriation)

1925   **Lord Grenfell, Field Marshall Francis Wallace Grenfell (died
        January 1925 in Windlesham, Surrey, buried in Beaconsfield,
        Buckinghamshire)

1928   Douglas Haigh, 1st Earl Haigh, Field Marshall (born 1861 in
        Edinburgh, died 1928 in London. Body sent by train from Waterloo
        station (verified) to Edinburgh for burial at Dryburgh Abbey)

1930   R101 disaster (major airship accident in France, forty-eight coffins
        taken by train to Bedfordshire for group burial at Cardington)

1942   Prince George, Duke of Kent (1902–1942) (died on active service
        in Scotland, by train to London, motor van to Windsor) (JHK
        funeral)

1944   Exercise Tiger victims (unverified reports that some victims were
        taken by train to Scotland, ostensibly for repatriation to USA – see
        book on Exercise Tiger by Richard T. Bass; also details in J. Clarke's
        BNR book that some victims were initially taken to Brookwood
        Cemetery)

1948   ***Sir Arthur Brown (1886–1948) pioneer transatlantic aviator
        with Jack Alcock (died in Swansea, buried in Tylers Green,
        Buckinghamshire, his wife's family place of origin)

Conscientious Objectors in Great War

1918   Henry William Firth (died at HM Work Centre, Dartmoor, by train
        from Princeton to Plymouth, then on to Norwich for burial in
        Earlham Cemetery)

Arts/Culture/Sports/Etc

1870   Charles Dickens, writer (died in Higham, Kent, by train from
        Higham station to Charing Cross, buried in Westminster Abbey)
        (Simon Bradley, p.159)

1871 Pablo Fanque (aka William Darby) Britain's first black circus proprietor (born Norwich, died in Stockport, commemorated in a Beatles song, buried in grave in St George's Field Leeds)

1874 David Livingstone, explorer (died in Africa, repatriated to Southampton, by train to London, buried in Westminster Abbey)

1882 ★Charles Darwin, naturalist (died in Downe, Kent, buried in Westminster Abbey)

1888 Matthew Arnold (1822–1888) writer and poet (died in Liverpool, by train to London, next day by train from Waterloo to Staines for burial at Laleham)

1890 ★Sir Richard Burton, explorer and writer (died in Trieste, buried in Mortlake Cemetery, London) (Garstin)

1892 Alfred Lord Tennyson (1809–1892) writer and poet (died at home, Aldworth, near Haslemere, Sussex. Taken by train from Haslemere to London, buried in Westminster Abbey)

1896 ★Lady Tennyson (in her 84th year) widow of Lord Tennyson (died at home at Aldworth, buried in churchyard at Freshwater, Isle of Wight)

1896 William Morris (1834–1896) Arts & Crafts movement (died in London, by train to Lechlade, buried at Kelmscott in Gloucestershire; more details in Stanley Jenkins' book, *The Fairford Branch*; probably also his wife Jane, died in Bath 1914)

1898 Edward Burne-Jones (1838-1898) artist and designer (died in London, buried in St Margaret's churchyard, Rottingdean, Sussex, close to his home in later life)

1899 William Ryder (18??–1899) young actor (died in Middlesbrough, by train to London as 'theatrical properties') (Simon Bradley, p.101)

1904 George Frederick Watts (1817–1904) artist (died at home in London, special funeral train to Woking where body was cremated, remains eventually buried at Compton, Surrey)

1904 Henry Morton Stanley (1841–1904) explorer and journalist (died in London, buried at Pirbright, Surrey, near Brookwood Cemetery, by train to Brookwood)

1905 Sir Henry Irving (1838–1905) major theatrical figure, first actor to be knighted (died in Bradford, by train to London, cremated at Golders Green then ashes buried in Westminster Abbey)

1910   Jem Mace (1831–1910) champion boxer, links to Norwich where a Blue Plaque commemorates him (died in Jarrow, Tyne and Wear, buried in Liverpool)

1935   *Tom Farndon (1910–1935) speedway rider, winner of competitions (killed aged 24 at event in New Cross, London, buried in St Paul's cemetery, Holbrook Road, Coventry, family's home, unusual motorcycle-shaped memorial on grave)

1963   Sylvia Plath (Hughes) (1932–1963) poet, wife of Ted Hughes, Poet Laureate (died in London, by train from Kings Cross to Hebden Bridge, cost £30, buried in Heptonstall) (Leverton)

Politicians/Leaders, etc.

1852   Duke of Wellington (1769–1852) (died at Walmer Castle, by train from Deal station to London for major state funeral – many trains used to bring mourners and public to London for funeral) (Simon Bradley, p.100)

1867   *Walter Coffin (1784–1867) colliery owner and Mayor of Cardiff 1848, MP for Cardiff 1852–1857, Deputy Chairman of Taff Vale Railway 1848, Chairman 1855 (died in Kensington, London, buried in Bridgend, Wales)

1879   Louis-Napoléon Bonaparte, Prince Imperial (1856–1879) (died in Africa, repatriated to Woolwich Arsenal, initially buried in Chislehurst, Kent, then reinterred in 1888 in Farnborough, Hampshire, train from Chislehurst to London Bridge, then gun-carriage to Waterloo, then train) (Garstin)

1884   2nd Duke of Wellington (1807–1884) (died on Brighton Station, body kept in waiting room overnight, by train to London then to Stratfield Saye, Berkshire, the family estate, for burial)

1891   Charles Stewart Parnell (1846–1891) leading politician and Irish Nationalist (died in Hove, Sussex, by train to Holyhead, then ferry across Irish Sea, buried in Dublin)

1898   William E. Gladstone (1809–1898) Prime Minster (died at family home, Hawarden, North Wales, by train from Broughton Hall to London for burial in Westminster Abbey)

1908   ★Frederick Arthur Stanley, 16th Earl of Derby, politician and Governor General of Canada, May 1888–July 1893 (died aged 67 at Holmwood in Kent, buried at family's home in Ormskirk, Lancashire)

1912   Emily Wilding Davison, suffragette (killed during Epsom derby by King's horse, by train to London for funeral, then by train to Newcastle upon Tyne, Northumberland, for burial at Morpeth, family home)

1913   ★★ Henry Matthews, 1st Viscount Llandaff. (1826–1913) barrister and politician, Home Secretary 1886–92 [longest serving until Theresa May] (died in London. Catholic, no family, buried Belmont Abbey [Catholic, Benedictine] Clehonger, Hereford)

1925   ★★George Curzon, 1st Marquess of Kedleston, Viceroy of India 1899–1905, Secretary of State for Foreign Affairs 1919–24 (died in London at Curzon House, 1 Carlton Terrace, buried in All Saints Church, Kedleston) [Note his first wife, Mary Curzon, Vicereine of India, died 1906, aged 36, at 1 Carlton House Terrace and is also buried in All Saints Church, almost certainly transported by train]

1930   ★Arthur Balfour (1848–1930) Prime Minister 1902–05 (died in Woking, Surrey, buried in Scotland near family home)

1936   Dr Leopold von Hoesch, German Ambassador (1881–1936) (died in London, by train to Dover then by UK navy ship to Germany; Pullman cars in train)

1940   ★★★Neville Chamberlain (1869–1940) (died at Heckfield, Hampshire, ashes buried in Westminster Abbey)

1965   Sir Winston Churchill (1874–1965) also his father, mother, grandfather (7th Duke) and aunt before him, also his cousin, 9th Duke of Marlborough in 1934, and his distant cousin, Viscount Churchill, 1934 and Viscount Churchill's mother, 1900

2001   Jimmy Knapp (1940–2001) RMT leader (coffin by train from Euston to Glasgow for burial in Kilmarnock)

Royalty
(UK and Foreign but had their coffins transported in UK)

1840 ★★★ HRH Princess Augusta Sophia of the United Kingdom (b. 1768) second daughter of King George III (died at Clarence House London, buried in St George's chapel, Windsor; train may not have been used to transport coffin, but train hauled by loco *Leopard* used to take mourners back to London from Slough)

1844 HRH Princess Sophia Matilda of Gloucester, first cousin of Queen Victoria (died Blackheath, by train to Slough, buried in Windsor; first confirmed use of train to transport royal coffin)

1857 ★HRH Princess Mary, Duchess of Gloucester and Edinburgh (b. 1776) fourth daughter of King George III (died in Gloucester House, either in London or Weymouth, buried in St Georges Chapel, Windsor. If in Weymouth almost certainly by train from there to London)

1878 ★King George V of Hanover (died in Paris, buried in Windsor)

1883 John Brown, (b. 1826), Royal servant to Queen Victoria (died at Windsor Castle, buried in Crathie Kirk, Aberdeenshire, close to place of birth)

1884 HRH Prince Leopold, Duke of Albany, youngest son of Queen Victoria (died in Cannes, France, by special train to Cherbourg, then by Royal Yacht to Portsmouth and train to Windsor)

1892 HRH Prince Albert Victor ('Prince Eddy') grandson of Queen Victoria, second in line to the throne (died at Sandringham, train from Wolferton, buried in Windsor)

1893 ★Duleep Singh, last Maharajah of Lahore, Queen Victoria's Godson, has links to Koh-I Noor diamond (died in Paris, buried in Elveden, Suffolk; also wife and son buried next to him, were there first, almost certainly transported by train)

1894 Prince Philippe, Comte de Paris, Pretender to the French throne (died at Stowe, Buckinghamshire, by train from Buckingham to Weybridge, Surrey, for burial in Chapel of St Charles Borromeo Catholic church, then reburied in 1958 in Dreux Royal Chapel, France, traditional burial place of members of the Orleans family)

1901   HM Queen Victoria (coffin transported twice by train, Gosport to Victoria, then Paddington to Windsor)

1902   Prince Edward of Saxe-Weimar, not royal by birth but related to Queen Adelaide (Royal train conveyed Prince of Wales from London to Chichester for Prince's funeral and burial in cathedral – believed that Prince's body also conveyed by same train)

1910   HM King Edward VII (died at Buckingham Palace, train to Windsor)

1910   Prince Francis of Teck, brother of Queen Mary (died in London, buried in Royal Burial Ground, Windsor; King and Queen used GWR royal train to Windsor for funeral)

1911   Sir Nripendra Narayan, His Highness the 19th Maharajah of Cooch Behar (died in Bexhill, Sussex, coffin taken by train to London for cremation at Golders Green; NB son Raj Rajendra Narayan (20th Maharajah) died 1913 in Erpingham, Norfolk, possibly by train to London for cremation?)

1918   Prince Jafar Mirza of Persia (1902–1918) pupil at Harrow School, (died in Llandudno, coffin taken by train to Euston, collected by J.H. Kenyon, body embalmed, initially (March 1919) deposited in catacombs at Kensal Green Cemetery, then in January 1920 removed, transported to Glasgow for conveyance to Kazemein for burial within shrine of two Shia Imams)

1918   *Prince Antonio Gastao de Orleans-Braganza (1881–29 November 1918) French-born Brazilian member of Orleans family, Pretenders to French monarchy. Served in British armed forces, including Royal Flying Corps. Awarded MC in 1917 but killed in air accident in Edmonton, north London shortly after end of the Great War (remains taken to France – almost certainly by train – and buried in Royal Chapel at Dreux with other members of Orleans family)

1925   HM Queen Alexandra (died at Sandringham, train from Wolferton, buried in Windsor. Van used to transport her coffin later used for King George V)

1936   HM King George V (died at Sandringham, by train to London with B17 2947 *Helmingham Hall* loco, then separate train from Paddington to Windsor with GWR 4082 *Windsor Castle*)

1931   HRH Princess Louise, Princess Royal, (b. 1867) daughter of King Edward VII, widow of Alexander Duff, 1st Duke of Fife (d. 1912) (initially buried in Windsor but later reburied in St Ninian's Chapel, Braemar, alongside husband – almost certainly taken by train. Her husband had died in Egypt and was initially buried in Windsor but was then taken in a special saloon by overnight train to Ballater, via Aberdeen, for re-burial at Braemar)

1942   HRH Prince George, Duke of Kent, fourth son of King George V (died in air accident on active service in Scotland, by train to London, then by 'red painted commercial van' to Windsor for burial)

1952   HM King George VI (died at Sandringham, by train to London with BR Standard loco, 70000 *Britannia* then separate train from Paddington to Windsor with GWR 4082 *Windsor Castle*, actually 7013 *Bristol Castle* in disguise)

1953   HM Queen Mary (1867–1953) (died in London, buried in Windsor, not train. Kenyon funeral but train used for her Lady in Waiting, Lady Elizabeth Dawson, daughter of 4th Earl of Clanwilliam, wife of the Honourable Edward Dawson, died in accident at Balmoral in 1924, train from there (Ballater) to London, then burial at Bray, Berkshire, motor transport from London)

1956   Princess Marie Louise, granddaughter of Queen Victoria (died in London, buried in Windsor, coffin taken by train)

1979   Earl Mountbatten (killed in terrorist attack in Northern Ireland, by train from Waterloo to Romsey for burial in Romsey Abbey)

Previous (1977) plans for royal funeral train for HM The Queen – Operation 'London Bridge', possibly might still be carried out in updated form.

The Great and the Good

1858   Wife of George Moore, Cumbrian merchant and philanthropist (died in London, by train to Carlisle, overnight stay at hotel)

1867   *Walter Coffin, colliery owner, Mayor of Cardiff 1848, MP for Cardiff 1852–57, Chairman of Taff Vale Railway Company 1855 (died in London, buried in Bridgend, Wales)

1883   ★Francis Close, Dean of Carlisle Cathedral, former Rector in Cheltenham (Dean Close School, Cheltenham, is named after him) (died in Penzance, buried in Carlisle cathedral)

1884   ★Richard Somerset, 2nd Baron Raglan (died in London, buried in Llandenny churchyard, near Raglan, South Wales)

1887   Father Alexander Mackonochie (1825–1887) famous Victorian Anglo-Catholic priest. First Vicar of St Alban the Martyr, Holborn, and founder of the St Alban Burial Society (died in Scotland, by train to London, then major funeral in London and by special train on Brookwood Necropolis service for burial in Brookwood Cemetery) (See also 1913, Father Arthur Stanton)

1891   ★W.H. Smith, expanded company business of bookseller and newsagent set up by his father, also called W.H. Smith, who is buried in Kensal Green Cemetery (died in Walmer Castle, buried in Hambleden, Buckinghamshire)

1891   ★Louis Lucien Bonaparte, philologist and politician, nephew of Emperor Bonaparte (died in Fano, Italy, buried in St Mary's Catholic Cemetery, Kensal Green, London)

1891   Basil Jayne, colliery owner/coal merchant, brother of Francis Jayne, Bishop of Chester, 1889–1919) (died aged 44 in London, brought by train to Abergavenny)

1892   3rd Duke of Sutherland (died at Dunrobin Castle, Scotland, buried in Trentham Mausoleum, Staffordshire; son, 4th Duke, also buried in Mausoleum)

1893   ★John Newton (reburial) hymn writer – 'Amazing Grace' – and anti-slavery campaigner (died and was buried in London 1807, reinterred at Olney, Buckinghamshire, 1893)

1901   ★Colonel Sir Henry Wilmot VC KCB, soldier and MP (died in Bournemouth, buried in St Mary's churchyard, Chaddesden, Derby (his home town) in 1831)

1905   Dr Thomas Barnardo (body taken to Woking for cremation, ashes back to London; coffin containing ashes taken by train to Barkingside on GER, now part of London Underground network, but was not at the time)

1906   Lady Howe, aunt of Winston Churchill (died in London, by train to Shackerstone in Leicestershire for burial in nearby Congerstone)

1906   Edward Arnott JP, colliery owner (died in Monmouth aged 65, coffin put in special carriage at Monmouth Troy station attached to 9.35 a.m. train to Pontypool Road and Aberdare, on Saturday, 1 September 1906, burial took place in Trecynon cemetery)

1908   *Sir George Livesey, philanthropist and Chairman of South Metropolitan Gas Company (died at home in Reigate, buried in Nunhead cemetery)

1910   Florence Nightingale (1820–1910) nursing pioneer (died in London, by train from Necropolis Railway station at Waterloo to Romsey, buried at East Wellow, Hampshire)

1910   Constable Walter Choat, police officer murdered with two other officers during robbery that led to the siege of Sidney Street, London (after major funeral in London body taken by train for burial in churchyard in West Byfleet, Surrey, the family home town)

1911   (November) Sir William Grantham (b. 1835) Barrister, MP and High Court Judge (died in London, coffin by train to Barcome, near Lewes, for burial near country estate)

1912   *Octavia Hill, social reformer and co-founder of the National Trust (died in London, buried in Crockham Hill, near Edenbridge, Kent)

1912   Lady Sykes (aged 56) famous society lady (died in London, by train to York then on to Sledmere and Fimber for burial in Sledmere, on the family estate)

1912   Alexander Duff, 1st Duke of Fife, son-in-law of King Edward VII (died in Egypt, initially buried in Windsor, by train to Ballater for reburial at Braemar; note: his widow, Princess Louise, Princess Royal, died in 1931 and was initially buried in Windsor but later reburied in Braemar – probably taken by train)

1913   Father Arthur Stanton, popular Anglo-Catholic priest at St Albans, Holborn, London (born 1839 and died in same building in Stroud, Gloucestershire. By train to London then by special train on Brookwood Necropolis service for burial in Brookwood Cemetery) (see also 1887 Father Mackonochie)

1914   William Scott, 6th Duke of Buccleuch (1831–1914) (born and died in London, but buried in family crypt, Buccleuch Memorial Chapel, Dalkeith, Scotland).

1915   ★★Sir Richard Everard Webster (Viscount Alverstone) Lord Chief Justice of England 1900–1913 (died at home in Cranleigh, Surrey, buried in West Norwood cemetery)

1919   Edith Cavell (1865–1915) executed in Belgium (remains repatriated May 1919 by train from Dover to London on SECR, then London to Norwich on GER)

1919   Captain Charles Fryatt (1871–1916) executed in Belgium (remains repatriated July 1919 by train from Dover to London on SECR, then London to Norwich on GER)

1920   Unknown Warrior (remains exhumed and repatriated by train Dover to London on SECR)

1921   ★★Francis Jayne, Bishop of Chester 1889–1919 (died in Oswestry, Shropshire, buried in Bowdon, Cheshire)

1934   Viscount Churchill, Chairman of GWR, 1908–34 (died in Scotland, by train to London, then on to Finstock, Oxfordshire, for burial) (NB Also his mother, Lady Jane Churchill, Mistress of Queen Victoria's Bedchamber, died at Osborne, Isle of Wight, overnight 24/25 December 1900, was buried at Finstock on 29 December 1900)

1934   9th Duke of Marlborough (died in London, by train for burial in Blenheim Palace, *Dean Goods* loco 2395 used on Woodstock Branch)

Funeral Directors

1880   George Attree (Brighton to Victoria, burial in Norwood Cemetery)

1891   James Harold Kenyon, founder of funeral firm J.H. Kenyon (Victoria to Brighton, burial in Extra Mural Cemetery)

Heritage Railways

1989   Hugh Jones (Talyllyn Railway)

1991   Margaret Warner (Ffestiniog Railway, though ashes only, but hearse van used)

1999   Mike Goodwyn (Manx Electric Railway)

2003   Jack Rowell (Keighley & Worth Valley Railway)

2009   Tony Beard (Isle of Man Steam Railway)

2011   Brian Cocks (South Devon Railway)

2012   Richard Eagle (Dean Forest Railway)

2012   Bernard Holden (Bluebell Railway)

2012   Mary Molesworth (Gloucestershire Warwickshire Steam Railway)

2013   Chris Woodland (South Devon Railway)

2014   Jack Owen (Bluebell Railway – ashes only but special train was run)

2015   Mike Stollery (Swanage Railway)

2016   Bob Washington (Welsh Highland/Ffestiniog Railway)

2016   Simon Brown (Bluebell Railway) (killed on Gatwick Express)

2017   Frank Mead (Swanage Railway)

2018   David Knowling (South Devon Railway)

2018   Sir William McAlpine (see *Heritage Railway* Issue 240 for more details)

2019   John Bunting (South Devon Railway)

Miniature Railways etc.

2006   Brian Collins (Lavendon Narrow Gauge Railway, Buckinghamshire)

2017   Lord Braybrooke (Audley End Miniature Railway)

2020   Richard Batten (Romney Hythe & Dymchurch Railway)

BIBLIOGRAPHY, SOURCES OF INFORMATION AND FURTHER READING

Books & Booklets

ADAMSON, Rob & NETTLETON, Chris. *'Winston Churchill' and the Bulleid Pacifics.* York. Friends of the National Railway Museum. 2014.

ALLEN, Cecil. *Trains Annual 1953.* London. Ian Allan Ltd. 1953.

ANDERSON, R.C. *Great Orme Tramway: The First 80 Years.* Broxbourne. Light Rail Transit Association. 1982.

ANON. *The Railway Traveller's Handy Book, 1862.* Oxford. Old House Books. 2010. (Originally published in 1862 by Lockwood & Co., London)

ARNOLD, Catharine. *Necropolis: London and its Dead.* London. Simon & Schuster UK Ltd. 2006. (Pocket Book edition, 2007).

BEAUMONT, Jonathan. *Rails to Achill: A West of Ireland Branch Line.* Usk. Oakwood Press. 2005.

BRADLEY, Simon. *The Railways.* London. Profile Books. 2015.

BRANDON, David & BROOKE, Alan. *London: City of the Dead.* Stroud. The History Press. 2008.

BRASS, Richard T. *Exercise Tiger.* Eastbourne. Tommies Guides. 2008

BROWNE J.H. & THEOBALD H.S., *The Law of Railway Companies*. London. Stephens and Sons. 1899.

CLARKE, John M. *The Brookwood Necropolis Railway*. Usk. Oakwood Press. 2006 (4th Edition).

CLARKE, John M. *London's Necropolis. A Guide to Brookwood Cemetery*. Stroud. Sutton Publishing. 2004.

CLARKE, John M. *London's Necropolis. A Guide to Brookwood Cemetery*. Catrine. Stenlake Publishing. 2018.

COLLINS, Paul. *The Kinver Light Railway: Echoes of a Lost Tramway*. Stroud. The History Press. 2012.

COLSON, Ben. *A Short History of Wolferton Station*. Published privately. 2010.

CRICHTON, Michael. *The Great Train Robbery*. London. Jonathan Cape. 1975.

CROFT, Rodney. *Churchill's Final Farewell, The State and Private Funeral of Winston Churchill*. Croft Publishing. 2014.

CURL, James Stevens (Editor). *Kensal Green Cemetery*. Chichester. Phillimore & Co. 2001.

DAWES, Martin. *The End of the Line. The Story of the Railway Service to the Great Northern London Cemetery*. Barnet. Barnet Local History Society. 2003.

FOLEY, Michael. *Britain's Railway Disasters*. Barnsley. Wharncliffe Transport, an imprint of Pen and Sword Books. 2013.

FRISBY, Helen. *Traditions of Death and Burial*. Oxford. Shire Publications. 2019.

GARFIELD, Simon. *The Last Journey of William Huskisson*. London. Faber and Faber. 2002.

GAVAGHAN, Michael. *The Story of the British Unknown Warrior*. M&L Publications. 2006 (4th edition).

GRAINGER, Hilary. *Death Redesigned: British Crematoria, History, Architecture and Landscape*. Reading. Spire Books. 2005.

GOULD, David. *Southern Railway Passenger Vans*. Oxford. Oakwood Press. 1992.

HAMILTON ELLIS, C. *The Royal Trains*. London. Routledge & Kegan Paul. 1975.

HANSON Neil. *The Unknown Soldier: The Story of the Missing of the Great War*. London. Doubleday. 2005 (Corgi Edition 2007).

HARDING, Peter A. *Branch Lines from Brookwood*. Woking. Peter A. Harding. 2008.

HOBBS, Christopher. *Windsor to Slough. Royal Branch Line*. Headington, Oxford. Oakwood Press. 1993.

HOEY, Brian. *The Royal Train*. Sparkford, Yeovil. Haynes Publishing. 2008.

HOOPER, Collette. *Railways of the Great War with Michael Portillo*. London. Transworld Publishers. 2014.

HURREN, Elizabeth T. *Dying for Victorian Medicine: English Anatomy and its Trade in the Dead Poor, c. 1834–1929*. Basingstoke. Palgrave Macmillan. 2012.

JANES, Brian. *The Unknown Warrior and the Cavell Van*. Tenterden. Kent & East Sussex Railway. 2010 (reprinted 2015).

JENKINS, Stanley C. *The Fairford Branch: The Witney and East Gloucestershire Railway*. Headington, Oxford. Oakwood Press. 1985.

JENKINS, Stanley C. *The Ross, Monmouth and Pontypool Road Line*. Usk. Oakwood Press. 2009 (Second Revised Edition).

JOBSON, Christopher. *The Welshampton Railway Disaster 11 June 1897: A Commemoration*. Wem, Shropshire. Published privately. 1997.

KEAT, Peter. *Goodbye to Victoria: The Story of Queen Victoria's Funeral Train*. Usk. Oakwood Press. 2001.

KINGSTON, Patrick. *Royal Trains*. London. Guild Publishing. 1985.

KUMAR, Amba. *Stately Progress: Royal Travel since 1840*. York. National Railway Museum. 1997.

LACY, R.E. & GEORGE, G.O.W. *Midland Railway Carriages Vol. 1 (of 2)*. Didcot. Wild Swan Publications. 1986.

LESTER, James (Jim). *Southern Region Engineman*. Southampton. Noodle Books. 2009.

LITTEN, Julian. *The English Way of Death*. London. Robert Hale. 1991. (Reprinted in paperback with corrections 2002).

LINGARD, Richard. *The Woodstock Branch*. Oxford. Oxford Publishing Co. 1973.

LOUDON, J.C. *On the laying out, planting and managements of Cemeteries, and on the improvement of churchyards* (with an Essay by James Stevens Curl). Holywood, Northern Ireland. Nerfl Press. 2019. (Originally published in 1843, with a facsimile edition published in 1981 by Ivelet Books, Redhill).

McCARTHY, Colin and David. *Railways of Britain: Norfolk and Suffolk*. Hersham. Ian Allan Publishing. 2007.

MARSH, Phil. *The Full Works: Celebrating the 175th Anniversary of Wolverton Works*. Cleckheaton. Cleek Railway Solutions. 2013.

MARTIN, Andrew. *The Necropolis Railway*. London. Faber and Faber. 2002. (paperback 2005).

MATHESON, Rosa. *Death, Dynamite and Disaster: A Grisly British Railway History*. Stroud. The History Press. 2014.

MAY, Trevor. *The Victorian Undertaker*. Oxford. Shire Publications. 1996.

MELLER, Hugh & PARSONS, Brian. *London Cemeteries: An Illustrated Guide and Gazetteer*. Stroud. The History Press. 2008 (4th edition). (First published 1981 by Avebury Publishing, Amersham).

MOODY, Jeremy B. & FLEMING, George. *The Great Salisbury Train Disaster Centenary 1906–2006: Voices from the Boat Train*. Salisbury. The Timezone Publishing Group. 2006.

NICOLSON, Juliet. *The Great Silence: 1918–1920, Living in the Shadow of the Great War*. London. John Murray. 2009 (paperback 2010).

O'BRIEN, Sean & PATERSON, Don (Eds). *Train Songs: Poetry of the Railway*. London. Faber and Faber. 2014.

PARSONS, Brian. *The London Way of Death*. Stroud. Sutton Publishing. 2001.

PARSONS, Brian. *J.H. Kenyon: A Short History*. London. Dignity Funeral Services. 2014 (Revised edition).

PARSONS, Brian. *From Brooke Street to Brookwood: Nineteenth Century Funeral Reform and S Alban the Martyr Holborn Burial Society*. London. Anglo Catholic History Society. 2014.

PARSONS, Brian. *The Undertaker at Work: 1900–1950*. London. Strange Attractor Press. 2014.

PARSONS, Brian. *J.H. Kenyon and the State Funeral of Sir Winston Churchill*. London. J.H. Kenyon Funeral Directors. 2015.

PARSONS, Brian. *The Evolution of the British Funeral Industry in the 20th Century: From Undertaker to Funeral Director*. Bingley. Emerald Publishing. 2018

PARSONS, Brian. *W.S. Bond, Funeral Directors: A Brief History*. London. Dignity Funerals. 2018.

PATTENDEN, Norman. *Salisbury 1906: An Answer to the Enigma?* South Western Circle Monograph No.1. 2006, new edition 2016.

PATTENDEN, Norman. *Special Traffic Arrangements*. South Western Circle Monograph No.4. 2008.

PEEL, David. *The Unusual and the Unexpected on British Railways*. Stroud. Fonthill Media. 2013.

QUINN, Tom. *Tales of the Old Railwaymen*. Newton Abbot. David and Charles. 1998.

QUINN, Tom. *Railway's Strangest Journeys*. London. Portico. 2010 (first published 1999).

READER, Dean. *A Pictorial History of the British Hearse*. Published privately. 2008.

RICHARDS, Jack & SEARLE, Adrian. *The Quintinshill Conspiracy*. Barnsley. Pen & Sword Books. 2013.

ROLT, LTC. *Red for Danger*. London. The Bodley Head. 1955.

ROYAL PARKS (The) and FRIENDS (The) of BROMPTON CEMETERY. *Brompton Cemetery: An Illustrated Guide*. London. The Royal Parks. 2002.

RUTHERFORD, Sarah. *The Victorian Cemetery*. Oxford. Shire Publications. 2008.

SCHIVELBUSCH, Wolfgang. *Railway Journey: Trains and Travel in the Nineteenth Century*. Oxford. Basil Blackwell. 1980 (First published: Berkeley. University of California Press. 1977).

SIMMONS, Jack. *The Railways of Britain: A Journey Through History*. Thornbury, Bristol. Book Promotions Ltd. 1986 (3rd Edition). (First published 1961).

SMALL, Terry. *Don't Tell the Management!* Wellington, Somerset. The Carly Press. 2011.

SNELL, John. *Tamar Valley Trains*. Tavistock. Published privately, printed by Ottery Press. 1997.

STOKER, Bram. *Dracula*. London. Penguin Popular Classics. 1984 (First published 1894).

THE STATIONERY OFFICE. *Tragic Journeys*. London. The Stationery Office. 2001.

TURNER, Keith. *The Great Orme Tramway: Over a Century of Service*. Llanwrst. Gwasg Carreg Gwalch. 2003.

TURPIN, John & KNIGHT, Derrick. *The Magnificent Seven: London's First Landscaped Cemeteries*. Stroud. Amberley Publishing. 2011.

VOICE, David. *Freight on Street Tramways in the British Isles*. Brora, Sutherland. Adam Gordon. 2007.

VOICE, David. *Last Rides: Funeral Trams Around the World.* Brora, Sutherland. Adam Gordon. 2015.

WESTCOTT JONES, Kenneth. *Rail Tales of the Unexpected.* Nairn, Scotland. David St John Thomas. 1992. (Book Club Associates edition).

WHEATLEY, Nicolas. *Final Journey: Funeral Trains and the Untold Story of Coffin Transport by Train in England and Wales.* Long Essay produced for Institute of Railway Studies and Transport History, copy in Search Engine, National Railway Museum. 2014.

WHITEHOUSE, Patrick & ST JOHN THOMAS, David (Eds). *The Great Western Railway: 150 Glorious Years.* Newton Abbot. 1984 (paperback edition 1985, reprinted 2002).

WILKINSON, James. *The Unknown Warrior.* London. Tudsbury Press. 2013. (First edition 2006).

WILLIAMS, Nick. *The Blue Plaques of Norwich.* Norwich. Norwich Heritage Economic and Regeneration Trust (HEART). 2010.

WRIGHT, Geoffrey. *Discovering Epitaphs.* Oxford. Shire Publications. 2010 Second Edition. (First Edition 1972).

Magazines and Journals

Archive, *The Quarterly Journal for British Industrial and Transport History.* Issue 63, September 2009. Lightmoor Press. '*Unknown Undertaking*'. Brian Parsons (Article on Dottridge Brothers).

Back Track, August 2018. Vol.32, No. 8, pp.502–8. 'Carrying them Home' Railways and State Funerals. Geoffrey Skelsey, LVO.

Back Track, May 2019. Vol.33, No.5, pp.292–6. 'Place on Rail' – The Transport of the Dead by Train in the UK. Brian Parsons. (Part of a longer study of the same name by this author which is available (to members only) on the website of the Railway & Canal Historical Society, www.rchs.org.uk).

Branch Line News (BLN) (published by the Branch Line Society).

1. BLN 585 of 5 May 1988, pp.144/88, Item 81. (ending of coffin transport on BR).

2. BLN 642 of 4 October 1990, pp.296/90, Item 73. (ending of coffin transport for BR staff).

Funeral Services Journal (FSJ), November 2008, Vol 123 No 11, pp.80–99. *Transport to Paradise – Part 3: Unusual and Novel Funeral Transport.* Article by Brian Parsons.

Funeral Services Journal (FSJ), May 2011, Vol 126 No 5, pp.88–94. *From Here to Eternity: The Brookwood Cemetery Railway.* Article by John M Clarke.

Great Eastern Journal (magazine of the Great Eastern Railway Society):

    1. 1981 No.81 (October, pp.10–11) (*Article by John Watling on GER hearse vans, with photos*).

    2. 1998, No.94. (*Large size photograph from Stratford Works Collection (NRM ref SX407) of locomotive D56 No1849 decorated for Captain Fryatt's funeral train in 1919*).

    3. 2020 No.182 (April)

        i. Pp.10–13. *Article by Ron Gooch on 'the funeral train of HM King George V and its driver Frederick Collis'.*

        ii. Pp.14–15. *Article by John Watling on 'the funeral carriage: GNR Saloon No.6'.*

        iii. Pp.15–25. *Article by Brian Parsons on 'proposed siding at City of London Cemetery'.*

Great Eastern Railway Magazine:

    1. Vol 9, No.102, June 1919. Page 104, (Photo of '*Guardsmen conveying coffin [of Edith Cavell] to the train at Liverpool Street Station*' and poem, *Edith Cavell's Last Journey*).

    2. Vol 9, No.102, June 1919. Page 103 and pp.125–6, (*Report and letters about Memorial Service [for Railwaymen] at St Paul's Cathedral 14 May 1919*).

    3. Vol 9, No.104, August 1919. pp 143-151 (Report and photographs of funeral of Captain Charles Fryatt, including, on p.150 a photograph of '*G.E. engine 1849 used to draw funeral train to Dovercourt'*).

Great Western Journal. No.58, Spring 2006, p.62 et seq. 'Leamington Spa Part 2'. Chris Turner & John Copsey. (Reference on p.71 to sending coffins by passenger trains).

Heritage Railway magazine:

    1. Issue 197 December 15, 2014- January 14, 2015 Letter by Alan Dibb on Churchill Funeral Train (CFT).

    2. Issue 198 January 15- February 11, 2015 p.98 'Star Letter' by Nicolas Wheatley about Churchill Funeral Train (responding to inaccuracies in letter from Alan Dibb).

3. Issue 199 February 12- March 11, 2015 p.85 Letter from Brian Higgins and 2 photos of *D1015* on return working of CFT to London, also photo of 34051 with train on way to Handborough.

Journal of Transport History. Vol 29/1. March 2008. *Applying the Life Cycle Theory: The rise and fall of railways*. Zdenek Tomes.

Mortality, Vol.12, No.1, February 2007. 'Embalmed Vision'. Dr John Troyer. (Article on embalming, includes reference to the transport of corpses by train in USA).

Railway Archive magazine No.49, December 2015, pp.2–24. Article on *'The Railways at Trentham Part 1: Trentham Station, The Dukes of Sutherland and the Florence Colliery Railway'*. Allan C Baker & Mike G Fell.

Railway Archive magazine No.50, December 2015, pp.2–24. Article on *'The Railways at Trentham Part 2: Trentham Station, The Dukes of Sutherland and the Florence Colliery Railway'*. Allan C Baker & Mike G Fell.

Railway Magazine:

1. October 1938, p.295. *'Private carriage LNER'*. (Reply to JB Dawson in '*The Why and the Wherefore*' about hearse vans on Great Eastern Railway).

2. June 1953, pp.363–72. *'Royal Railway Journeys'*. (Article with photographs).

3. October 1954, pp.713–15. *'Kings Cross Cemetery Station'*. (Article with photographs)

4. March 1965, pp.132–4. *'Sir Winston Churchill's last journey'* (Article with photographs).

5. December 1965, p.727. *'Churchill van goes to America'*. (Article with photograph).

6. August 1998, pp.55–7. *'Is this shabby 'bus shelter' a proper tribute to Diana's memory?'* (Article with photographs).

7. October 2001, p.15. *'First funeral train since 1979'*. (News item on Jimmy Knapp's coffin being transported to Glasgow from Euston).

Railway Magazine publication, *Royal Trains of the British Isles*. 1974, (includes material on royal funeral trains).

Steam Railway magazine No.440, January 29-February 25, 2016, pp.48–54. Article *'Engineers at rest'*.

Steam Railway News, Issue 173, 29 November 1991, page 2. Article '*Ffestiniog run funeral train*'.

Steam World Magazine, Issue 211, January 2005, pp.16–22. '*Operation Hope Not*'. Steam World Publishing. (Article on 40th anniversary of Churchill's funeral train).

Talyllyn News, no.144, December 1989. '*Hugh Jones, an appreciation*' by Roy Smith, (includes reference to transport of coffin on Talyllyn Railway).

The Golden Way, Journal of The Pullman Society:
1. Issue 103, 2015/1. pp 4-9. Article by Nicolas Wheatley on Churchill Funeral Train and repatriation of vehicles from USA. Also photos (p.29) of Van S2464S being restored at Shildon.
2. Issue 104, 2015/2. pp 59-62. Article by Nicolas Wheatley, with photos, of launch of exhibition at NRM of Churchill Funeral Train.
3. Issue 107, 2016/1. pp 12-15. Article by Nicolas Wheatley, with photo, on use of Pullman cars in other funeral trains (apart from Churchill Funeral Train).

The Locomotive magazine, February 15, 1936, p.42. (Photograph of locomotive 4082 *Windsor Castle* decorated for hauling royal funeral train on 28 January 1936, and report on '*Workings of Royal Special Trains in connection with the Funeral of the late King*').

The London Journal, Vol.34 No.1, March 2009, pp.1–15. *Houses for the Dead: The Provision of Mortuaries in London, 1843-1889*. Dr Pam Fisher.

Underground News. May 1998, pp.248–9. *The District and a Melancholy State Occasion*. RE Rodrigues. (Article on train journey of coffin of WE Gladstone).

Warwickshire Gardens Trust Journal, Autumn 2003, pp.12–17. '*The Next Train is for Knowle Necropolis Only*', J.M.L. Lovie

Board of Trade/Ministry of Transport Accident Reports

14 December 1906. Report into accident on 24 November 1906 at Ulleskelf, Yorkshire.

12 July 1912. Report into accident on 21 June 1912 at Hebden Bridge, Yorkshire.

8 November 1946. Report into accident on 15 July 1946 at Hatfield, Hertfordshire.

NOTES

Introduction

1 On the track entitled 'Being for the Benefit of Mr Kite'.

Chapter 1

1 After this accident, in 1876, various improvements to signalling were introduced, including requiring signals to show 'danger' unless they were cleared for a train to pass. Previously the default position was 'clear' unless a train was in the section.

2 After this accident, in 1889, several safety measures were made compulsory, such as continuous brakes.

3 The Stockton & Darlington Railway had opened in 1825 but was not built to carry fare-paying passengers, whereas the Liverpool & Manchester Railway did carry passengers from its opening.

4 Wolfgang Schivelbusch, Chapter 3.

5 For example returning the Honourable Charles Rolls back to Llangattock, near Monmouth in 1910, see pp.152–4.

6 In a curious indirect link to Captain Charles Fryatt (see Chapter 4), Huskisson was MP for Harwich 1807–1812.

7 The episode is mentioned on p.31 of Foley, *Britain's Railway Disasters*, see Bibliography.

8 Quoted in Schivelbusch, p.129.

9 It is named as 'Eclipse' by Rolt in *Red for Danger*.

10 Quoted in Bradley, p.150.

11 William Ewart Gladstone, who had his own final journey by train after his death in 1898, see Chapter 8.

12 Schivelbusch, p.130.

13 At the time the Board of Trade was the body responsible for investigating railway accidents.

14 Quoted in Rolt, 1955 edition on pp.45–6.

Chapter 2

1 Such as Arnold Van Gennep, who first articulated the concept in his 1906 book *Rites of Passage*.

2 Funeral liturgy in Scotland is believed to have broadly similar wording, though the author is not familiar with this.

3 For example in the academic field of Death Studies.

4 The author is grateful to Ian Hunter, Historian of the Worcester, Birmingham & Droitwich Canals Society, for information provided by him during an email exchange with the author in July 2019.

5 See Bibliography for details of this book.

6 In Volume 948/3, pp.112–15.

7 Euston station opened in July 1837, St Pancras station did not open until October 1868.

8 Olivia Bland, *The Royal Way of Death*, p.151.

9 Earl Mountbatten was related to the royal family and had a ceremonial funeral train in 1979, which took his coffin to Romsey rather than to Windsor.

10 Naylor, 2013.

11 This accident is reported in Foley's 2013 book on railway accidents, though some of the factual details (particularly the direction of the train's travel) do not match the information recorded in the Board of Trade Report.

12 A modern copy is in the Author's Collection. It has not been possible to trace a copy of the fireman's Death Certificate.

13 The author is grateful to Dr Helen Frisby for providing this phrase, which originates from Charles Cowling, at a Death Day conference at the University of Winchester in October 2010.

Chapter 3

1 The author is grateful to John Clarke for allowing the use of this information from his book *The Brookwood Necropolis Railway* (4th Edition, 2006).

2 For example, in *Bleak House* (1853) and *The Mystery of Edwin Drood*.

3 See Bibliography.

4 At the time it was proposed it was referred to as the London Necropolis as Brookwood did not then exist. It became known by its more familiar name later.

5 Loudon, 1843, p.47.

6 Loudon, 1843, p.49.

7 The London and Southampton Railway was built from 1834 onwards and opened as far as Woking Common (which became Woking after the town was expanded) in May 1838. The railway changed its name to the London & South Western Railway in June 1839 and reached Southampton in May 1840.

8 Loudon, 1843, p.49.

9 Clarke, 2006, p.15.

10 *Ibid.*

11 In his *Gatherings from Graveyards, Particularly those of London: with a Concise History of the Modes of Interment amongst Different Nations, from the Earliest Periods. And a Detail of Dangerous and Fatal Results produced by the Unwise and Revolting Custom of Inhuming the Dead in the Midst of the Living* (1839).

12 Supplementary Report on the Results of a Special Inquiry into the Practice of Interments in Towns (1843).

13 The 1848–49 outbreak caused 14,600 deaths in London alone.

14 Its proposed location is shown in figure 3.19 and a view of it is shown in figure 3.20, both on p.66 of Curl, 2001.

15 See Fisher, 2009, p.3 and Note 20.

16 See Fisher, 2009, for an explanation of the reasons why.

17 'An Act to amend the laws concerning the Burial of the Dead in the Metropolis', often called 'the Burial Act 1852'.

18 The others were at Woronora Cemetery, in Sydney's Sutherland Shire, which operated 1900–44, and at the Spring Vale Cemetery at Fawkner, Melbourne, which operated 1904–43. There was also a cemetery at Sandgate, Newcastle, served by funeral trams until 1933, though visitors were carried on a Sunday only service until 1985.

19 It is incorrect to refer to this service as the 'London Necropolis Railway', a term with no historical validity.

20 4th Edition 2006, Oakwood Press. It is believed that a reprint of this book is possible and that a new 5th edition is being planned (as of February 2020).

21 www.tbcs.org.uk (last accessed 09/02/2020).

22 As mentioned above.

23 A type of locomotive designed by Dugald Drummond (born 1840) and built between 1897 and 1911. After his death in 1912 his coffin was transported to Brookwood Cemetery by a train hauled by another locomotive designed by him, D15 Class 4-4-0 number 463. He is buried near the site of the South Station.

24 Page 164.

25 There was also an article by Eric Neve in the March 1982 edition of the Great Northern Railway Society Newsletter.

26 The author is grateful to David Hyde for supplying a copy of the article in its original printed form.

27 The origin of this name is explained in Dawes on p.36.

28 Published by Shire Publications, Oxford, 2008.

29 As quoted by Lovie from the Minutes of the Corporation of Birmingham Burial Board Committee, 10 December 1858.

30 It is this unusual turn of events which is mentioned by Rutherford, on p.56.

31 www.smithsonianmag.com/history/london-graveyard-s-become-memorial-citys-seedier-past-180953104/, last accessed 09/02/2020.

32 *The Victorian Cemetery*, p.55.

Chapter 4

1 Nurse Edith Cavell (executed 1915, repatriated May 1919) and Captain Chares Fryatt (executed 1916, repatriated July 1919).

2 This expression is used in this chapter as it was the name given to the conflict at the time, which has only become known to history as the First World War after the later major conflict in the twentieth century, now referred to as the Second World War.

3 R38 was this airship's British designation but at the time of its crash agreement had been reached for its sale to the US Navy, which designated it ZR-2.

4 Others will doubtless come to light when more research is undertaken on this subject. In the meantime Colin Fenn has published a blog inconvenientdead.wordpress.com/2018/12/01/the-mass-mobilization-of-corpses-during-world-war-i/ (last accessed 22/02/2020) detailing some of the known cases. There is clearly much more information to be discovered.

5   blog.maryevans.com/officers (permalink, last accessed 18/02/2020).

6   www.mmtrust.org.uk/mausolea/view/509/Champion_de_Crespigny (last accessed 18/02/2020).

7   W.E. Gladstone's remains had the benefit of a final journey by train, being transported from Broughton Hall, near Chester, to London in May 1898.

8   According to Richard Van Emden, in *The Quick and the Dead*, 2012, London, Bloomsbury, pp.131–3.

9   The VC medal is held at the Fleet Air Arm Museum in Yeovilton, Somerset.

10 For a biography of Captain Liddell see *With a Smile and a Wave* by Peter Daybell, 2005, Pen & Sword, Barnsley.

11 These were the bodies of Rachel Nimmo, aged 28, and her baby son, Dickson. See *The Quintinshill Conspiracy*, pp.235-6.

12 See *The Quintinshill Conspiracy*, p.37.

13 See *The Quintinshill Conspiracy*, p.41, Note 8.

14 2013, Pen & Sword, Barnsley.

15 Page 38.

16 See *The Quintinshill Conspiracy*, p.41, Note 8.

17 There is a report of this accident on a New Zealand government website, nzhistory.govt.nz/page/bere-ferrers-rail-accident, last accessed 20/02/2020.

18 www.cwgc.org/find/find-war-dead/results/?cemetery=PLYMOUTH+(EFFORD)+CEMETERY&fq_warliteral=1&csort=dateofdeath&tab=wardead&fq_servedwithliteral=New+Zealand, last accessed 20/02/2020.

19 The line from Plymouth is still operational, though it terminates at Gunnislake, a few miles south of Tavistock.

20 He became an acting Admiral in December 1916, later being made a full Admiral and eventually became First Lord of the Admiralty. He was ennobled as Earl Beatty in October 1919.

21 www.iwm.org.uk/history/boy-1st-class-john-jack-travers-cornwell-vc, last accessed 21/02/2020.

22 Information from the June 2019 Newsletter of the Cheltenham & Gloucester Branch of the Western Front Association.

23 There is a certain irony to this, as the building was opened in 1809 to house French prisoners of war during the Napoleonic Wars.

24 See the records published on the website of the Peace Pledge Union, menwhosaidno.org/men/men_files/f/firth_henry.html (last accessed 22/02/2020).

25 A modern copy of his Death Certificate is in the author's collection. The research confirming the rail transport of his remains was carried out by Colin Fenn, who has carried much research on the deaths of conscientious objectors during the Great War. The author is grateful to him for sharing his findings with the author.

26 The Great Western Railway had operated the Princetown Railway from its opening in 1883. It closed in 1956.

27 www.kesr.org.uk.

28 preservation.kesr.org.uk/wagons-vans/cavell (last accessed 22/2/2020).

29 Quoted in Brian Janes' booklet.

30 Nothing has been discovered about this person and it is believed the poem is now out of copyright.

31 This is an oblique reference to Captain Charles Fryatt, from Dovercourt, Harwich. By May 1919 Captain Fryatt, who had been executed in July 1916 causing much outrage, had not yet been repatriated.

32 A report of this service was made in the *Great Eastern Railway Magazine* in June 1919, Vol. 9, No. 102, pp.102–3.

33 This is the figure reported in the *GER Magazine* in 1919 but the Programme for the Centenary Memorial Service in 2019 gives a figure of 7,000.

34 On 6 November 2019 the author was privileged to attend the 'Railway Workers World War 1 Centenary Memorial Service' held at Southwark Cathedral, London, which, in part, commemorated the service held in 1919. It also 'looked to the railway industry of today as a conduit, a channel through which a message for love, peace and reconciliation can flow' – words from the Welcome to the congregation from The Reverend Canon Michael Rawson, Sub Dean and Pastor.

35 *Railway Magazine*, July 2019, p. 68, from the *Railway Magazine* archive.

36 Published in 2016 by Amberley Publishing, Stroud.

37 This watch is now is now in the collection of the Imperial War Museum, having been donated by one of Captain Fryatt's grandchildren. www.iwm. org.uk/collections/item/object/30106824 (last accessed 23/02/2020).

38 In an ironic twist of history, *U-33* was one of Germany's submarine fleet that was surrendered to the British at Harwich, Captain Fryatt's home port, in January 1919; it was subsequently broken up. (Information from Carver, p.75).

39 Noted in the booklet by Brian Janes, *The Unknown Warrior and the Cavell Van*, p.13.

Chapter 5

1 There is more information about these events in *Death from the Skies: The Zeppelin Raids over Norfolk, 19 January 1915* by R.J. Wyatt, Gliddons Books, Norwich. 1990.

2 See Chapter 10 for a report on a funeral of several people killed on a tram in Streatham in September 1916 by a bomb dropped from a Zeppelin airship.

3 In December 1914 142 people had been killed in Hartlepool, Whitby and Scarborough when five German battleships shelled those towns from the North Sea. These were probably the first civilians killed in Britain by enemy action.

4 Sadly the Hindenburg crashed spectacularly and very publicly in May 1937 in the USA, causing thirty-six fatalities, fewer than the forty-eight of the R101 accident.

5 This phrase became the title of a booklet, subtitled 'The Tragedy of the Airship R101', by Ronnie Barclay, published by St Mary's Cardington PCC, which is only available from St Mary's Church, Cardington; published 2000, reprinted 2010.

6 For more information on Edith Cavell and her railway repatriation see Chapter 4.

7 Many of the details of the repatriations and funeral are to be found in an article by Dr Brian Parsons, printed in the *ICCM* (Institute of Cemetery and Crematoria Managers) *Journal*, Spring 2011, Vol. 79, No. 1. The author is grateful to Brian Parsons for providing and allowing the author to use this information.

8 For more information, see the report at www.airshipsonline.com/news. R101-memorial.htm (last accessed 10 January 2020).

9 This is mentioned in Brian Parsons' article for the *ICCM Journal*, see Note 7.

10 There is an excellent contemporary report of the accident and rescue operations in *Flight* magazine, 1 September 1921, Vol. XIII, No. 35, pp.589–92.

11 There are several Pathé news films on YouTube of the rescue efforts.

12 On the R101 the fire risk had been reduced by using diesel-powered engines. The fire in that case may have been caused by calcium phosphate flares being drenched in water when the airship hit the ground, thereby causing their ignition, see *We're Down Lads*, pp.26–7.

13 E.M. Maitland, then a Brigadier-General, had been on the R34 airship which made the first powered east-to-west crossing of the Atlantic, also making the first two-way crossing on its return in July 1919.

14 *Flight* magazine, 1 September 1921, Vol. XIII, No. 35, p.591.

15 *Ibid.*, p.589.

16 historicengland.org.uk/listing/the-list/list-entry/1096014, last accessed 17 January 2020.

17 historicengland.org.uk/listing/the-list/list-entry/1203258, last accessed 17 January 2020.

Chapter 6

1 An image of her funeral procession appears in Chapter 2.

2 Dave Knowling, one of the people featured in Chapter 13, wrote in his informal memoirs in the South Devon Railway's magazine *Bulliver* in the Spring 2015 issue, No.208, about a time 'in late 1956' when as a loco fireman he shunted the hearse van from a train transporting 'one of the old princesses' to Windsor. The date ties in with the death in December 1956 of HH Princess Marie Louise.

3 Information correct on 03/30/2020. stenlake.co.uk/book_ publishing/?page_id=131&ref=907&section=

4 For examples see *The Royal Trains* by C. Hamilton Ellis, 1974; *Royal Trains* by Patrick Kingston, 1985; and *The Royal Train: The Inside Story* by Brian Hoey, 2008.

5 *Windsor to Slough: A Royal Branch Line* by C.R. Potts, 1993, Oakwood Press.

6 As recorded in *Names and Nameplates of British Steam Locomotives 2. GWR and Absorbed* by Gordon Coltas, Heyday Publishing, Crosby, 1985.

7 The early locomotives from this class were named after stately homes in the region served by the LNER, though some later members of the class were named after various football clubs and became known as 'Footballers'.

8 The level crossing, over what is now the A1123 road, still exists, though the siding has gone, as has the signal box from which the photograph was probably taken.

9 The B17 SLT has no connection with the Sandringham Estate.

10 Information from a B17 SLT publication *History of B17 Locomotive Helmingham Hall*. The information on B17 locomotives comes from *The*

power of the B17s and the B2s by Peter Swinger, Oxford Publishing, 1988 (2004 impression).

11 www.steam-museum.org.uk, last accessed 05/03/2020.

12 Hoey, p.121.

13 The transportation of Jimmy Knapp's coffin in 2001 was on a scheduled train.

14 Hoey, p.120.

Chapter 7

1 The name of the nearby village is 'Long Hanborough' with no letter D in its middle.

2 This was a courtesy title as the son of a duke. Winston did not qualify for a courtesy title, but was invested as Knight of the Garter (KG), the highest ranking British form of knighthood, in 1953. He twice refused the offer of a peerage, one title reported to be 'Duke of London'.

3 For more information on this train see Chapter 6.

4 It was initially numbered 21C151 when built by the Southern Railway and was renumbered on the creation of British Railways in 1948.

5 This is referred to by Jim Lester on p.72 of his book *Southern Region Engineman* (2009, Noodle Books, Southampton), which contains a chapter on his experiences of being fireman on the funeral train from London to Handborough.

6 *Flying Scotsman* is now (February 2020) running with its British Railways number of 60103.

7 A photo of the train, including *Lydia*, appears on p.63 of James S. Baldwin's book *Flying Scotsman*, 2013, The History Press, Stroud.

8 This information is correct as at February 2020, though *Lydia* did have a brief spell at the West Somerset Railway in early 2017, though it never ran in service there.

9 This information is correct as at February 2020.

10 www.glenloabbeyhotel.ie/en/pullman-restaurant-galway/history-pullman (last accessed 16/02/2020), though note that some of the history of the restaurant car's former use is slightly incorrect. It has never been known to travel abroad, nor was it used in the Pullman service to Brighton, nor was it used in the making of the film *Murder on the Orient Express*.

11 Author Tom Quinn, 1998, David & Charles, Newton Abbot, pp.100-1.

12 Blenheim Palace could still be seen from Bladon church at the time of Sir Winston Churchill's burial, but trees have since grown to obscure this view.

13 Information taken from Brian Parsons' booklet *J.H. Kenyon: A Short History*, 2014.

14 Coincidentally the same age as her brother, Lord Randolph Churchill, Sir Winston's father.

15 www.battlefieldline.co.uk.

16 2001, The Oakwood Press, Usk.

17 Information reproduced in Pullman Car Services Newsletter 23, January 2005. A guinea was a unit of currency equating to £1 and 1 shilling (21 shillings), though it was abolished in 1971 when the UK converted to decimal currency.

Chapter 8

1 *Brookwood Necropolis Railway*, 4th Edition, p.113.

2 2012, Palgrave Macmillan.

3 These were a basic double coffin enclosed in an elm or cheap pine chest, of the same design for everyone, each containing one cadaver.

4 Hurren, p.306.

5 Hurren, p.189.

6 Contemporary reports, as collected by R.E. Rodrigues and published in *Underground News* in 1998, show some variations on certain facts.

7 This is not the 0-4-2 locomotive of the same name that is preserved and on display, ironically with Royal Train decorations, at the National Railway Museum in York. However, the locomotive *Hardwicke*, which gave its name to the class, is preserved and is on display at the Locomotion museum in Shildon.

8 Originally opened in 1849 as 'Broughton', renamed 'Broughton Hall' in 1861 and renamed 'Broughton & Bretton' in 1908. It closed in 1964. www.disused-stations.org.uk/b/broughton_and_bretton/index.shtml

9 Now known just as 'Westminster'.

10 Article by Brian Parsons, 'Place on Rail' in *Backtrack*, May 2019, pp.292–6. A fuller version of this article is on the website of the Railway & Canal Historical Society, rchs.org.uk/wp-content/uploads/2019/09/FINAL-Parsons-Coffins-by-Train_1-2.pdf, though it is only accessible to members of RCHS.

11 On the former Malton and Driffield Railway, closed 1950.

12 www.parishofmorpeth.org.uk/stmary.htm, last accessed 13/03/2020.

13 historicengland.org.uk/listing/the-list/list-entry/1445426, last accessed 14/03/2020.

14 The most likely explanation is that the crew experienced a 'micro-sleep', losing awareness of their situation. See Norman Pattenden's publication produced as a Monograph for the South Western Circle, *Salisbury 1906: An Answer to the Enigma?*

15 As recorded by Parsons in the booklet *J.H. Kenyon: A Short History*, 2014.

16 As reported in the *Western Times* on 13 July 1906.

17 en.wikipedia.org/wiki/Pablo_Fanque, last accessed 14/03/2020.

18 Personal comment made to the author during a visit to Cardiff City Hall by an unnamed member of staff.

Chapter 9

1 Considerable research has indicated that this poem is no longer in copyright.

2 *The Brookwood Necropolis Railway.*

3 Lacy, R.E. and Dow, George (1984-86) *Midland Railway Carriages Volumes 1–2.* Upper Bucklebury, Wild Swan.

4 The transport of corpses by train is rarely covered by academic literature but a rare example is Dr John Troyer's article 'Embalmed Vision' published in *Mortality* journal, Volume 12, No.1, 2007. This article about the development of embalming in the USA makes some reference to embalming corpses prior to sending them by train after the American Civil War, 1861–65.

5 Hutchinson, Col. Sir Eric A.O. (1945). 'Some prototype vehicles: No.2: NBR Corpse Van'. *The Model Railway News* February, p.35. A 7mm scale model of one of these vehicles was illustrated in *The Model Railway News*, June 1952, finished in LNER livery and numbered 9203. See also Chapter 11 for more details on a proposed 00 4mm scale model of the NBR corpse van.

6 A drawing of this carriage appears on p.60 of *Goodbye to Victoria, The Last Queen Empress: The Story of Queen Victoria's Funeral Train*, by Peter Keat, 2001, Oakwood Press, Usk.

7 As noted on p.38 of *Stately Progress: Royal Train Travel Since 1840*, Amba Kumar, 1997, National Railway Museum York.

8   These details are taken firstly from p.154 of *The Royal Trains* by C. Hamilton Ellis, 1975, Routledge Paul & Kegan, London, and secondly from p.161 of *The Royal Train – The Inside Story* by Brian Hoey, 2008, Haynes, Yeovil.

9   These details are taken from p.164 of *The Royal Train – The Inside Story* by Brian Hoey, 2008, Haynes, Yeovil.

10   www.festipedia.org.uk/wiki/Hearse_van, last accessed 28/02/2020.

11   There was an obituary of Hugh Jones with a report of his funeral train in the *Talyllyn News* No.144, December 1989. The author is grateful to Roger Whitehouse of the Talyllyn Railway for bringing this report to his attention.

12   This information is recorded in Hoey, p.123.

13   *Great Western Journal*. No.58, Spring 2006, p.62 et seq. 'Leamington Spa Part 2'. Chris Turner and John Copsey. (Reference on p.71 to sending coffins by passenger trains.)

14   Quoted by Brian Parsons on p.111 of *The Evolution of the British Funeral Industry in the 20th Century*, 2018, Emerald Publishing, Bingley.

15   The author is grateful to Brian Janes of the Colonel Stephens Museum at Tenterden for providing a copy of this notice. The use of capitals is as in the original, though the initials of the railway companies have had the intervening full stops removed.

16   The author is grateful to Brian Parsons for finding and sharing this document.

17   The author is grateful to Brian Parsons for sharing this advertisement. He is not related to the company, which has long since gone out of business.

18   The author is grateful to Peter Rance of the Great Western Trust at Didcot for bringing this Notice to his attention.

Chapter 10

1   Published by Adam Gordon, Brora, Sutherland, 2015.

2   The author is especially grateful to David Voice for permitting him to use much material from *Last Rides*, including using several sections that are quoted verbatim.

3   Information from history section of unofficial website, www.greatorme-tramway.org.uk last accessed 05/01/2020.

4   Information from official website, www.greatormetramway.co.uk, last accessed 05/01/2020.

5 His Death Certificate records the cause of death as 'Rheumatic disease of the heart, 1 year 3 months'.

6 As noted in Chapter 13 in relation to the Achill & Newtown Railway in Ireland, this was not the only occasion when the carrying of a coffin was the first use of a tramway or railway line.

7 Sadly his grave has no headstone and its exact location has been lost.

8 A single deck tram.

9 Voice, p.13.

10 Voice, p.10.

11 The author is grateful to Richard Dodge from the Isle of Man for supplying this information, some of which had been printed in the MERS journal, the *Manx Transport Review*. The photo agency that supplied the photos no longer exists but it has not been possible to trace any current copyright holder.

12 Made by the firm Colourful Coffins, www.colourfulcoffins.com, to whom the author is grateful for the supply of the image of 'Eric's Tram' coffin, though note the destination in this image reads 'Triangle'.

13 See David Voice's book, *The History of the Worcester Tramways*.

14 Information from www.disused-stations.org.uk/b/botanic_gardens, last accessed 04/01/2020.

Chapter 11

1 This information is recorded in *The Royal Train: The Inside Story*, 2008, Brian Hoey, Haynes Publishing, Sparkford.

2 www.nbrstudygroup.co.uk/modelling/products.php.

3 The information about the kits of the LSWR hearse vans was kindly provided by John Clarke in a personal exchange of emails with the author.

4 Information kindly provided by John Clarke during a private exchange of emails between him and the author.

5 www.hmrs.org.uk.

6 Information correct as of 20/01/2020.

Chapter 12

1 Simon Mullen, (1968), London, Herbert Jenkins, pp.143–4.

2 Board of Trade report dated 12 July 1912 by Lt Col E. Druitt into accident at Hebden Bridge, Lancashire and Yorkshire Railway.

3 Bradley, 2015, p.100, refers briefly to this incident, saying it was a purpose-built corpse van, but it is more likely that the corpse was just being carried in a separate van, not purpose built.

4 Ministry of Transport Report dated 8 November 1946 'Report on the derailment which occurred at Hatfield on 15 July 1946 on the London and North Eastern Railway' by Lt Col G.R.S. Wilson.

5 The book *Rail Tales of the Unexpected* by Kenneth Westcott Jones (published by David St John Thomas Publisher, Nairn, 1992) mentions this story on p.66, though many of the details are given incorrectly.

6 There are more details about this in Chapter 10 'Following Death: Pauper Bodies and the Medical Schools of Aberdeen, 1832–1914' by Dr Dee Hoole, within the book *Death in Scotland*, Jupp and Marland (eds) published in 2019. THe author is grateful to Dr Hoole, Honorary Research Fellow, Department of History, Kings College, University of Aberdeen, for providing the author with much information about the transport of corpses to the medical schools in Aberdeen.

7 In *The Railways, Nation, Network and People*, 2015, Profile Books, London, pp.101–2.

8 This was the railway's spelling of the place name, which was sometimes also spelled Mulranny.

9 There are more details about this railway in Jonathan Beaumont's book *Rails to Achill: A West of Ireland Branchline*, 2002 (revised 2005), Oakwood Press, Usk.

10 It is possible that more than forty-eight coffins were transported at a time by train to Brookwood Cemetery, especially in the early years of its operation, but these did not arise from a single source or accident.

11 The author is very grateful to Brian Parsons for bringing this news report to their attention.

12 The author is very grateful to Roger Whitehouse of the Talyllyn Railway for bringing this report to their attention.

13 The last train ran on 29 September 1935.

14 The line from Taunton to Barnstaple closed in 1966.

15 The author is grateful to Colourful Coffins for permission to use the images of their coffins in this book.

16 www.crazycoffins.co.uk

17 The coffin was also displayed at the South Bank Centre during another exhibition in March 2017.

18 www.manchestereveningnews.co.uk/news/greater-manchester-news/decade-ago-brian-designed-coffin-13684884 (last accessed 15/02/2020).

19 Understandably, the cost of this coffin was something that neither Brian Holden nor its makers would disclose.

20 The author is grateful to Terry Bye and Antony Ford, both members of The Pullman Society, for some of the information about the Pullman cars mentioned in this story.

21 Diligent research has revealed that this poem is no longer in copyright.

Chapter 13

1 Parsons, p.241, *The Undertaker at Work: 1900–1950*, Strange Attractor Press, 2014.

2 Parsons, *W.S. Bond, Funeral Directors: A Brief History*, Revised Edition, 2018. London, Dignity.

3 Parsons, *ibid*.

4 Spire Books, Reading.

5 Grainger, p.24.

6 Article by Brian Parsons 'Cremation in England: The Legacy of Sir Henry Thompson Part 2. Arrangements for the First Cremations; Coffins and Transport'. (2006) *International Cemetery and Funeral Management*, Vol 66 No.2, pp.23–37.

7 The building in which this operated is now a museum, www.ragged-schoolmuseum.org.uk (last accessed 12/03/2020).

8 The report of his funeral and train transport is taken from Parsons, *The Undertaker at Work*, p.306. Strange Attractor Press, London, 2014.

9 The only person who did have his coffin transported on what even then was part of the underground railway system was William Ewart Gladstone, Victorian Prime Minister, in 1898.

10 See p.49 of Parsons, *The London Way of Death*, 2001, Sutton Publishing, Stroud.

11 It closed in 1998 but the cemetery still operates, run by a trust. It is one of the best Victorian garden cemeteries outside London.

12 Grainger, p.24.

13 Published by Her Majesty's Stationery Office, 1963, with a facsimile reprint published by The National Archives and Harper Collins in 2013.

14 The author is grateful to Ian Pope for providing this image and allowing its reproduction in this book.

15 Information supplied in a personal communication by Andrew Leverton, Director of the funeral director firm Leverton & Sons, which arranged the transportation. www.levertons.co.uk (last accessed 06/03/2020).

16 See Chapter 7 for more information.

17 A railwayman working in the industry at the time.

18 *Branch Line News*, 5 May 1988. Vol. 585, item 81, pp.144/88. 'Ending of Coffin Transport on BR.'

19 *Branch Line News*, 4 October 1990. Vol. 642, item 73, pp.296/90. 'Ending of Coffin Transport for BR Staff.'

20 Parsons, p.110 of *The Evolution of the British Funeral Industry in the 20th Century*, 2018, Emerald Publishing, Bingley.

21 First published in 1991 by Robert Hale, London, and reprinted with corrections in 2002.

22 The author is greatly indebted to Peter Rance, Chairman and Collections Manager of the Great Western Trust, Didcot, who alerted the author to this document in the GWS archives, and has permitted its inclusion in this book.

23 *The Railway Magazine*, August 1998, pp.55–7, 'Is This Shabby 'Bus Shelter' A Proper Tribute to Diana's Memory?'.

24 Article in *Journal of Transport History*, March 2008. Vol. 29/1. 'Applying the Life Cycle Theory: The Rise and Fall of Railways.'

25 This is the supporters' organisation for the SDR, of which the author has been a member for several years.

26 A report of this funeral train is available online www.dailymail.co.uk/ news/article-2218581/Bernard-Holden-Final-stop-Bluebell-Railway-founder-aged-104-coffin-draped-medals-carried-tracks-ahead-funeral. html, last accessed 19/03/2020.

27 A report about Mike Stollery's funeral train appears on the Swanage Railway's website, www.swanagerailway.co.uk/news/detail/pioneering-swanage-railway-founder-makes-his-final-journey-on-the-line-that-he-helped-to-rebuild, last accessed 19/03/2020.

28 A report of his funeral was carried in the August 2017 issue of *Funeral Services Times*, on p.10, though it does not appear to have been reported in the railway press at the time.

29 Just as this book was going to press the author was notified of an event in 1997 when a coffin was transported on the North Yorkshire Moors Railway, but further details are not available.

30 Since 30 March 2018 the railway has been open to Broadway and the run-round loop at Laverton has been removed; there was never a station there.

31 Personal communication to the author by a person associated with the FR who is knowledgeable about its history.

32 A report of this event, as recounted by Brian's wife Kathleen, appeared in the magazine *Full House*, Issue 25 on 22 June 2006. The magazine is no longer being published.

33 The author was privileged to visit in July 2018, meeting with Tony and Pam Collins, and being able to discuss some background information to this very special funeral train.

34 lavendonconnection.co/home/lngr/, last accessed 20/03/2020.

35 Lord Braybrooke had eight daughters but no sons, so his title passed to a distant cousin. The AER continues to operate.

36 www.iomsra.org, last accessed 21/03/2020.

37 The author is grateful to Richard Dodge for providing the details of Tony Beard's funeral train.

38 Their website should be consulted for further details. fawleyhill.co.uk/, last accessed 21/03/2020.

39 One of the locomotives on this delightful railway is No. 6, called *Norfolk Heroine, Edith Cavell*.

40 www.wwlr.co.uk/, last accessed 22/03/2020.

41 www.west-somerset-railway.co.uk/funeral-services, last accessed 22/03/2020.

42 www.midlandrailway-butterley.co.uk/funerals/, last accessed 22/03/2020.

43 www.peacefunerals.co.uk/railway_funeral, last accessed 22/03/2020.

Chapter 14

1 www.bbc.co.uk/news/magazine-34442302, (last accessed 23/02/2020).

2 An email was sent (to subscribers to their emails) on 15/01/2020 by London Transport Museum titled '10 Things You Didn't Know About the Underground' which stated as item 7 that 'people have also lost items including a coffin and a skeleton' – though presumably this was not within the coffin!

3 This was the funeral train on 17 January 2020 for Richard Batten, a volunteer driver on the Romney Hythe & Dymchurch Railway. The train was driven by his son, Simon.

4 Andy Seatherton was a train driver for First Great Western Trains, based in Exeter. His father was also a train driver, retiring in 1983 after forty-three years' service. This poem, adapted by Andy Seatherton from its American origins, was used by Alison Orchard, a humanist funeral

celebrant, at Arch Seatherton's funeral in 2009 and was later emailed by her to the author. It is used with Andy Seatherton's permission.

5   White was used at night to indicate 'all clear'. The risk of confusing such a signal with other lights led to the Board of Trade requiring green to be used to indicate 'all clear' though this did not become a formal requirement until 1892. (Rolt, *Red for Danger*, 1955 edition, p.100).

6   This poem was printed in the Order of Service for John William Mumby (11 February 1950–31 May 2018); his funeral service took place on 2 July 2018 at Bedford Crematorium. It is used with permission from Jessica Green, Funeral Celebrant who conducted the funeral service.

7   The tombstone refers to an accident that occurred in 1845, 175 years ago.

8   Poem © Katrina Porteous, taken from *The Lost Music*, 1996, Bloodaxe Books, used under licence.

INDEX

Figures in bold refer to photographs and CS refers to photographs in the Colour Section.